Blood
Stain

Blood Stain

PETER LALOR

A SUE HINES BOOK
ALLEN & UNWIN

First published in 2002

Allen & Unwin
83 Alexander Street
Crows Nest NSW 2065
Australia
Phone: (61 2) 8425 0100
Fax: (61 2) 9906 2218
Email: info@allenandunwin.com
Web: www.allenandunwin.com

National Library of Australia
Cataloguing-in-Publication entry:

Lalor, Peter, 1963- .
   Blood stain.
   ISBN 1 86508 878 1.
   1. Knight, Katherine. 2. Women murderers - Biography.
   3. Cannibalism - Australia. I. Title.
   364.1523

Cover and text design by Phil Campbell
Edited by Margaret Trudgeon
Typeset by Pauline Haas
Printed by McPherson's Printing Group

10 9 8 7

The names of children in this book who were
under 18 at time of the event have been withheld.

To my Sue
for her wise counsel, faith and beauty.

And to Bob Wells
a good copper and a good bloke.
Bobby, you won the last rubber!

Contents

Acknowledgements

Writing a book is like driving a formula one car, you sit down and steer while an enormous team of people build the engines, change the tyres, provide the petrol, wipe your brow and give you a push in the right direction when you spin off the track. I must thank some of them.

My wife Sue's help was invaluable. She worked double time so I could get a few hours in here and there. She also provided good counsel and emotional support. The kids were fantastic. Harry, I owe you five zillion kicks of the footy and Lucy you'll get an equal amount of bed time stories, but never this one.

I met Bob Wells in Aberdeen one day while covering Katherine's trial and remember thinking he was the nicest copper I'd ever met. He is. Bob and his wife Cath were always friendly, helpful and hospitable. It's an honour to know you.

Thanks to David Kellett and family for their genuine hospitality and friendship. Thanks to David Saunders for the sore heads and all those late nights in the pubs of Scone and Muswellbrook. Also, thanks to John Chillingworth who is an intelligent man and gave good advice.

This book wouldn't have happened if Liz Deegan (now deputy editor of the *Adelaide Advertiser*) had not insisted I turn my attention to the case right back in March 2000 or John McGourty who sent me up the valley with Bob Barker to cover the trial and ran the stories.

Sue Hines saw the germ of a book in the *Daily Telegraph* coverage and I thank her for making the phone call, accepting so many mad phone calls in return and making this as painless as possible. Sue, we got on so well it was almost like I'd met you before. Andrea McNamara provided similar support and counsel. Thanks for that Andrea.

There were so many other people who offered advice and support that are too numerous to name.

Rebecca, you are a great girl and your dad would be so proud of you.

Introduction

At 6 pm on the night she killed John Price, Katherine Knight sat singing nursery rhymes with her granddaughter on her lap, her youngest children at her feet. *Round and round the garden like a teddy bear . . . This little piggy went to market.* She hugged and kissed her children before taking them out to dinner at the local Chinese restaurant. The happy family scenes are captured on a video she made. To watch it is disconcerting, as there is a second video that was made the next day. It shows the indescribable horror of what Katherine does next and as you watch Katherine playing happily at home with the kids you know that the hands that hold the little grandchild will soon pick up a knife and stab John Price 37 times before skinning, beheading and further mutilating his corpse. Those hands then prepare parts of his body, including his head, for his children's dinner. Each video informs the other in a feedback loop. She looks so normal but will be so evil. She is so evil but can be so normal.

The murder of John Price defied the imagination. After the crime the outside world was drip-fed information via the media, detail by terrible detail, as though it may be too much to comprehend in its entirety. He was beheaded. He was mutilated. He was skinned. He was cooked. Served on plates for the family.

What of the woman who did it? She was his defacto. A mother of four. An abattoir worker. The grandmother who sang about the little piggy and the teddy bears.

And, she must have been mad. Of course she was. The sane do not behave like that. She was a monster. Less than human, less than sentient. Wasn't she? It seemed important to us that she was because it was too horrible to contemplate otherwise.

Murders are common. Gratuitous mutilation, even cannibalism, isn't unheard of. In June 1988, as a young reporter I went to a warehouse in South Melbourne where a vagrant had been murdered. For some reason the police invited me inside for a look. It was a peculiar crime and solved a puzzle that had begun weeks before when a penis was found in a hand basin at Flinders Street Station. It transpired that one homeless man had killed another inside the derelict building the month before and had sliced off his genitals. He placed the testicles on a tram track, then he disposed of the corpse in a fire. It was a small fire and it took about a week to burn the man. A week crouched on the dirt floor, in the draughty space with its broken windows and strange light. Some time during the process the killer had become hungry and eaten slices of his victim's buttocks, cooking them in a wok. On an old bench sat recently purchased packets of tomato sauce, salt and rice—the condiments. The killer was never tried; he was an escapee from a psychiatric hospital and he was duly locked up again. I have some memory that he was sent back to New Zealand, his home country.

It was a macabre murder, but easily dismissed as the work of a madman. Nothing too disturbing.

Katherine Knight was not mad when she killed John Price. She was sane according to the measure of our justice system. She planned it and she did it knowing that it was wrong. She wasn't mad either when she used her abattoir knives to remove his skin and head. She was of right mind when she cooked him with vegetables. Made a soup with his head. Prepared the gravy. It was all about revenge. And possibly even pleasure. She had dressed in a black nightie and had sex with him beforehand. She turned the night into a performance. And that is what makes this murder so worthy of examination.

How can somebody be so bad? So immoral? And yet not be mad?

You know Katherine Knight the mother. Four kids from three blokes. You've parked outside her home, seen her emerge red-faced and furious. Move ya fuckin' car, ya stupid cunt! Ya can't fuckin' park there! Unreasonably angry over the slightest thing. You've seen her battling with a gaggle of children, a smoke dangling from her mouth as she ushers them into a van. Seen the family unit at caravan parks and country RSL clubs, or queuing with forms at the welfare office, clutching duplicated doctors' letters to prove her incapacity. Stood behind her at the counter as she counts out change for white bread and milk. Cringed as you watched her thump one of the kids a little too hard, thought of saying something but backed off the moment you saw that look in her eye. Totally uninhibited. Couldn't give a fuck what you thought. Katherine would swerve the car to hit cats or dogs that strayed onto the road and cackle herself silly. She's like a stray dog herself. You can't tell if she'll bite or lick.

You don't know the world in which she was raised. The Petri dish of dysfunction which nurtured her badness. Katherine Knight is a woman who left the family home with few basic moral constructs beyond a sense of justice. An understanding that if you erred you must be punished. One psychiatrist referred to her 'primitive conscience'. The red-headed twin cowered in the dark while incest, violence, paedophilia and rape stalked the corridors of her childhood. She knew more about sex and violence than she ever did of love.

In Katherine's world an absence of love enabled evil to take root and murderous resentments to flourish.

She wasn't a total monster by any means. Katherine had a heart of gold. Dressed her kids up and sent them to Sunday school. Sewed dresses for friends' babies. Visited the sick. Ran people around in her car. She would do anything for anyone, her family say. You just didn't cross her.

To examine her past is not to give her an excuse. Katherine is one of eight children and the only one with a serious criminal record. The others have their demons and their failings, but nothing in Katherine's league.

Katherine suffers from a serious borderline personality disorder and there are suggestions of other personality disorders, but that was not why she killed John Price. She had been sexually and physically abused as a child, which seems to almost inevitably cause problems in people, but that is not why she killed him either. Katherine killed her lover and did those terrible things in that long, vile night because it was her nature to go one step further. To go over the borderline.

John Price will die today
29 February 2000

Tonight Katherine Knight is going to kill John Price. She's had her knives sharpened, she has everything ready, but she's not in any hurry. She'll take her time, and anyway, she's got something to prove first. She's been to the welfare shop and bought a black nightie with buttons down the front and she's going to surprise him, wake him up and seduce him. They can never say no to sex. None of them. Sex and violence have always gone together in Katherine's world. They'll do it slowly and gently, one last time. Then, when they're finished, when he's lying back and listening to the airconditioner droning away, she'll make her move. She will have her justice. She'll force some order on this emotional chaos. And, as he screams and runs for the door, as the knife plunges in and out and his blood sprays up onto her face, he will be every man who has ever crossed her. Katherine will have her payback. She'll settle the score against them all. Against John, for casting her aside; against the siblings who soiled her with saliva on their groping fingers; against the violent father who forced sex on her poor mother. All of them. Even the no-good husband who took off up the highway

25 years before and left her scared and alone with a baby, locked up in a cold concrete psychiatric ward so drugged out any man could take her. She'd always been abandoned. Abused and abandoned. And they've always been fumbling under her clothes in the night. Getting their way. *I was always afraid of being raped . . . I picked the wrong ones. They're all drunk and violent.*

And, when her anger is done, when the frenzied stabbing and slashing and chasing is over, when John is lying in a congealing crimson pool, she'll take a rest. Smoke a cigarette, put on the kettle, listen to the coal trains that pass through town, and think about happier times. The thrill of the slaughterhouse. *I always wanted to follow my father's footsteps . . . scraping the congealed blood out of them, the marrow out of their body . . . I loved doing all that.* Loved being young and free in a place where the animals screamed and died, where the hides were peeled from the bleeding carcasses and long razor knives sliced through sinew and flesh, transforming the living into the dead. Where the red meat was packed in vacuum packs and the white of the bones exposed.

The abattoir has been closed for nearly a year, but Katherine will go back to work tonight. Just for the hell of it.

She has been so upset for so long; she's been taking pills for her nerves. John wants her to go and the thought is terrifying. She is calm now. She knows what has to be done. She's waited her whole life for this.

This morning, in the pre-dawn stillness, she stood at the end of his bed, her hands behind her back. Just stood there smiling and cold, savouring the moment, knowing she could finish it here and now. And John sensed it, felt the gooseflesh form on his skin even as he slept. He almost died of fright when he opened his eyes and saw her there. He jumped up and ran for his life, convinced she had a knife and this was it.

Sick bitch.

And John knows he is about to die. He has seen his murder rehearsed, heard his death foretold. It's been coming for so long now and it is a wicked torment. The police can't help. He can't tell his mates. It was too much for them when he took her back last time after she'd got him the sack from the mines. They'd lost respect for him. Now he's trapped. She told him back then that if she took him back there was only one way out.

Today is a leap day, the 29th of February 2000. The last day of his life.

He's got a job now with Bowditch and Partners Earth Moving and it's turned out well. He was out of work for a while and drank like a bastard, but then this came up. They made him a supervisor after twelve months. He eased off the grog.

He can't get out of his home quickly enough this morning. His heart's still pounding as he drives down the New England Highway past Muswellbrook to Bowditch's. With the early morning wake-up call he's arrived even earlier than usual, and when the crews and work are organised for the day he sits down in the office with Geoff Bowditch, the young boss, and Peter Cairnes, one of the managers. Pricey's always been one of the boys and management hasn't come naturally to him, especially as he can't read or write, but today he feels that maybe these two are removed enough from his life to let him open up a little. He's rattled and he's got to talk to somebody about this shit. A bloke can't keep it bottled up forever.

He tells them how things are difficult at home. How he wants Kath—he calls her the Speckled Fucking Hen (she has red hair and freckled skin)—to get out of his house, but she won't go. He tells Cairnes and Bowditch about a vicious blue with her on Sunday. She'd gone for a knife and he'd run for his frigging life. The cops came and he asked them if they'd get her out of his house, but they weren't interested. Then, last night, they came around and served a bloody apprehended violence order (AVO) summons on him for assaulting her. He tells Bowditch and Cairnes she has form, a history of violence. She's a sick bitch and capable of anything. There was an incident with an axe and a baby years ago. Her eldest. She'd put her on the railway tracks. She'd cut the throat of a bloke's dog. She can throw a punch as good as any man. She'll just snap and God help you if you are in her way. She's a fucking maniac when she gets worked up. Strong as a man.

It all comes pouring out. Bowditch and Cairnes take a while to catch on to what Pricey is saying. They've seen her around; she's a little strange, but nice enough. Doesn't she run him round to the pubs, look after his house? Surely she's not that bad. It's not the usual early morning chitchat, but as they listen they realise the little fella is dead serious. He says he's even keeping in contact with a mate down the coast, telling him what's going on at home—In case something happens to me, somebody'll know.

Cairnes has only worked with Pricey for two years and is surprised that this rough little bloke is so rattled by a woman.

—Has she had a go at you, mate?

Pricey opens his shirt and shows them a scar on the right side of his chest where she stabbed him a few months ago. He's never shown anyone before, just stuck a bandage on it and let it heal by itself. It wasn't so bad, but it shows you what she's capable of.

He'd lost it on Sunday night, she was pushing and pushing and when she said something about his mother he cracked and tried to throttle her. Had her by the tit and was twisting and she was clawing at his face as they rolled around on the couch in front of the telly. Her kids and a niece were cowering in the bedroom. It was so fucking pathetic. Then she went for the knife.

He tells Cairnes and Bowditch about waking up that morning and thinking she was going to stab him.

—Ya don't know what to fuckin' do. You're half awake and half asleep and the mad bitch is just staring at you. What sort of woman stands at the end of your bed in the middle of the night looking at you, anyway?

She's driving him out of his mind. Anyway, the cops reckon if he wants to get her out he has to go to the court-house and see about getting an order against her. He wants some time off, if it's okay with the boss. Of course it is. Bowditch likes Pricey and is horrified by what he's just heard.

Pricey drives up to the courthouse at lunch time. The bloke he speaks with, Glenn Dunning, is the one who dealt with the AVO from Sunday night's fight. He recognises the name. Pricey says he needs to get her out of his house. Dunning tells him he'll have to wait until the original order goes to the court in three weeks' time. Pricey figures he'll probably be dead by then. He wants the bloke to know how bad it is and shows him the stab wound. It's a mark of how desperate he is. Up until that day nobody has seen it—Dunning is the third person now in a few hours. Pricey says he's worried that if she doesn't get him she'll get his kids. The court officer isn't going to be any help. Realising how futile it is, Pricey lightens up a bit and jokes that she's threatened to cut his old fella off. Says it's caused him a lot of trouble in the past but he'd hate to lose it. Dunning remarks later that he found him 'friendly and like-able'. John Price's charm was not muted by his fear.

Concerned about what he's heard that morning, Bowditch comes looking for Price that afternoon. The little fella tells him it's been a waste of time. He's been fobbed off. The young boss offers Pricey a place to stay. He has a self-contained flat up at his house that a lot of the blokes have used at different times.

—No. I don't want her to think I'm running away. If she

can't find me, she'll go for my kids and I'd rather she got me than them.

—Don't put yourself in danger, John. If you're worried, come and stay with me. I've got a big house up there and I'm in it by myself.

—Mate, if a bloke can't stay in his own fucking house . . .

Of course it would be nice to escape, but he knows, as he's told Dunning, she's after blood and if she doesn't get him she'll get his kids. Katherine hates the eldest, Johnathon Price, who lives nearby with his fiancée. She is so bloody mad and vindictive that she even reckons his youngest, a 14-year-old girl, has sexually assaulted her two little ones. It's absolute bullshit, but she will say and do anything, especially if he throws her out.

—It's gonna cost me $10 000 to get rid of her.

That was her price. Bowditch repeats the offer of the flat but Pricey doesn't want to think what would happen if he runs away. After their chat Price knocks off. It's only 3 pm, earlier than usual. He heads for the pub. He's a particular friend of the managers, Sharon and Jim Simmons. Sharon has had a soft spot for him and she can see he's not himself. He's mentioned to her that he has blood pressure problems and is seeing a doctor.

He pulls up a stool in the corner and they chat.

—Is work getting ya down?

—Nah, it's not that.

He doesn't know if he can go into it all again, but it's a heavy weight to carry alone. Fuck, he's depressed. A mate, Frank Heap, comes and joins them and notices something on Pricey's face.

—The Speckled Hen been at it again?

—Yeah, congratulations. You're the first to notice, mate.

Sharon sees that Pricey has a scratch mark under his eye.

It's from Sunday's blue. He tells them about all the shit that has happened and seems to get himself into a bit of a state. Heap suggests they change the subject. Sharon says she's got to go upstairs to do some cleaning. Pricey doesn't want her to go; he grabs her hand in his. She can feel it shaking.

—Thanks for listening, love. Thanks for such a gentle time.

The poor little bastard seems so down, she thinks as she trudges up the stairs.

At 6 pm Pricey heads home for some tea. She isn't there when he gets back. Thank God. It's a hot night and he's not in the mood for being alone so he takes a few beers across the road to young Keego's place. Anthony Keegan was at school with Pricey's son; he's a truck driver and they became mates when he bought the house across the road two years ago. They often drink together in the shed or on the verandah. Pricey loves his kids and Anthony's missus Jill. She thinks he's one of the nicest blokes in town and is glad to have him as a neighbour.

Price shows Anthony and his father, Larry, the court papers from Sunday's incident. Can you believe they served an AVO on him and not her? They ask where she is. He doesn't know, but he figures she'll be back. Like Bowditch, Keegan is worried and says he can stay with him and the kids if he wants.

—Thanks mate, but if a bloke can't live in his own fuckin' house . . .

It's becoming a mantra.

He has to go, but pauses before leaving.

—I love youse forever.

He seems so bloody sad as he wanders back across the road.

*   *   *

At the same time Katherine has driven to her home and opened the side gate in preparation for a midnight return. She should be tired. It's been a big day and she's had a lot to do. There have been police, solicitors, doctors and family to see. And she's taken back the video camera from her sister's, the one he banned from the house after she used it to get him sacked from the mine, and she's made a tape of her grand-daughter. *Nana's gonna get ya . . . Nana's gonna get ya.* Then she shot some more footage with the camera sitting on the televi-sion. She got her two daughters in one shot and kissed and hugged them. Then, when they were all out of the room she sighed and turned to the camera. *I love my children . . . and I hope to see them all . . .* Somebody came back in and she stopped.

Anthony Keegan has his tea and is in bed by 10.30 pm, but he can't sleep. At 11 pm he's sitting at the kitchen table when he hears a car pull up across the road. Through the window he sees Katherine's red Lite Ace van. It's parked next to Pricey's work truck. 'The Speckled Hen must be home,' he says to Larry and then goes back to bed.

Katherine lights a cigarette outside and prepares to go in.

All hell is about to break loose.

Where is Pricey?
1 March 2000

Lisa Logan gets up and goes to the toilet. It's about 3.30 am. On the way back she opens the front door to let the little Maltese terrier out so it can relieve itself on the front lawn. It's a warm night and she wanders out onto the front verandah for some air. In the darkness Lisa sees a figure walking up from the railway tracks. Hears the slap of thongs against feet. She bends down to pick up the dog before it starts barking and wakes up everyone in St Andrews Street. Looking up, she sees a woman in a light coloured shirt and top walking towards John Price's place. Despite the darkness she can see it's Katherine Knight. Knight doesn't see her; the verandah is shielded by a big shrub. When she's gone Lisa lets the dog go. She goes back to bed thinking nothing of it.

Katherine keeps walking. She has a job to finish.

* * *

John Price's steel-capped work boots sit on the front verandah of 84 St Andrews Street like a pair of dogs waiting for their master. It's after 6 am but the place is quiet and the curtains are drawn. There's a stillness to the unremarkable little house. The thermometer climbs sharply in the valley that Wednesday morning and the air is already sticky and thick. The sort of day you're better off watching from inside an air-conditioned office, although they don't run to that sort of thing round here. It's all coal mines, tanneries and dusty paddocks.

Price's house looks like it needs a woman's touch. A bland, brick, modern-style house, it sits there like it's been plonked on the block. A transplant that hasn't taken. A half-hearted effort at a garden in the front does little to diminish the effect. If you look around the back you'll find a Hills Hoist, a shed and a brick barbecue, but it all seems a bit barren. A range of cars lines the driveway.

John Price wasn't just punctual, he beat the clock. It was nothing for him to get to work at 5.30 am for a 6.30 am start. He liked the quiet of the morning to clear his head from the night before and plan for the day ahead. Everybody knew that and when he didn't rouse, when the work ute stayed cold in the driveway and the boots remained unlaced on the verandah it was like a small cog seizing in a large machine, throwing everything else out of whack before bringing the whole damned factory to a stop.

* * *

Peter Cairnes arrives at work early. Pricey isn't there. It's not unusual for his co-worker to have headed out to a job before anyone else, but he gives him a call anyway, just to see what's happening. He gets no reply.

The first thing Geoff Bowditch does when he climbs into the work truck is pick up the radio and give Pricey a call on the two-way. The bloke has been on his mind all night. God knows it sounded silly, but ...

He sends out a call on the two-way.

NOT HOME

The company's two-way radios have an LED display that spells out that message when the other radio isn't on. Bowditch keeps trying.

NOT HOME ... NOT HOME ...

Then he tries again.

NOT HOME

It's a little unnerving. Bowditch persists as he drives toward the depot.

*   *   *

Anthony Keegan gets out of bed around 6 am. He looks through the window and sees Pricey's truck still in the driveway. Pricey is always on the road before Keego. Something isn't right. His wife Jill has heard about the troubles and says she'll call Pricey and see if he's okay. She's concerned too. The phone rings, and rings, and rings. Like Bowditch, she keeps at it, calling and calling and calling. Fear rising.

After a while Keegan goes out to start up his truck, thinking that its enormous engine will wake him up. If he's still with us. He turns over the motor and looks across the road for a movement at the curtain, a figure at the door. He goes back inside and then decides he'd better go over. He's been putting that off.

Crossing the road is like walking towards a car crash; your heart thumps and your legs are like soft lead, as though they're protesting against what you might find.

Keegan bangs on the door and there's no answer. Looking down he sees blood on the handle but doesn't even want to contemplate what it means. Hopefully it's from Sunday night when she scratched his face. He bangs on the bedroom window, softly at first, then louder. Nothing. He notices the work boots and then spots something else too awful to contemplate.

By this time Bowditch has arrived at work and discovered Pricey isn't there. He's told Cairnes to try Price's home number, then he gets him to find Keegan's. Before Bowditch's arrival Cairnes has already called the top pub, thinking maybe Pricey has got on the piss and stayed the night or headed off to someone else's house. There's no panic from Cairnes: blokes in the construction industry drink hard and mess up some-times. His only real worry is that Price might have got a belly full and stacked his car somewhere.

Bowditch gets Jill on the phone and she's just saying that Keego is over the road when he walks back into the house. Keego is more worried than ever. Bowditch asks if Kath's little van is there? It's not. Which is strange. Keegan's sure he saw it parked there the night before. Keegan says he's going to pop up the road and get Ron Murray. Murray and Pricey are good mates—he might know something.

Bowditch tells Jill he's going to call the police. He hangs up and begins to look for the number for the Muswellbrook station. One of the drivers, Jon Collison, is a neighbour of Price's. There's been a mechanical breakdown with one of the trucks so he's going home until it's fixed. He says he'll drop in and see what's wrong.

Ron Murray was up earlier to drop his son off at work and noticed Pricey's ute at the house. It was 6.30 am and Ron had said to the boy that his mate must be having a day off. He'd never sleep in. Now Keegan's at his door saying he's worried about John. Could he come down and check it out? They both walk down to the house together. They again try knocking and yelling and peering through the windows. Ron thinks his mate is asleep, but thinks it odd that all the curtains are drawn. They're never closed like this. Later he'll thank God they are.

Everybody fears the worst, but they can't just stand around. Ron Murray goes back home to get his car and drives around to Kath's house to see if her van is there. He can't see it (it's hidden behind the shed). He comes back and goes to see Kath's twin sister Joy, who lives just up from Pricey's, closer to Murray's place. As he knocks on the door the school bus comes down the street as it does every morning around 8.15 am. He tells Joy they couldn't find Kath or Pricey. Joy doesn't know where they are, doesn't seem that interested. Later she jumps in the car and drives off, apparently oblivious to the drama going on within eyesight of her home. Joy and her sister-in-law Val Roughan are taking Ken Knight, the twins' father, to Newcastle for a doctor's appointment.

Jon Collison arrives from Bowditch's and sees the others out the front of Price's house. Pricey told him on Monday he was crook and he assumes he must have gone up to the hospital during the night. Still, he does the rounds of the windows like everyone else. He sees the blood on the door and starts to wonder. The police come around the corner just as Ron Murray walks back from Joy's house. They arrive in two cars. Collison takes them around the house and they go through the same futile motions. Banging on the door. Peering through the windows. Yelling out.

One of the cops thinks he's seen a bunched curtain hanging in the archway from the kitchen to the lounge and makes a mental note of it. It doesn't look right. The others haven't seen it, or haven't mentioned it if they did.

Collo gets a crowbar from Pricey's work truck and they pop the laundry door at the back of the house. He's about to follow the cops inside, but for some reason doesn't. It's a decision he's never regretted. He waits outside on the landing.

The cops are inside for a few minutes, long enough for Collison to work out that something is wrong.

There's a small commotion, then they bring Kath out. She's ruffled, but clean like she's just had a shower. They're supporting her and she looks out of it on drugs or something. She looks at Collo and seems to recognise him. He's known her for nearly 30 years. The cops look pale and agitated. They ask him to move out of the way and the two lead Kath around to the side of the house, sitting her on the ground behind the police car.

One of the police takes Collison aside. 'Sorry mate, he's dead.' Collo looks over to Ron Murray who is watching from a distance. He turns a thumb towards the ground to let the neighbour know what he's heard. He doesn't need to say any more. Ronnie understands straight away. *The little fella was gone. That was it.*

Cairnes gets onto Bowditch and tells him they had better head down to Aberdeen.

—What's happened?

—The absolute worst possible thing.

Keegan has called young Johnathon Price even before the police arrived and has told him there's blood on his dad's front door.

—It was weird 'cos as I was driving over I was thinking, God, I'll have to organise the funeral ... I drove straight in the driveway and they pulled me up to stop ... By this stage Katherine was laying down on the ground on all fours, crouched down like a dog and I said to the copper, 'He's gone, hasn't he.' Graham Furlonger sat me down on the step and he said 'Yeah, mate, yeah,' and that was it.

Somebody asks where the kids are.

What kids?

The two young ones always stay if she does.

Oh fuck.

3

Bob Wells drives up
1 March 2000

Bobby Wells is belting up the New England Highway with Mick Prentice in the passenger seat. The older detective always drives when there's a need for speed; he is a nervous passenger. Mick has to defer to his more senior partner and hangs on as they race up the road. Hurtling towards a horror they could never imagine. The pair started work in Singleton that morning when a call came through at about 8.30 am about a possible murder further up the valley at Aberdeen, a small town between Muswellbrook and Scone in the heart of the coal mining country. It's an odd place.

If you look at a map it's hard to figure out what geographic–economic imperative led to the establishment of Aberdeen. It's squeezed between Muswellbrook to the south and Scone to the north on a 30 kilometre stretch of the New England Highway and it is overshadowed by both centres. The nearest major town is Newcastle, about 120 kilometres down the New England Highway. Sydney is another world.

Muswellbrook is big enough to be the place where the young migrate towards. It's got drugs and parties—all the embellishments of the city right there in the bush. If that's not enough they move down further to Newcastle. Scone's a bit

more pony club, what with Kerry Packer's polo estate nearby
and a lot of horsey types wandering around. It's got boutique
charm. Packer is Australia's richest man. And Aberdeen? Well,
it's got an abattoir and a tannery, or it had an abattoir up until
a few years back, and recently they got another coal mine.

Aberdeen was first settled in the mid-1820s by white
Australians hungry for grazing lands, only weeks after its dis-
covery by British explorer Henry Dangar. The Great
Northern Railway Line reached Aberdeen in 1870 but didn't
have any immediate impact on the population. After World
War I the larger properties in the district were broken up and
parcelled off to returned soldiers, who established dairy farms
where once wool, cattle and sheep had held stead.

Aberdeen really kicked on when the Australian Meat
Cutting and Freezing Company built an abattoir by the railway line in 1891. The factory slaughtered sheep and sent the
frozen mutton by train to the port at Newcastle. The population expanded rapidly after it opened—whereas only 36
people lived there in 1892, by 1894 the meatworks alone
employed 200.

The town struggled to accommodate the influx of
workers and the company built barracks on the meatwork's
grounds to accommodate new arrivals. In the early 1900s its
owners built a row of cottages on McAdam Street for young
workers to buy on a hire–purchase basis when they got married. The strip became known as Honeymoon Lane and many
decades later Katherine Knight and her family would live in
one of the cottages on the strip.

In the latter part of the twentieth century the abattoir
became the main supplier of beef patties to McDonald's and
at some time you may well have eaten a burger prepared by
one of the knife-wielding Knights. At its peak there were over
600 people slicing throats, skinning carcasses and scraping

out foul smelling offal. More than a third of the town's population spent their days like this.

For a century Aberdeen was a slaughterhouse town and Katherine Knight's people were a slaughterhouse family. Every local knows the Knights and their kin. They had some notoriety in the area for their rough ways, but an abattoir town is never going to be picket fences and cosy two-by-two families saving to put the kids through university. Meatworkers tend to be a little itinerant and the fact that most places will hire casual labour from a morning line-up meant you would get your fair share of drifters coming through to pick up a bit of work.

Lloyd Lyne was the local sergeant from 1969 to 1976. He worked a lot of small towns with tough reputations but says that Aberdeen was the worst of the lot. He was always busy with hot-headed kids who, he said, turned to trouble and drugs early. The meatworkers were a tough lot who drank hard and he says the casual employment attracted a lot of passing criminal trade in need of some quick money. The sergeant never had a slow day in sleepy old Aberdeen.

These days Aberdeen is quiet. The main employer, the meatworks, is now closed and once it went there was bugger all left. If you're driving up the highway, there's hardly a road sign until you almost reach town and it tells you there are 1750 people living at an elevation of 190 m.

This morning there are 1749. The slaughterhouse has taken one last victim.

As Wells and Prentice drive they pass slag heaps that form their own minor mountain ranges. Coal sidings and conveyor belts follow the road. It's a strange piece of countryside. Part rural, part industrial. Before Muswellbrook there are two enormous power stations, one on either side of the highway. Their oversized chimneys pump towering clouds of steam into the sky. The mines release poisonous gases into the atmosphere. The locals reckon that their fences and cars rust at twice the rate of anywhere else in Australia because of chemicals in the air. By the side of the road is a permanent protest camp, where miners picket one of the multinational companies.

This morning the two cops are happy to get out of the office. There's a sense of excitement as they drive shoulder to shoulder with the coal trains. A local copper, John Alderson, has called from Aberdeen and said it looks like murder. Wells is the area's senior detective, so he has to come up and supervise. Wells and Prentice are keen to get there as quickly as possible. To be honest, they're going flat chat through the morning. The adrenalin is flowing. You don't get that many big jobs and a murder is as big as it gets. You don't join the force to write speeding tickets. This is what it's all about. The big league.

They phone for directions as they approach town and are told to go over the bridge and take the first right. They hit Aberdeen and are through the town in a minute. They cross the bridge over the Hunter River and can't find the turn-off.

Shit.

They call the locals again, do a U-turn and came back through town, taking the railway bridge before the top pub. Pretty soon they find what they are looking for.

It's 9.15 am, give or take five minutes, and it's getting hot.

Eighty-four St Andrews Street is surrounded by blue police tape. The bunting of death. There are cop cars on the street, cars in the driveway and an ambulance. A small group of people are gathered on the lawn across the street.

It proves to be a morning that none of the cops, ambos or locals will ever forget. A glimpse into the dark, cockroach corners of the soul. A lot of the blokes there that day are never

the same again. Even now they have nightmares, angry outbursts, depression. They avoid each other because they don't
want to be reminded of what they've been through together.
There are murders and there are murders. There are bodies
and there are bodies, and then there's what lies waiting for
Bob Wells and the others behind the front door of this little
brick house with its blinds drawn and airconditioner working
against the oppressive Hunter Valley heat.

As Wells and Prentice get out of the car two ambulance
officers close the doors of their van and begin to drive
off. Muswellbrook detective Graham Furlonger and John
Alderson are waiting. They try and bring the pair up to speed:
the suspect's in the back of the ambulance. A suspected overdose.

—You're not going to believe what's going on in here,
mate. It's fucking crazy.

What else could they say? It *is* fucking crazy. There aren't
words for it. Frankly, Furlonger and Alderson are not even
sure exactly what they've seen. Furlonger looks rattled. The
four men walk down the western side of the house and
Furlonger points out something on the grass in front of a
Ford Mondeo.

—Check that out, mate.

—Fuck. Is that what I think it is?

—Mate, I told you this was fuckin' bizarre.

—God!

—You don't know the half of it.

It is a piece of cooked meat, fatty and dark like mutton.

4

Inside the slaughterhouse
1 March 2000

Inside 84 St Andrews Street are horrors those who stand outside can never imagine.

John Price's watch rests on a shattered picture frame, the
face smeared with blood, its second hand ticking like a faint
heartbeat in a car crash. A photograph of his son lies beneath
the shards of glass. Flies on a blood stained knife. An ocean of
blood on the cork tiles and a body of raw flesh. A severed neck
with gaping windpipe. An arm propped on a softdrink bottle.
A pelt on a hook. Bloodied coffee mugs and twisted cigarette
butts. Vegetable peels in the sink and a baking tray on the
stove. Congealing fat and a cup of gravy. A soup pot on the
stove. An airconditioner and a snoring sound. It's a nightmare swirl of images.

John Price's death is shocking beyond comprehension.
To enter 84 St Andrews Street is to lift the grate and descend
to a lower world. Others, like Jon Collison, could choose not
to go there, could turn back at the door, but professional
imperatives force a small number of people into that home
over the course of the day to witness the congealing crimson
detail.

After they'd cracked the lock on the back door with a crow bar, Duty Officer Graham Furlonger, followed by Senior Constables Scott Andrew Matthews and Robert James Maude, were the first outsiders to witness this vision of hell. They emerged shaken and horrified, unable to describe or understand what they'd seen.

At 9.10 am Furlonger leads Wells and Prentice inside. Nothing he can say will prepare them.

Outside the March sun is stark and blinding and inside the curtains are drawn and the darkness contained. Bob Wells' pupils dilate slowly, images emerge like photographs in a developing tank. A nightmare lifting from the nothingness. Reds from the blackness.

—Mate, I told you this was fucking bizarre.

Wells' heart pounds a crazed drum beat warning. Turn around now, while you can. Get out and don't look back.

Something hangs in the archway between the kitchen and the living room, contorted and shapeless. Some sort of drape. It's the first thing you notice. It takes a moment, then you realise. It's him. John Price. At least it's his skin hanging like a wetsuit on a nail. A man melted like a Dali clock. A human curtain. The face a sick rubber mask without a skull to give it shape. The eye holes vacant under an exaggerated eyebrow arch. His mouth twisted and distorted, falling in a silent scream. There are his ears, or what remains of them. His scalp is crowned by bloody curls. The rest is slashed and punctured, hanging in porcine strips right down to his flanged feet. A patch of pubic hair offers some orientation.

Price faces the kitchen, the butcher's hook hung on the lounge side of the architrave and poking into the back of his scalp. There's an unopened stubbie of beer lying on the floor in front of the fridge. Just out of reach.

Beyond the curtain John Price's denuded body lies on the

carpet, headless and skinless. Furlonger points it out to Wells and Prentice.

A steady drone comes from the eastern end of the house. It is an airconditioner and when the first officers approached, gasping and retching, another sound, guttural and bestial, announced itself. Guns drawn, they had inched past the punch holes in the corridor plaster and generous gesticulatory patterns of blood, searching for the source of the strange noise. They had found her lying on the crumpled bed, clean and oblivious. The bed cover was pulled down and a sheet led from the bed towards the door. Katherine was snoring loudly.

Now she is gone and there is no life save the airconditioner droning on and on. A large bed is squeezed into the small space, a mirrored built-in robe on the west side, a dressing table at the foot of the bed. A pair of thongs on the floor, a packet of Winfield cigarettes on the table, three spent butts and a stubbie cap in the ash tray. There are tissues, noname massage oil, baby powder and an oil burner on the bedside table. Clothes on the floor. Female lotions on the dresser, framed photographs of a baby and a young girl. Empty tablet strips. A bedroom in summer disorder.

It must have started here. The first drops of blood on the sheet, fountain and spray above the bed head and onto the mirrored robe. Palm smears by the door and coagulated teardrops on the light switch where a man in the middle of his murder has frantically groped about, trying to turn on a light to protect himself from the homicidal darkness.

The corridor is sprayed with arterial patterns and desperate, lurching smears. Failing to get the light on he has run this way, then turned left into the entrance hall and tried to get out the front door. She's followed him every step, stabbing and hacking. Relentless.

There are roughly five litres of blood in the human body.

On this corked floor behind the front door John Price has bled to death. The scale is profound. He appears to have lost almost every drop. There is just so much blood here. Just so damned much of it. Now it's darkening from the outside in and reflecting the light bulb above it. Here, on the wall, are the butterfly smears of John Price's last struggle and dying fall. Wide bloody sweeps at shoulder height, repeated as he slipped down. Delicate arterial sprays and long dying drops.

Perhaps the pool seems so confrontingly large because it is empty. Drag marks lead towards the loungeroom but you do not have to peer in to know what's there, for his skinless legs protrude into the entrance hall with the left crossed over the right. Casually reclined.

Tiptoe around the sticky pool.

John Price lies on his back with his head towards the kitchen; his body like one of those anatomical illustrations you see stripped of skin so that students of life can study the major muscles. The clean anatomical detail is destroyed by the presence of yellowing fat, drying flesh and gaping puncture wounds.

John Price has no head. A certain blood pattern near the neck on the carpet suggests he has been dragged from the hall and beheaded here.

His left arm is propped up on an empty 1.5 litre bottle of lemon soda squash. By the body is a large plastic handled knife that has scratch marks on the blade as if it has been recently sharpened. Part of the knife edge is missing, it has broken off during the attack. Later, when the crime scene video zooms in on this knife a fly lands on the blade as if this were some strange Hitchcock film.

Nearby a small piece of hairy flesh lies alone. It must have been cut free from the skull in a clumsy moment of savagery. A sharpening steel with a dark black handle sits on the cushion of a chair near the knife with a packet of Winfield cigarettes.

Across the room is the coffee table with two framed photographs that have been smashed. One is of Price's son, Johnathon. A photograph of his youngest daughter has been similarly vandalised. Under it is a piece of tissue paper that contains random hastily scrawled notes, written with an obviously bloody hand. The ticking watch.

Then there is the kitchen. Hell's kitchen.

There is an empty stubbie on the servery, a pack of cigarettes, a Walkman, an ash tray with two butts, a paring knife and a sharpening stone. Details. There are also empty pill packets and a wallet. A bloody coffee mug is filled with fat.

A meal has been prepared and served on two plates, but whoever cooked it has worked hastily and not cleaned up. There are vegetable peelings in the sink, a small cutting board, a bloody knife. Two used bowls. The microwave door is open and his thermos flask is on the bench next to an electric kettle with blood smears on it.

A metal roasting tray sits on top of the cooker, filled with uncongealed fat. Nearby are two plates with a heavy and unappetising meal on them. Coarse chunks of zucchini, potato, squash, cabbage and big cuts of dark, fatty meat. The meals are lying on towelling paper with the names of his two children on them, some sort of hasty name card for a place setting. It is only later that the true horror of this begins to sink in. The cold, calculated spite. The layers of payback. The fact that she has done all this and then cooked and served him for his children.

Then there is a cup of gravy that has not been poured. On the stove is a still warm aluminium cooking pot. Inside is a skinless head, the flesh detaching into a fatty, soupy stock of onions and vegetables. One cooked eye looking up. It is just so sick.

Pricey's work bag is on the table with a cap and a work shirt. There's also a strange little gorilla sitting there. It's a cute touch.

To this day Bob Wells can reel off every detail of the scene in perfect recall. It could be considered an advantage for an officer heading up a case, but for Wells it is a terrible burden he cannot shake. It's as if somebody has downloaded the images onto the hard-drive of his brain. Too many times he has closed his eyes and been transported back into that darkness. The skin and the pot and the skinless torso. An ocean of blood, a continent of flesh. Cigarette butts and gravy cups. Wells was catching a giant wave that day. He was the senior investigating officer and one of the few to see the crime through from start to finish. He lived and breathed the savagery of Katherine Knight from this first morning of March 2000 until the end of the following year when she faced a court. He never stopped, limping around on a gout-swollen foot, a screaming pain in his temples, insomnia and nightmares that wouldn't go away. One cooked eye looking up.

Wells becomes agitated as he recalls the events. He shifts in his chair, the eyes glaze up a little and he begins to speak faster and faster, the ideas running off at tangents.

The blood they've all encountered so many times before, but it was the skin that really made the initial impact.

At first I sort of saw it and I was going ...

It wasn't until you go up to have a look at it that it ...

And I just, mate, I don't know how I felt. I've done a few murders and that sort of thing, especially out west and violent Aboriginal situations, stabbings, things that are easy to work out. This human skin, mate, with the hair, hanging from the architrave by a butcher's hook on the other side and it was hanging right down. The scalp, the hair, right down and just touching the floor.

It just took a while to register and I thought that this is something right out of left field, right out of the ordinary.

I looked around the kitchen and there was the pot. I think Furlonger had brought it to my attention along with the drops of blood on the floor and he said, 'The body's in there, but there's no head', and so I looked in, brushed past the skin and I could see Price's skinned body and I said, 'Mate, this is just . . .' You sort of lose your senses for a minute or so.

You didn't have to be a brain surgeon to work out where the head was.

Three days after Christmas, 1989, Newcastle was rocked by an earthquake which flattened parts of the city and left thirteen dead. Wells was in Maitland prison interviewing a prisoner. Later, he says the feeling of the ground lifting in waves, the terrible noise and the complete incomprehension were much like what happened inside 84 St Andrews Street that morning. You knew something was happening, but your senses were overwhelmed. You couldn't find a nail to hang the sensation from. How do you comprehend the earth twisting and tormenting itself? How do you comprehend what was inside that house?

He came and went many times that day. Standing there with the others, bouncing about theories, piecing together a jigsaw. And there was the smell. Human death has its own odour, it's not like a butcher's shop. Cops will tell you that a dead human smells different to a dead animal. And in St Andrews Street the whole thing was complicated by the last supper that Katherine prepared. As the day dragged on it started to get very ripe. Some of the crime scene boys say it is the most profound memory and they've smelt death more than most.

What saved Wells initially was the need to behave like a policeman. To do his job no matter what was going on.

You reel a bit then reality kicks in and you say, mate, this is a major crime scene and I'm in charge.

'I want everybody out of here.' This is not our job at this stage. 'I want nothing touched until the crime scene blokes get here'—they were on their way—so my concern was to preserve that crime scene.

On leaving the house Wells learned that Knight had two children. He sent the other police off to check around town with a sinking feeling. To have a dead bloke was one thing; a couple of dead kids would have really topped off what was already a shitty day.

Fortunately they found the pair safe at Natasha Kellett's place in Muswellbrook. She was Katherine Knight's second daughter and a fine piece of work herself.

Then the cavalry arrived. The boss, Superintendent Blanche, showed up along with the crime scene guys, Senior Sergeant Neil Raymond and Peter Muscio, and Wells gave them the guided tour. They spent a lot of time inside, trying to fit together the pieces of the crime. The video unit came up from Sydney with the forensic pathologist in tow and started to make a crime scene film that will go down in the annals as one of the worst anybody is ever likely to see. Crime agencies also came up, two homicide detectives, but they weren't too interested. The homicide boys would have jumped in if there was no suspect or at least not one in custody; as it was they offered a bit of advice and headed home.

The cops had a conference outside the house. The moment has been captured by a photographer for the *Newcastle Herald* and was published the next day under the headline 'Slaying of a Battler'. You can see it was getting really hot and uncomfortable. There's an air of unease in the way the police are arranged, some with hands to heads, others staring at the ground. They worked out a plan of attack.

Wells and the other cops started to talk to the crowd of friends and picked up straight away that Knight had threatened to kill Price, that he had been in fear of his life. Didn't look like this case was going to be too hard to solve, but that didn't mean it was going to be easy either.

The investigation began.

You have got to get stuck in straight away, get people on paper because, mate, it was bizarre, just bizarre, I looked at it and knew this brief was going to be something, it was going to be something. Everything was pointing at her. I knew that it was on.

And Bob Wells could feel a knot forming in his gut, a tightening in the temples that started to beat an urgent rhythm in the relentless March heat.

5

Ex-boyfriends and husbands
1 & 2 March 2000

Dave Saunders and a mate were heading down the New England Highway towards Muswellbrook early that Wednesday morning. They had just passed Aberdeen when Dave saw two cop cars go flying past. 'Something must be on,' he said. They got to town, did their business and were heading back up the road when Saunders saw one of the cars headed back in the opposite direction. 'It couldn't have been too much, here comes one of 'em back.' They kept driving to Scone and his mate headed off. It was still early, about 9.30 am.

They were heading out to do a few things but his wife Jenny hadn't had a shower yet. While she did that Dave went outside to start up the Falcon. Listened to it run. Just then a copper came walking down the driveway. A highway patrol bloke.

—Are you Dave Saunders?

—Yeah. What have I done?

—Do you know where your daughter is?

—No, she should be at school. Why?

—Well, she's not at school.

Dave had a daughter to Katherine Knight from a relationship a decade before. He knew that Kath would send her to school come hell or high water. These kids would have to be at death's door before they'd be allowed to stay home for a day and mess up their mum's routine. Saunders started to panic. At first the cop wouldn't say anything, but he could see the fear in the father's eyes.

—What's Kath done?

—We think she's done Pricey in.

—Well, where's me daughter?

—We don't know. Can you give us any names to ring and check?

—Oh, no.

Saunders was terrified. He ran in and got some numbers. He yelled to his wife to get out of the shower.

—We've got to go and look for the girl. I think Katherine's killed Pricey. No one knows where the kids are. C'mon Jen, we've got to go!

He asked the copper to ring him on the mobile if they found her. Saunders drove around for the next four hours. Up and down the highway. From town to town. Place to place, panic rising. His mind going a million miles an hour. He knew Kath was violent. She'd killed one of his dogs, hit him with an iron and a saucepan, even stabbed him with scissors, but he never thought she'd go this far. Where's my little girl? What's she done to her?

By early afternoon he'd run out of places to look and rang the cops back. They told him they'd found the girl and she was okay. They'd found her a couple of hours before. Nobody had bothered to tell him. He was pissed off but relieved. Then he began to think about Pricey. He was a top bloke. They were mates. He'd been chatting with him on Saturday night at a party. Kath had been giving him a hard time. Poor bastard, he didn't deserve that.

*   *   *

John Chillingworth, father of Katherine's youngest son, was in his cab just outside the Gold Coast Hospital when his mum called on the phone telling him to pull over. She had some news.

—It's Dad, isn't it? What's happened to Dad?

—Nothing's happened to your father. Pull over and I'll tell you.

—Yes, Mum.

He keeps driving. As you do.

—John, Katherine's killed Pricey.

Christ almighty, that was one out of the blue. He should have pulled over.

—Killed him?

His mum said something about not being able to find the kids and that's when Chillingworth started to panic. It was just momentary confusion. The shock of the news, the mobile phone, an elderly woman. His mum reassured him that Katherine's daughter Natasha had called and the boy, his son, was with her. He was okay. A crossed wire, but still Chillingworth was frightened.

—He should be with you, Mum. Why haven't you got him?

After she got off the phone, his mum drove from Scone with Chillingworth's sister and picked up the boy from Natasha's place. Chillingworth dropped the cab off, went back home and hit the highway as fast as he could, driving with an intensity he hadn't experienced since making a similar trip six years earlier when she'd first taken the boy from him. He had plenty to think about on the way down. He figured what happened wasn't that surprising. He always believed Katherine was always going to kill or maim somebody, but he was beside himself with worry about what the boy had seen. What had he been through? Poor little bugger.

Chillingworth arrived in the early hours of Thursday

morning, shaking and agitated. Back in his old stomping ground. He was just so happy to see the boy, but of course things turned to shit the next day, as was usual from his experience of past dealings with the Knight women. He just wanted to get his son away from the place, but the kid had to make a statement to the police and it took an hour and a half. Then they couldn't leave because Knight's daughters and family were making trouble about him taking the boy's things back with him. Making appointments and changing their mind. They were Kath's relatives allright. Always worried about what was theirs. The women finally agreed that he could pick the boy's things up from Kath's house early on Saturday morning. Then they insisted he find a justice of the peace to sign a statutory declaration about what he took and they filmed him taking the things. Usual shit.

And, in the middle of it all, there were bits and pieces of news floating around the place. People were saying to him that she'd cut him up, but he didn't believe it. Johnny Hinder, who was married to Katherine's twin sister Joy, had a chat with Chillingworth on the Friday night and passed on some of the detail.

—What really happened to him?

—Just imagine in your wildest dreams what anyone could do to a man with a knife and that's what happened.

—What, she hacked him up?

—Worse than that.

—Shit, she couldn't have done what I'm thinking.

—Mate, it's ten times worse than what you're thinking.

Chillingworth thought that the mother of his son had cut off Pricey's penis. God knows she'd threatened similar things many a time.

—No, she fuckin' skinned him and cut his fuckin' head off.

—You're joking.

He didn't say too much more because Joy was there looking daggers. Chillingworth couldn't get out of that town fast enough.

*   *   *

David Stanford Kellett was the last of the fathers to find out. The news drifted back through time and relationships to him. He was her first real boyfriend and the man she had married when she was still a teenager. Kellett was driving to his in-laws' place on Thursday morning with his second wife and their two kids; a thousand kilometres and nearly two decades on from that wild red-headed woman who had fractured his skull, burned his clothes, bore him two children and left him.

His wife was reading the local paper. Something caught her eye.

—David, there's been a murder in Aberdeen. What was the name of Kathy's boyfriend?

—Pricey. John Price.

—God, David. It says here a woman in Aberdeen has killed him. He's been beheaded and mutilated by his girlfriend.

—What?

Kellett wasn't sure if Kath was still with Price, but he was sure there was only one woman capable of doing that. He'd been on the wrong end of her knives once or twice himself. When they got to his parents-in-law's place Kellett called Ken Knight, his former father-in-law, and asked him if it was true.

—Yeah, that's fuckin' right, Kellett. Buy yourself a lottery ticket, son!

Kellett rang the Muswellbrook police, told a policewoman he was Katherine Knight's first husband and she put John Alderson on the phone. They spoke for a while and he learned a little more. He's never slept right since. On reflection, Kellett knew, or thought he did, every second of Price's miserable last minutes. He knew Pricey; they'd had a beer together a couple of years before and the poor bastard had told him he was having troubles with her, that he wanted to get out of the relationship.

Two years later, sitting in a club, eating a steak sandwich, Dave Kellett's voice starts to break.

I get so close to tears every time I even think about it. I don't know, I get so emotionally upset, not to think that it could happen to me. Probably because she was the mother of my children. I was married to her for the first ten years of our life. Holidays we went on together, things we did together. I try to hide everything, always have. I get emotionally ... I could sit down and cry sometimes when I think about it. What he's gone through. I can actually see her doing it, I really can. I can see what she's doing, I know how she'd go about it and I can see her talking to herself and talking to him and abusing him as she's doing it. I can see her abusing him. To hold a knife at my throat like she did ... If something comes on the TV about a murder I don't sleep that night, still don't because I think of her. I even wake up some nights and I can hear the knife going into the flesh, I can hear that noise that happens when you tear the skin off a rabbit.

Kellett has an unlisted number and doesn't let anybody know where he lives. He thinks that she'd come for him next. The thought terrifies him. All three think that. Each man feels as if he has been given a guided tour of hell and somehow found the way back.

6

Katherine grows up
and marries David Kellett
1955–74

Katherine Mary Knight and David Stanford Kellett were married in 1974. The big day could have been a Bruce Springsteen song. There was drinkin', marryin', lovin' and fightin'. A slaughterhouse couple at the courthouse. The roguish little groom wore a purple paisley shirt, purple flairs and tortured bangs; the bride looked sweet, if a little gawky. A tall, thin 18-year-old girl with wire-framed spectacles in a sleeveless pink dress, a bow hanging from the bodice and a man on her arm. She is a fiery, good-time local lass with a dark history and a darker future, as her new husband would discover before the night was out.

The couple arrived at the Muswellbrook courthouse on Katherine's Honda 250cc trail bike, Kellett hanging on desperately to the back. He'd recently lost his licence and anyway he was smashed. Profoundly pissed. He'd been out all night and kept drinking into the morning. It was almost 10.30 am and they were half an hour late because his mates had tried, vainly, to sober him up.

This was no *Woman's Weekly* white wedding. The two abattoir workers had opted for the $20–20 minute slap-up with a few friends from work in attendance. Kellett says the fact that he was actually marrying her had most of the town whispering that this must be a shotgun affair. She'd asked him during a lunch break at work, just as years later she'd buy a ring and announce that John Price was her fiancé. Despite their predictions she was not pregnant.

Kath and Dave made a shambolic picture standing in front of the justice of the peace. Him swaying as if the ceremony was held on a yacht, her nervous and tall. A good head taller in fact. Her height gave her an advantage, if he tried to kiss her she could lean her head back and he was left puckered up and stretching. It also meant, as he was to discover, that she could lord it over him physically. When the justice of the peace was all done, however, she leaned down to kiss him and it was official. Man and wife. Kellett and Kath. Till death, or serious physical assault, do they part . . .

From the courthouse the couple wove their way—Knight hardly ever drank and was supporting her diminutive groom—to the pub across the road, where they spent their first hours as Mr and Mrs David Kellett. There was no honeymoon. In fact, they had to be back at work the next day.

Knight thought she was in love, Kellett wasn't so sure but went ahead with it anyway. He thinks now he may have caught her on the rebound, that she raced him to the altar because there was a chance he'd get back with his ex. Still, she was a good girl, who knew how to look after a bloke, and they got on well together. She seemed to like fishing and shooting as much as him. She could skin a rabbit as good as any bloke and wasn't too fussy about his drinking or wild nature. She stood by him if things turned nasty in the pub, sometimes stepping up front and telling people to fuck off and leave her bloke alone. She was ready to back it up with her fists if necessary. A chip off the old block, Kath. A roughrider's daughter.

The wedding day dragged on. And on. Later that night, at their rented flat, the groom was called on to perform his conjugal duties and says he made a reasonable go at it. They did it three times, but the new Mrs Kellett wasn't satisfied. Her mum and dad had done it five times on their wedding night. Her mum told her that and what her mum said was gospel to Katherine. Kellett was buggered, all that rooting and 24 hours of drinking had exhausted the little fella and he rolled over to go to sleep.

—Geez, three times was enough with her!

Still, they had gone for it like rabbits during their romance. 'Ten times a day was nothin'; behind the chook shed, in the car . . .' They'd even run back to her parents' during lunch break at the abattoir, stripping off their overalls and rolling around in a lusty frenzy, shrouded in the sickly sweet smell of blood and dead animals. Bucking like bunnies. Kath had her first orgasm with Kellett and the experience frightened her a little.

But the night of their wedding her new husband was asleep and as she lay there listening to his laboured breathing she started to get worked up. It just wasn't the way the world was meant to be. Mum and Dad did it five times and she was bitterly disappointed. The new Mrs Kellett's blood was starting to boil. He knew she had a bit of temper, she was a redhead after all, but that was half the fun with Kath. She could be fiery.

Suddenly he was wrenched from sleep. She was at him, hands around his throat. Choking and shaking him. She was well worked up. Fuckin' furious.

My parents did it five times!

She was shaking the shit out of me. I was pissed. Asleep. What do you expect? I'd been drinking all fucking day.

Five fucking times!

She was shaking him like he was one of the dolls she used to play sex games with as a little girl. 'Five times!' He was shirking his duty, undermining the order of things. And at that moment they *were* like Katherine's mum and dad.

He had to get it together fast. Get the voice down into those sweet, apologetic tones. He eventually got her calm, but he had been warned: much of their ensuing marriage was dictated by what Katherine's mother, Barbara, said. In fact, Barbara Knight had given him a little advice before they fronted the courthouse.

The old girl said to me to watch out. 'You better watch this one, she'll fucking kill ya. Stir her up the wrong way or do the wrong thing and you're fucked—don't ever think of playing up on her—she'll fuckin kill ya.' And that was her mother talking!

She told me she's got something loose, she's got a screw loose somewhere.

Her mother used to tell me things, the crazy things she used to do, so headstrong and just crazy, not playing with a full deck.

Barbara told Kellett how the red-headed twin daughter could snap like a dry twig. She was prone to murderous rages that began without warning and blew over just as quickly. You had to watch that one, she had the Thorley gene that had come down from the women on Barbara's side of the family— Barb was one of the Thorleys of Muswellbrook. A tribe, like the Knights, not to be taken lightly.

Kellett wasn't the only person Barbara Knight warned about Katherine. Many years later sitting in her kitchen with Colleen Price, she offered a similar assessment. Barbara knew that this one was capable of unimaginable anger and unspeakable acts.

My daughter Rosemary was about nine, I went out there to pick her up. She was playing with Joy's kid, and we went in for a cuppa and a chat. Barbara used to make these gorgeous cakes and scones, and right out of the blue, we were talking about nothing, she said, 'Whatever you do, keep an eye on Kathy. Don't cross her'. Kathy was always weird. We were both only young then. Her birthday is the 17th, I'm the 10th.

* * *

The personality problems demonstrated in the history of Ms Knight's life are not in my view psychiatric diseases—they are her nature. These personality problems did not stop her from knowing what she was doing, or whether it was right or wrong. Nor did they stop her from exercising control of her actions ... The main effect of Ms Knight's personality probably was to cause difficulty for others. I question whether that should be regarded as an 'aberration of mind' and think, or believe, it is not, but it is probably an issue for the court to decide.

Dr Rod Milton 14.10.2001

What she did on the night was part of her personality, her nature, herself ... It is probable that she thought about doing things like that for a long time, perhaps many years ... It is more than just stabbing, cutting, the knife going in and out many, many times. The skill, the time, the focus that must have been required ...

Dr Robert Delaforce 26.10.2001

Despite the warning from his potential mother-in-law, David Kellett had little hope of knowing what sort of a girl he had married in those wild and woolly days. She was fun, she was devoted, she was sexually compliant, and she was also damaged goods. Seriously damaged. A time-bomb that would explode violently, time and again, without warning. Even before she turned 21 the path of Katherine Knight's adult relationships was laid out clearly. She would fall in love suddenly and totally, and fall out of it with equal haste and venom. It was almost guaranteed that she would have a string of kids to a string of partners. She would react with inappropriate anger to minor upsets, was impulsive and restless. Any man who took her on was in for a rollercoaster ride marked by violent outbursts, suicides, love and hate. A lot of hate and dreams of revenge.

When Barbara Knight warned Kellett about the consequences of doing the wrong thing by her little girl, there was every chance that she was speaking with more than just a mother's intuition. She knew this twin child like she knew her own damaged self. To understand her daughter you don't have to dig very deep or travel very far. The red-headed girl's secrets and fears lay buried in a shallow grave in the family's backyard, covered by a sprinkling of earth that could be disturbed by the slightest wind.

When Katherine throttled David on their wedding night because he didn't make love to her five times, she was revealing so much about her past and her future. Like all the Knight children, she knows the details of her parents' sex life because her childhood was set against a backdrop of physical conflict, overt sexual behaviour and violent sexual demands. Fucking and fighting were never far apart and sometimes there didn't seem to be any distinction.

Little Katherine Knight grew up in a home where Mum and Dad didn't lock the door and make love on Sunday morning. For a start there was very little love. And unlike most 1950s Australian families, the Knights didn't treat sex as a secret, or something to be ashamed of. Katherine's childhood memories are painful and vivid. She told psychiatrists she remembers her dad, Ken, chasing Barbara around the house demanding sex, using violence and intimidation to get his way. The kids grew up watching their horny slaughterhouse father bailing Mum up with a broom. They would see fists fly in drunken, randy rages and black eyes in the morning. There was no discretion. One visitor remembers going around to the Knight house in the 1970s—after Katherine had married and left home—and seeing Barbara with bruises on her face. 'The old cunt knocked me out for sex again' the mother of eight explained in a bitter flat tone.

Barbara wasn't the retiring type either; she could stand up for herself. And Barbara, it seems, confided in her daughters. She told Katherine how much she hated men and sex. The brutal demands. And later, when Katherine's time came and one partner upset her by insisting on anal sex, she turned to her mother for advice. Barbara told her to put up with it. Stop complaining.

Inevitably, the charged sexual atmosphere of that dysfunctional household filtered down to the children, and the boys, who began to eye their developing little sister with that same horny look Dad had. The girls began to fear the night. Katherine clung to her mother's skirts and her twin sister's hand; the only two women who could understand her fear in an aggressive, testosterone-charged male world.

Katherine Knight has two words for her childhood: sad and bad. She has attempted to draw a curtain across it, but the sinister shadow play has continued her whole life. These aren't memories that are easily suppressed. Like most victims of childhood trauma she spent the first half of her life trying to forget them and the latter half trying to deal with them. Time and again after the murder she hints at the troubles. Opens the door a crack and then closes it again.

Barry Roughan, Katherine's half-brother and Barbara's fourth child, understands something of the landscape that nurtured Kath's darkness. Driven out of Aberdeen after his half-sister, Joy, ran off with his wife, Barry offers an opinion about this slaughterhouse family's history.

—If you dig deep enough it's as grubby as all shit, our family. As grubby as shit. Mate, the family is rotten to the core.

*   *   *

Katherine Knight's mother was born Barbara Thorley, a tough talking, dirt poor Muswellbrook girl who escaped from the deprivations of home when she moved up the road to Aberdeen and married the hard drinking abattoir worker Jack Roughan in the 1940s. Every small town has a family like the Thorleys and they always have a daughter like Barbara who marries a bloke like Jack and the relationship sticks to the script as surely as water flows down a hill.

Barbara had a hard childhood. Her father left when she was young and she was raised in a small, crowded house with an extended family. They were poor and her mother struggled to put food on the table. One of Kath's siblings remembers Mum saying that as a child she was never 'loved or cuddled or nursed—her mum was busy and there was no time or room for affection or love'. There is a suggestion that Barbara was sexually abused by relatives. At one stage she found herself in a home for wayward girls. The traumas of Mum's youth were something her kids were aware of, but not something Barbara went into great detail about. There was too much sadness.

Barb was hurt so much as a child and a teenager. She had some very bad things happen to her within her wider family; she was abused and she was in a girls' home and was run around a bit. She never talked about it much. She mentioned it sometimes in passing, but you knew it was always there.

Locals remember Barbara as highly strung and foul mouthed. She was a woman you didn't cross. She was physically sturdy, but mentally fragile. On a number of occasions she was hospitalised for her 'nerves'. She told her children (and others like Colleen Price and David Kellett) that there was a madness running through the female side of her family. It was something she recognised in Katherine.

Barbara would say, according to her moods, that she was part Aboriginal. Sometimes she told the family they were descended from a Maori princess. Other times Mum would tell the kids that their great-great-grandmother was an indigenous woman from the Moree area and their great-great-grandfather was an Irishman. 'When she was feeling good we were Aboriginal. She knew all along, she just didn't say. There was a lot of racism in those days. It was a secret if it was in your family.' Even today in Aberdeen, people might whisper to you that so and so has got a bit of Aboriginal blood, as though it might explain certain behaviour. When Katherine's first granddaughter was born the family sat around and made jokes about her 'little boong nose'. Somebody even suggested they call her Little Boong.

Barbara's first husband, Jack Roughan, was the manager of the Aberdeen abattoir's pig farm—a job he'd inherited from his father. When the pig farm closed Jack got a job inside the abattoir. He was older than Barbara and sired four boys with his young bride in the first ten years of marriage. Old-timers can remember the family being raised in the barracks, an extended boarding house type arrangement for the meat-workers.

Later, they moved to a small worker's cottage near the abattoir. Barbara became increasingly unhappy. Her husband, they say, drank too much and gambled away his money. The last two boys, Neville and Barry, were born in quick succession. Raising four kids in a rough cottage was not easy and the marriage ended in sensational circumstances. With the youngest, Barry, only a few months old and Neville not even two, Barbara took up with another tough young abattoir worker, Ken Knight.

The Knights were legend in Aberdeen. Ken's father, Charlie, maintained the council's water supply before the Glenbawn Dam was built and rode about town on a horse to do his job. There were a lot of sons and most of them, Ken included, became well-known roughriders, hurling their bodies about on the backs of buck-jumping horses and rodeo bulls. The old family home sat like a pimple on your nose in a hollow next to the outdoor cinema on the main street of town, across from the barber, tailor and pool hall. The Knight boys were a tough lot and you didn't mess with them.

Some say that Barbara Roughan was driven into Ken Knight's arms by Jack Roughan's drunken, neglectful ways. Others say they just fell in love. It depends on which side of the family you listen to. Even today adultery still manages to raise an eyebrow in most circles, but in old-world rural Australia, in a fly-speck community like Aberdeen, the affair between Barbara Roughan and Ken Knight was an enormous scandal. It's a town small enough for everybody to know everybody and the story of Ken and Barbara's elopement is still remembered half a century later. Katherine and her siblings grew up knowing there was talk about them and scandals past. Katherine acted like she didn't care, but in truth she always carried baggage about issues of paternity and fidelity.

It must have been impossible for Ken Knight to keep

working at the same place as Jack Roughan and so he and Barbara decided to get away from the heat and headed up to Gunnedah where he got a job as a butcher in the meatworks. The Roughan family was torn apart by their mother's affair. Some say the church stepped in and forced Barbara to hand over her two youngest to Jack's family; others says she just left the four behind. Whatever happened, Barbara's four boys were split up. Patrick and Martin were left with their dad and ran wild, raising hell around the paddocks and streets of Aberdeen. Barry and Neville were raised in Sydney by an aunt on his father's side and were schooled in the Roughan contempt for Barbara. Barbara was soon pregnant with a child to Ken. Kenneth Charles Knight (he was obviously named after his father and grandfather, but they called him Charlie) was born less than a year after his half-brother Barry Roughan.

Joy Gwendoline and Katherine Mary were born in Tamworth Hospital in October 1955. Two girls to complement the five older boys. In just over five years Barbara had given birth to five children in quick succession.

In June 1957 Jack Roughan died. On top of his drinking, Jack, like many in those days, consumed Bex Powders with abandon. Family lore is divided over whether it was the grog or the medicine that killed him. He died of hypertension, leaving his two motherless sons, Patrick and Martin, now fatherless. With Jack's death, the two Roughan boys moved back to be with their mother in Gunnedah, while the two younger boys remained in Sydney. Barbara Knight suddenly had five kids on her hands, with two more farmed out to relatives. Katherine says that her mother told her Ken was an alcoholic in those days, which can't have made family life any easier. To make matters worse, he didn't seem to appreciate the stepsons being around.

After the twins, Barbara Knight gave birth to one last son,

Shane, and was done. The eight kids had taken a toll on her nerves and life with Ken and the kids around the house was always a little fraught. Both parents were strict disciplinarians and had nasty tempers. According to two of the sons, Ken was especially hard on Patrick and Martin, his two stepsons. Patrick had worked in the abattoir at Gunnedah and then did his national service before coming back to Moree.

Around this time Neville Roughan came up to visit his mother from Sydney and decided to stay. He and his brother Barry had never had much to do with her during the first fifteen years of their lives. Although Ken was a little more receptive at this time to the children of his wife's first husband, one friend remembers him punching out Neville after he gave his new stepfather a bit of lip. The roughrider was never shy with his fists when it came to the boys or Barbara, but according to the kids she gave back almost as good as she got. There was constant sexual and physical tension between the two from the time they met until she died. Ken demanded sex like it was a bad debt. One visitor remembers him chasing his wife up and down the corridor in the last year of her life. 'Give us a root, come on, fuck ya, give us a root.'

The kids had to keep their heads down while the parents went for it. Hammer and tongs.

Barbara was the softer one, but she could be equally hard on the kids and didn't put up with any nonsense. She told you something once and if you needed to be told twice you suffered the consequences. She liked a neat house and the children all had to make the beds so tight that a five cent piece could be bounced on them. If the five cent piece didn't bounce she stripped your bed and you had to start again. It didn't take long to learn the lesson.

Barbara wasn't an affectionate woman. She was damaged and, like her mother before her, she couldn't show the children much love. A son remembers her cringing away from his hugs. It frustrated the children. Especially Katherine, who craved her mother's love and complained that she didn't get it. She always believed that Joy was the family favourite.

When Katherine has spoken about her childhood, she hasn't recalled the good times. She remembers her childhood through a fog of misery and violence. *I used to get belted a lot but I can't remember the beltings.*

Katherine says she does not remember her parents saying they loved her. Family members recall she would become depressed at times, worrying and fretting. She had a vicious temper and had to be held back when she lost her cool. At other times she and Joy were carefree and self-contained. The kids stuck together. Life can't have been all bad and children are pretty resilient. Living in the country they made their own fun. The older brothers paid the girls to clean their rooms and would look out for their sisters. The girls remained best friends all their lives—young Katherine failed to make many strong relationships outside the family.

The Knights lived in a run-down old home on Boston Street in Moree that had been divided into two flats. They lived in one half, with rough furnishings and not enough rooms. The verandahs had been converted into extra bedrooms when somebody nailed up some timber and corrugated iron to keep the weather out. It was a forbidding place and the kids who went to school with Katherine and Joy can remember the home had a chilling atmosphere.

Her mother and father weren't loving, they didn't seem to care for the kids or take any notice of them. Even if there wasn't an argument going on in the place you could still slice the air in there with a knife. You could smell the violence. It was a terrible atmosphere. There just seemed to be no love.

As a small girl, Katherine was close to Ken's brother Oscar Knight, another champion roughrider. In 1969 Oscar shot himself. He was only 34 years old. Katherine was devastated. It was her first experience of death and it terrified her to think someone she loved could be taken away from her. Later she said she wished it had been her father because she loved Oscar more. She has kept items owned by the uncle with her all her life and says he appeared to her as a ghost. Sometimes she says he was an angel.

People who knew the twins said they would do anything to gain some attention, good or bad, because they were neglected by their parents. When they started at Moree High School the two long, thin, red-headed girls immediately attracted attention for their violence.

If there was a fight in the playground it was usually either Kathy or Joy, but it was more likely to be Kathy and she would fight anyone. She wouldn't go looking for fights but she never ever backed down.

The twins used to fight each other with a viciousness that left the other kids at school cringing in fear. Katherine never seemed happy and always wore a threatening frown. One school mate remembers an argument between Katherine and Joy over who would ride and who would push their one bicycle.

Suddenly, they were at it, throwing punches like men. It was frightening. They were always together because they didn't have a lot of friends, but they fought like cats and dogs ... but if somebody fought Kath, Joy would be in there to help out and vice versa.

Katherine was a nightmare for her class teachers; she refused to do anything she was told and was always in trouble.

Katherine claims in interviews that she was the victim of repeated sexual abuse from within the family and some of the psychiatrists who have treated her accept this, although there is room for minor doubts. Most of the incidents appear to have happened when the family lived in Moree. She says two of her brothers abused her. She says the older brother would spit on his fingers and rub her vagina. She has trouble remembering the exact details.

She told the psychiatrist Dr Leonard Lambeth she remembered *his body climbing on top of me, and that's all. He reckons he stopped when I was six, but I remember him touching me when he was in the Army,* which apparently makes her seven or older.

I grew up all my life knowing them two have touched me.

Psychiatrist Robert Delaforce spent two days with Knight in June 2000. She painted a bleak picture of her youth. Although everything she told the psychiatrists in this period has to be seen as self-serving others confirm elements of what she says. Katherine was eager to portray herself as a victim. She claimed little memory of her childhood and found it difficult to discuss it, but she said her childhood was spoiled by physical violence and sexual tensions. Ken, she said, was brutal to all the children and her mother, forcing her to have sex with him. She says her father accused her of procuring men for her mother.

Katherine wet the bed until she was 11 years old—around the time the sexual abuse stopped. She was afraid of the dark and kept a doll that protected her.

One doll used to protect me. I was scared at night, they wouldn't let me have a light on.

I thought there was something wrong with me and that all boils down to my brothers touching me . . . I played with my dolls and things like that a lot. I had one doll I carried everywhere with me. It used to protect me ... Mine was like gold to me. It meant more to me than anything in the world, I suppose.

In the late 1990s Kath's cousin, Brian Conlon, moved in with her brother Charlie in Muswellbrook. Brian is almost a member of the family and has known the Roughans and Knights for most of his life. Kath's kids call him uncle Brian. He remembers Katherine dropping into her brother's for a chat about once a month. On one occasion she came by with her second eldest daughter, Natasha, and started asking Charlie if he knew anything about her being molested as a child.

Conlon thought that his cousin didn't know if she had been or not. Charlie told her she had. Today Charlie admits his family has dark secrets. He wanted $50 000 to tell the story, 'because what I know will mean I got to leave town'. Another sibling was also reluctant to talk about sexual abuse in the family. 'I can't really say. That's one of those questions I won't answer, it cuts too deep, just explaining it would ...' The sentence was too hard to complete.

Katherine's eldest daughter, Melissa, was willing to relay what her mother had told her about the sexual abuse she suffered as a child. She told the police:

I can recall from talking to Mum when I was 12 years old, she told me that she had been sexually molested by her half-brother ... Mum told me that this abuse was constant from when she was between the ages of five to nine years.

I also recall talking with Mum when I went to see her in Sydney about two weeks ago. I confronted Mum about things that I had been told by other family members. I told Mum that I had been told that Uncle Charlie Knight had also molested her when she was young. Mum said to me, 'Don't blame Uncle Charlie. He was too young. He was brought into it by . . .' This was upsetting for Mum and she did not want to talk about it further.

Melissa says now that Charlie discovered his sister being abused by his elder brother and was convinced to join in 'the game' by the older boy. Katherine says she told her sister Joy that she too was assaulted in a similar manner. In a statement to police, her twin said this:

> Kath has told me something about being sexually abused when she was very young, about five or six years old. It was by a family member, but I don't really want to talk about that.

Dr Milton, who examined her after the murder, casts some doubts on the veracity of Knight's claims of sex abuse because she cannot remember the details. He believes that victims of sexual assault rarely suffer suppressed memory. In fact, most crave to forget what happened to them. Still, there seems to be enough smoke to suggest that there was a fire.

*   *   *

The Knight family left Moree and made the move back to Aberdeen for good in the late 1960s when the girls were about 12 years old. They moved into a house in 35 McAdam Street when Katherine was at high school. It was a former abattoir property. They kept chooks and a couple of Ken's greyhounds in the backyard. Kath recalls around this time being belted with the dog lead and protected from her father by her mother, but she also remembers being belted by her mother with a jug cord. One visitor remembers a piece of wood above the door which was referred to as the killing stick. It was for disciplining the children.

Katherine's relationship with her father has remained volatile throughout her life. She says he hit her in sixth class and that he was charged with assaulting her many years later. In September 1984 she attended the local doctor with a bruise over her left breast which she claims was caused by her father.

> I know it gets me very emotional where he's concerned. I can't handle him ... I just remember him violent to Mum ... Dad used to bash Mum all the time. A lot of violence there but I can't remember it. Lots of little bits, and I was always afraid of being raped.

She said that she has a memory of Ken trying to get into her bed after her mother refused to have sex with him, but she never claimed he sexually abused her. However, her fear of rape, which clearly evolved from these early traumas, seemed to develop into a paranoia that manifested itself on many occasions. Katherine was forever making allegations that men had or wanted to abuse her children. None of these allegations was ever substantiated, but the fears were terribly real in her own mind, no matter how trivial or malicious they looked to anybody else. Katherine viewed all men as possible sex offenders where her daughters were concerned. *They rape them. They abuse them. They're helpless,* she told psychiatrists.

After shifting back to Aberdeen, Katherine had a lot of trouble with schooling. Locals remember she was a bully who stood over smaller kids. She was something of a loner who didn't fit in well and only mixed with her immediate family. All the kids knew about the Knights and were willing to give her a wide berth. She is said to have assaulted one boy at school with a bamboo pole. One teacher beat Katherine so hard she left bruises and Barbara came to the school to see what was wrong. The mother was sent away with the news that her daughter was uncontrollable, which was no news to her. Barry Roughan says his sister was *the wild one of the family*. However, she remembers washing the cups for teachers and getting lollies for being good. It appears Katherine didn't have as much difficulty in her early years at school as her later ones, which Dr Rod Milton, who interviewed her for the trial, said could indicate social rather than intellectual problems.

> Her personality problems were likely to interfere with her ability to concentrate, to relate to teachers and to other students, and resulted in her having very poor scholastic attainments, leading to the impressions that she was intellectually lacking.

Katherine managed to leave Muswellbrook High at the age of 15 without having learned to read or write, which wasn't that unusual. If you weren't a farm kid there was little else to do in Aberdeen than work at the abattoirs and Katherine was keen to follow in the footsteps of her father, her twin sister and older brothers. You didn't need a lot of education to wield a knife and Aberdeen kids knew that. It was part of the natural flow of things: fill in time at school until you're old enough to work at the abattoirs. One of Katherine's brothers learned to read the newspaper during lunch breaks at work, under the tutelage of a better educated colleague.

Katherine suffered an initial setback when she first applied and failed to get a job at the meatworks, so she took up work as a cutter-presser at a clothes factory for twelve months before finally getting a position in the offal room at the age of 16. She was in heaven, following in the family tradition and doing a job she loved.

Her job was towards the end of the chain or line and involved cleaning congealed marrow and blood out of the carcasses and cutting the animals into smaller pieces. Later she became a boner and the story is she was a mean hand with a blade. The best bit about the abattoir was she got her own set of knives. They were her pride and joy.

And it's here, among the blood and guts and gumboots that Katherine met the lovable rascal, David Kellett.

The young girl that set out on her first serious relationship brought with her a sordid collection of family images. And the teenage girl that rode to the courthouse with her husband on the back of her trail bike was spiritually and psychologically corrupted. She was anxious, tortured by phobias about sex and violence; she could not connect with the real world; she didn't understand love; she could never be stable in a relationship or deal with her problems. She was prone to violence and discord. Even though she would send her children to Sunday school and care for sick neighbours, she was a girl with the brittlest moral constructs. Katherine grew up with a void where love should have been; a place where evil could take seed.

Poor David Kellett. He was too drunk to realise.

Kellett was a hell-raiser in his younger days, a pint-sized torpedo they called Shorty or Ching, because he looked Chinese (it was short for Ching Chong Chinaman, a relic of less politically correct times). He was cute and could charm your pants off in a blink. Had a few run-ins with the cops, and the old sergeant still shudders when he hears the name, but that was par for the course for a young country bloke in those days. Hell, it was the 1970s. A time of weed and rock festivals, rootin' and cutting loose. He'd hit Aberdeen full of testosterone and an energy that possibly verged on the self-destructive. A little bloke with swagger and a job on the railways. He had been shunted down the tracks for falling asleep and derailing too many trains up around the Coffs Harbour area. They were glad to see the back of him. Dave was a long hair. A troublemaker.

He'd had a rough time in the job before he got to Aberdeen. At Grafton he'd supported the crushed body of one of his best mates who had got caught between the couplings of two carriages in a shunting accident. He was still conscious but was not in a good way. They brought the bloke's wife down, but when they pulled the carriages apart the man died. Another time he was just knocking off at South Kempsey railway crossing when a train hit a school bus at 4 pm, 9 December 1968. Kellett spent the next hours pulling school girls' broken bodies from the wreckage. Six were dead. Looking back he thinks the shock of the accident might account for the amount of drinking he did as a young bloke.

> You'd go to sleep and you'd hear the crash ... the sound of screeching brakes would scare the wits out of you. After that I just drank so much, sometimes I'd even drink after a shave. There was no counselling in those days, they just gave you a week off.

The railway job at Muswellbrook fell through because he got into trouble with the cops once too often, so he got himself a job at the abattoir in Aberdeen. There was nowhere else. At work Kellett fell in with a local, Charlie Knight, and they'd get on the piss big time on the weekends. Three-night binges, starting on Friday and staggering through until Monday morning, when they'd have to get their shit together for another stint in the slaughterhouse.

One night Charlie took him home for tea to his parents' place. His twin sisters, Kath and Joy, were 16 at the time. All

four started to hang out together. They'd have big nights at
the Muswellbrook Workers Club, where there was pool, darts,
music and all the limited fun of a country town on the
weekend. The girls knew how to have a good time. Both of
them swore like troopers and liked it a bit rough. There was
nothing pony club about the Knight girls. Kellett had been
shacked up with another girl around this time and when that
dissolved young Katherine was there waiting. 'People said I
got her on the rebound and I guess I probably did.'

Kellett was as close to Joy as he was Kath and would often
go out with one or the other. Even when he and Kath started
dating it was nothing to spend the night dancing with her
sister. One night Kellett got locked up for being drunk and
disorderly and found out in the morning from the copper
that his future sister-in-law had been in the next cell for dou-
bling on her motorbike.

Other times the four would head out to the Glenbawn
Dam and camp, go after the catfish at night or maybe do a bit
of shooting, get a rabbit or a 'roo. Sometimes they'd take pot-
shots at a passing train, although there'd been a bit of trouble
over that. It's strange how things that seem funny when you're
pissed really get up the cops' noses. One time somebody
knocked off a steer and Kellett cut it up with a chainsaw for a
barbecue. Kath insisted he skin it too; she was keen to have a
cow hide and loved all that sort of stuff: hides, skulls, horns.
When the farmer found out he called the cops and it got
serious. Kellett was on a bond over another incident and he
was going to go down but the local copper gave him a break
and didn't inform the magistrate about the bond. That way he
had one over Shorty and could maybe keep him under control a bit.

In those days Kellett, like most young blokes, figured he
was indestructible. Maybe he was. Easter 1973, he, Charlie

and another local were out shooting rabbits on a belly full of grog. Bullets starting flying everywhere. The details are sketchy, but it seems the other guy shot Kellett, smashing his shoulder blade and depositing shrapnel just above the heart. Charlie and the other bloke wrapped him up in a blanket, put him on the back seat of the car and rushed to the cop shop to get help. Kellett lay on the back seat, bleeding like a stuck pig and asking for beer and a cigarette. The copper, a sergeant called Lloyd Lyne, told him he'd been watching too many cowboy movies. To this day Kellett remains a big John Wayne fan and still keeps the piece of shrapnel close to his heart— the doctors weren't game to remove it. He's got a full set of John Wayne commemorative plates on display in his home too.

He recalls another time when he and one of the local coppers got pissed and played Russian roulette with a pistol. You can be pretty stupid as a young bloke, stepping up to the edge and poking the hereafter in the chest. Have a fuckin' go! Then, when the years have passed and it's stalking you, you lie in bed at night and think about the hammer falling and break into a cold shiver.

Somehow Kellett and the young cop survived that stupidity.

Young Katherine Knight stood by him as he raised hell. After all, her brothers were pretty wild and you wouldn't expect her to take up with the local bank teller. She got pretty worried when he was sentenced to five years in East Maitland Jail around 1972, but celebrated when he got out early on appeal. Years later, when she was jailed herself, their daughter showed him a scrapbook his young wife had kept of his brushes with the law at the time. He'd never seen it when they'd been together. She adored Kellett. Loved his notoriety and cheeky attitude.

Later Katherine told people they weren't in love when they got married; it was just that she didn't want to be left on the shelf. People grow up fast in country towns, babies have babies, and at 18 Kath was older than a lot of others. However, Kellett knew how to treat a woman well; he'd been brought up by his mother to show respect and on occasions did. It was something of a novelty to Katherine who'd never heard a bloke sweet-talk a woman before. Where she came from they demanded a root and got it. Five times on the wedding night, for God's sake! Dave had a gentle side and she liked that. She'd buy him presents, chocolates and beer. From the day they were married she took over the finances and she was real careful with their money. Still, there was room for the odd little treat. Sometimes he got a bottle of cheap scotch.

Kellett had worked on the killing floor when he first landed at the abattoir but got bumped from there for growing marijuana under the manager's office. He was transferred to the offal room. It was a foul place where the bags, or stomachs, came down the chute and needed to be inverted and cleaned. He'd much preferred the other job where he was responsible for stunning the animals before their throats were cut. That was a real buzz.

Katherine loved the knives and the camaraderie and the death. She had been happy to skin a rabbit when they went camping, like one of the boys, and the blood, guts and noise of the abattoir didn't worry her one single bit. And while she didn't have many mates there, all the Knights worked alongside each other. It was a family affair.

Later, she told a psychiatrist she loved talking to an old man whose job it was to stick the pigs with a knife and bleed them to death.

The slaughterhouse isn't for everybody, but some people get a kick out of that work. Young Dave Kellett certainly enjoyed it.

I was in charge of killing pigs for about twelve months. I had a big stun gun, a glove that fitted on your hand. It was leather with a trigger and two prongs and the pig would come down the race and you'd put it behind the ear and you'd keep it on until it knocked them out. If I had a pig that was giving me the shits I'd keep it on until it killed 'em, then they'd get shackled up before being stuck with a big knife.

Sometimes they'd shake off the shackles if I hadn't stunned them enough. You'd have to push 'em back with pipe and use the endless chain and then they go to the big boiler, but [Katherine] was in the next room over in the boning and slicing room.

I enjoyed doing it, I loved doing the pigs, watching them shake like shit, frothing at the mouth and [their] eyes rolling in the sockets.

We'd go rabbit shooting, me and Kath and her brother Charlie, just behind Ken's place and we'd come home with a dozen or so rabbits and she'd sit down beside us and skin 'em. She'd skin 'em as good as anyone, pick 'em up by the legs and pull. It was animals first and then she graduated to humans. She never did skinning at the meatworks; all she did was cut the fat off.

It was a marriage made on the killing floor and consummated in a night of fucking and fighting. Little Kath was over the moon. It was all she'd ever dreamed of. Almost.

Abandoned and anguished
1974–81

Katherine's wielding a crutch at a one-legged man. She's got a suitcase full of knives and scissors and bandages and money boxes. She's smashing windows and she says she's gonna kill the family huddled inside the service station. Whimpering among the broken glass. Says she'll cut them up because they ran away. If only she could have found the gun. The boy with asthma is watching from across the road. Petrified.

—The crazy lady is going to kill us. Where are the police? Somebody please help us.

The gun was on the verandah but it's not there now. Where the fuck is it? She's already slashed the girl. There's so fucking many of 'em. Nicked her cheek like she nicks the arteries of animals and watches them bleed. Yesterday she took on the town with an axe. That had them running for cover. She'll get this mob, cut them up. Get the one-legged prick too. He fixed the car. He knew the bastard was leaving her. The knife was under the blankets in the bassinette. The girl ran, stumbled and then ran for her life. She told the nurses at the hospital she was going to do the job right this time. She's gonna get Kellett's mum too. She's got a knife and she's got this bug-eyed little fellow by the footy jumper and the police are coming at her now with broom sticks. She's planned this. Lain awake at night plotting. Made sure nobody was home to hear the cries for help. If only she could have found that rifle she'd have been away by now.

David Kellett is gone. Done a runner. And Katherine's distress comes in hot waves of anger and anguish. She's unhappy and unhinged. Incensed.

Everything is just so out of control.

There's been sirens and police and psychiatric hospitals and there's a southbound train coming down the railway line and the baby is lying in its path. Lying there where a few decades later a young bloke loses his life after a night on the grog. They say he was asleep, or he fell and hit his head. Anyway, the train just came and ran him over. This time old Ted's wandered down and found the little thing lying on the tracks. Little Melissa. Ted picked her up and saved her life.

Ted had a plate in his head and worked at the abattoir for a while. Everybody in the town remembers old Ted and everybody in the town knows the story of Katherine putting her baby in front of the train. Just a few months old she was. Some say her mum tied her down. Everybody in town knows the story except Kath, who says it's not true. Maybe she took her by the ankles and spun her round and round. She don't remember, but that's what they reckon. They also say she put her pram in front of a parked truck.

And now the police are here again.

—Let the boy go. Drop the knife. Kathy, drop the knife.

—Don't take me back to the hospital again. Please don't take me back to hospital. I won't go.

Melissa has slept through it all, through the screaming and smashing glass, unbearable sorrow and madness. Years later, when she wakes up and hears the story, Mum denies it, starts to talk about pyjamas and anything but trains. Melissa knows when her mother is lying.

Everything is just so out of control.

Everything is just so bloody sad and tragic and veiled behind a crimson curtain of rage, so it's hard to see where it all started and where it all finished. Hard to know whether to cry or kill. The only thing everybody knows is that hell has no fury like Katherine scorned and Katherine has been scorned. Just when it all seemed so perfect. A nice little house, a nice little baby, a nice little loving husband. Got a job and place of her own and she wasn't left on the shelf like she feared. She's even been learning to cook a little. Got away from home and started on her own. Now this. Home is where the heartbreak is. There's nothing more certain. She's not even 21 and she's been abandoned. A single mother. She hates that baby. That's why he left. He wanted a boy. If only she were dead things might be right again.

* * *

The wedding night histrionics gave David Kellett some hint of what lay ahead. He'd already had a taste of Katherine's formidable sex drive, which was something he could handle. What young bloke couldn't? If you had a goer you thanked your lucky stars and Dave had a goer on his hands all right. Yet there was this idea she had that everything had to be done the way Barbara had done it. If Ken and Barbara fucked five times on the wedding night then they had to too. Things were always done the way Ma Knight said or there was hell to pay. That was a lesson that was reinforced with bruises on young limbs. You didn't give any lip back to Ken or Barb. Hell no. And now she does as they did. Forget the fact that this was the

1970s, a decade after the generation gap had apparently appeared. Barbara said a man should hang out the washing. Dave hung out the washing. She said a woman controlled the money. Kath controlled the money. Knickers were never to be hung on the outside of the line. Dave learned that lesson very early and was always careful about that. It sent her right off if you got the little things like that wrong.

She was paranoid about her knickers, you had to hang them inside the line surrounded by her other clothes. You couldn't hang them on the outside of the line. She was paranoid over that. If I hung clothes upside down or the wrong way she would rave and rant, scream and yell.

Kath turned to her mother for counsel on all manner of things, right down to the nitty gritty of the bedroom. 'She told her mother I was nothing short of an animal in bed—she confided in her mother with anything,' Kellett recalls.

Dave started having problems with this little matter of what he came to term her 'psychotic ways'. As the years went by the little bloke noticed his young bride's ability to switch from apparent equanimity to murderous rage in the blink of an eye. And then back again. Every time it was like a bomb blast. Glass shattered in nearby windows, eardrums popped and furniture shattered. Then she'd dust herself off and pretend like nothing ever happened. Maybe even buy you a nice present to make up for it. Oh, and gave you a wild ride in the sack too. That always took the edge off things.

It didn't take Dave long to realise he'd chained himself to a pit bull and when its moods turned to black he would be the closest thing to its snapping jaws.

Poor Shorty ended up, as his dear old mum said, 'wrapped around her little finger'. If not there, then on the end of her fists. At times he was like a clown with an enraged rodeo bull. He had placed himself in the line of attack and sometimes seemed to be doing his damnedest to provoke it. Egg her on. Ask her for one when she was worked up. And she towered over him, always having a crack at his head.

The first two years were good, plenty of fucking and fighting, camping and carousing. She was one of the boys and loved to get out and have a good time.

Kellett has fond memories of the early days. They lived in Muswellbrook before shifting up to Aberdeen, where he bought a house near the railway tracks on Short Street with money from his family. It wasn't much of a street, just a dirt track that ran off the highway. Between the road and the railway line near the top pub. You turned off at the service station near the silos. There were only two or three other houses there.

You had the trucks on the highway and the coal trains on the other side, but it was a quiet little cul-de-sac and it was theirs. You could pick up chunks of coal from the tracks for the fire and grain from the silos for the chooks. That saved a few bucks.

She was good company, she could be very, very loving—a marriage made in heaven. She could be so nice, buy me chocolate out of the blue, buy me a beer, always buy me a beer. Prefer me to drink at home rather than go out.

Maybe her young groom's idea of heaven doesn't quite tally with the one promised in the Bible, but he'd married a willing sexual partner and a good companion.

Sometimes when things got hot he'd get a backhander, but he says, and she confirms, he never hit back. It wasn't in his make-up to hit women; he'd been raised properly. He'd walk away or give her a cheeky line to square up.

—How's about a fuck?

—Go pull ya'self.

Kellett learned, like the others, that Katherine's explosions had a regular bonus for partners. To make amends she would turn on her sexual charm.

> She'd get down on her knees and look up at you with those loving eyes as if butter wouldn't melt in her mouth and she'd be so sorry. Everything would be right after that.

Katherine was learning the art of manipulation, learning to control others by fear or favour. A little present or a knife to the throat. A fuck or a fight. Whatever worked best. Emotionally stunted though she might be, she was cunning. And, she had learned to like the power fear gave her. It was something she knew at home and probably developed at school. A way to keep the smart kids down, to fend off the teasing.

Kellett was even more unsettled by her affection for her abattoir knives. She cherished them and wouldn't let him go anywhere near them. When they'd had a flat in Muswellbrook, Katherine went for them for the first time in his presence. The bloke in the flat next-door had pig dogs for hunting and if there was one thing she hated it was barking dogs. One day when Kellett was at work they really started to yap. She got herself into a right state before picking up the knives and heading over to sort them out. She was infuriated. She confronted the bloke and told him she'd 'cut their fucking throats' if they didn't stop. It was a big call; these were hunting dogs that would have made it pretty tough for her to get anywhere near them, but she wasn't being rational at the time. The bloke let her rant for a while and she left. He waited for Kellett to get home and told him the next time his missus came around threatening him he'd loose the dogs on her.

Kellett had the odd beer with him and they got over it. It was a woman's thing. Didn't come between the blokes. He didn't think too much about the incident. Barking dogs gave him the shits too. Still, she loved those knives.

The slightest little thing could send her off. It could be watching a TV program on the news or the next-door neighbour's dog barking and then she would just snap, totally snap and just throw something through the window at the dog—the closest thing at hand. It might be a fry pan, it might be a cup, anything, it wouldn't matter and then she'd be just . . . so calm. I always thought it would be something she would grow out of.

She was obsessed with those fucking knives from the moment she got 'em. She wouldn't ever let me use 'em. They were her life.

Later on she did cut a dog's throat. A little dingo pup. But that was another bloke. Another episode. Anyway, she said, he asked for it.

Kath was developing a menacing air. A worker at the meatworks remembers she used to nick the arteries on the animals to watch them bleed. She was a bit of a loner there, mainly mixed with her family, but there was one time in the packing room when she held another woman up with a knife. Held it to her throat. That was crossing the line big time. If there was one code among the workers, it was that you were careful with your knives and if there was a fight they were never raised. Too many people took bad cuts from slight accidents, just brushing one of those blades could open you right up. You had to respect them, but not Kath. She loved those bloody knives.

Mavis Paulger, Kellett's mother, remembers the first time she met Katherine the girl admitted to her new mother-in-law that she couldn't cook. Mrs Paulger was impressed by her honesty. She noted the thin young woman was fairly subdued, but apparently in control of her son and the family monies. The mother-in-law remembers the couple were very proud of the house at Short Street that she and her husband had helped them buy. Kath controlled the family purse and would walk a long way to save a couple of cents. She was a bit of a spendthrift and over the years developed a pawing love of money. That first time Mrs Paulger came down to visit, she went with Kath to her family home and Barbara told her the girl didn't know how to boil water and had never learned to cook. Her mum was wondering what they'd been eating at Short Street. Mavis tried to help and taught the young girl a little homecraft while she was at it. All the time wondering what sort of upbringing lets a young woman loose on the world without the ability to boil water.

During that visit Barbara told Kellett's mother that there was a wild streak running through the female side of the family. And, while it appeared to have missed Joy, it was as wide as the Hunter Valley in Katherine.

A visit to the Knight clan was something of an eye-opener for Mrs Paulger: her son had certainly chosen a colourful group of in-laws for himself. Hillbillies is what the Americans would call them. There was just a strange air about the place. Too many men.

After a year together, he and Kath decided they were ready to start a family and so she went off the pill. She was 19 when she got knocked up, spent her twentieth birthday vomiting. She had a lot of trouble with morning sickness. It knocked her about almost every time, but before she'd gone full term the world had started to turn away. Dave was starting to wander around town. 'I had a few morals in the early days of our marriage. I remained faithful up until she was four months pregnant.'

Although it seems she didn't know at the time, Kath had her suspicions. She was an intensely jealous girl who would grow into an intensely jealous woman. There were dark clouds gathering in the ranges, but nobody could have foretold just how long and fierce this storm would be, except Barbara, who had clearly warned Kellett of the consequences of playing around.

Strange things started to happen close to the birth of the child. While Katherine was in Muswellbrook hospital the house caught fire. Kellett was asleep in bed and got a little burnt before escaping. He didn't smoke in bed and there was no sign of an electrical fault. The police suspected arson. It looked like somebody might have kicked something through the back door. Many years later the whole place would burn down. Katherine was edgy and suspicious. Dave was cagey and nervous.

Melissa Ann Kellett was born 11 May 1976. Two days after Mother's Day, but close enough to make it a special thing for Katherine. There was some argument over the name, but Kellett won out and the girl was named Melissa Ann Kellett. Melissa was a girl he knew. Later Kath and her family would say he put on a right turn at the hospital because he wanted a boy, saying he turned the air blue with his language. He says the only argument was over naming the child. Whatever happened, it did not bode well for the first-time parents. This should have been a happy time but there were thunder claps and lightning in the distance.

A first-time mother can do it pretty tough, but Melissa's first months were very difficult for Katherine, who became more paranoid about her husband and his absences. She suspected something was going on and began to rumble. They were arguing and separated for a while. He seemed toey. She was getting agitated. She could sense something. Then, in early July, when the baby was only seven weeks old, things got really heated. There was an argument and she tried to stab him with a broken beer bottle. Or something like that. It's all become confused. Kellett sent her off to her parents, who gave her a gob full. She could be a mad bitch, the brothers would say. Kellett decided to escape. Life was just getting too hairy.

He planned it carefully, unwilling to face her with the news. 'She would've fucking killed me, I could never have told her.'

He gave in his notice to the manager at the abattoir, swearing him to secrecy about his plans and then jumped into his HR Holden 186 with his new girlfriend before anybody knew anything. Melissa was just two months old, Kath was 20. Dave had had the car fixed up at the local service station before he left; it was just at the end of Short Street, about 50 metres from the house. Old Hoppy Sullivan had done the job for him. And then he was in the car, checking the rear vision mirror as he raced up through the mountains toward Queensland.

I left her a note saying I was leaving ... I couldn't stand her mood swings, her psychotic ways.

I didn't set out to deliberately have an affair; I got sick of ... her psychotic ways, the mood swings. She could be as calm as Hannibal Lecter and then she could go into a frenzy and smash, it wouldn't matter what, and then she'd say sorry the next day.

I told her parents. Her mother told me she'll hunt me down.

And, in a way, she did. Katherine was crazy with despair. Broken and angry. Veering madly between the two states. Dave reckons she told the cops he was going to Queensland and he was carrying drugs. They stopped him and pulled the car to pieces at Wallangarra on the border but found nothing. If dobbing him into the cops was Katherine's attempt at pay-back it was half-hearted. However, her emotional turmoil was anything but. She was hysterical. Abandoned and anguished. A scorned woman. Ken and Barbara tried to help her, but even they couldn't cope. She was carting the knives around, talking nonsense and threatening to kill Melissa. They knew she could be like this, but this time it was real bad. Even Barbara couldn't get her back on the leash.

One day she went completely berserk. The police were called and she was admitted to St Elmos Psychiatric Hospital in Tamworth. She'd been saying she was going to kill Melissa. There were rumours she had swung her around by her ankles. She told the doctors she'd tried to stab Kellett with a beer bottle. He'd left her. Katherine was admitted to the hospital on a Schedule 2 because she was dangerous to others and not under proper care and control. She said she would kill her-self. They found her agitated and depressed and kept her there for two weeks. They treated her with antidepressants and then sent her home.

What else could you do? She was sad and angry, but she wasn't mad and over time she calmed down. There's no slot for people like this. You can't keep them in a straight jacket just in case. Katherine clearly had a personality disorder of some form and it was common for people like that to behave frantically when abandoned. It wasn't something you got locked up over. Still, she was an accident waiting to happen.

Around this time Mrs Paulger got a phone call from a Tamworth psychiatrist about her daughter-in-law and recalls the doctor saying that Katherine should never have had chil-dren. It made her wonder what the hell was happening down there.

After that it got really rough. Joy told Katherine that

Kellett had left with another girl. It was something she couldn't handle. Who could? There was a suggestion the girl was pregnant. It was like being chopped off at the knees.

Sergeant Lyne's wife, Betty, recalls standing on the verandah of the station house when Katherine arrived in an agitated state, talking nonsense. She pushed the baby into her arms. It was a Sunday, but Betty can't remember what happened after that, well, nothing until she was bringing Kath lunch in the cells a few days later. It was all so long ago. And so sad.

Katherine had never been a person to care what others thought and this would develop over the years to the point where she didn't give a flying F. *Let 'em look. Fuck 'em all.* Even if she did care, she had no control over her anguish and now she was ready to take it to town. After all, they had provided the girl and fixed the car. They knew about it. The little town of Aberdeen was to witness a storm it talks about to this day, whispering just in case a Knight walks in.

On Monday 2 August 1976 a terrible mournful sound disrupted the sleepy trade on the main street. A couple of men outside the old CBC Bank looked up and saw young Katherine Kellett coming up the road, dishevelled and wailing and throwing a pram from one side of the footpath to the other. Jagging it violently from left to right. She was out of her mind with grief and at any moment it looked like she would let go and the baby would fly into the path of oncoming traffic. The good citizens of Aberdeen turned their backs or ducked for cover. A mad woman had been let loose on the town and nobody knew what to do. You couldn't go near her, that much was obvious. She looked fearsomely strong.

The railway line runs through the heart of Aberdeen, but it's in a cutting so it's hidden from the top end of town. The locals say that Kath took Melissa down there and put her on the tracks, knowing the southbound train was due any minute and would finish her off. Lorna Driscoll, who's got a dusty old fashioned corner store with a petrol bowser out the front, reckons she saw Kath coming up the road. Lorna was outside her house on the other side of the tracks. Kath came over and grabbed an axe from her neighbour's woodpile and start to run around with it. Running amok, trying to punch a hole in her despair. Lorna struggles to describe the fury and energy Kath had at that moment. It was like nuclear fission. You wouldn't have messed with her.

Doors slammed closed and people ran for cover, pulling their curtains closed and putting their eyes to the cracks. Lorna's neighbour was hysterical with fear but Kath wasn't after them. Old Ted Abrahams came up from the track with the baby. Lorna saw him.

Ted was a war veteran who was doing it a little tough. He had a plate in his head and a short temper which was often baited by other men at the meatworks. He was laid off after hitting his head during a fight with another bloke in the showers. He spent a month in hospital with a fractured skull. He'd seen a terrible plane crash in New Guinea during the war. In 1943 a bomber landed on an Australian convoy killing 69 soldiers. It was the largest single accident of World War II involving Australian soldiers. It shook him right up. He'd been in Egypt and then New Guinea, where he got hurt and sent home. He didn't have a good war, but he was a harmless old bloke if you left him alone and he liked to keep to himself to wander the outskirts of town. Ted lived in a shack near the silos on the other side of the line from where Katherine and Kellett lived and would collect grain and coal from the sidings. Ted's shack burned down one year so he moved to a half-built house with no roof, but that burned down too. This particular day he emerged from the railway depression with

Melissa in his arms. Told people he'd found her on the tracks.

Over 25 years later Melissa heard the story from her family. She confronted her mother with it and says Katherine started to talk about pyjamas and nonsense. Melissa concluded she was lying. If ever asked, Kath said she was suffering post-natal depression, which suggests she didn't tell Melissa the truth. (Years later a truck driver would talk of another incident where he had come out of the top pub around this time and noticed something under the cabin of his truck before he'd driven off. He checked and found it was a little baby in a pram—Melissa.)

This day somebody called the police and Constable Daryl Mackell calmed her down. He decided she was having women's problems and drove with her up the highway to St Elmos Hospital Tamworth in the ambulance. She told the doctors her parents didn't love her and this had built up in her mind. It was her second visit and the doctors knew there was little they could do for her. For some reason Katherine was discharged the same night into her parents' care. When she signed herself out she promised to go berserk again. This time with a knife. Said she was going to do the job properly this time. She arrived home before Mackell, who'd had to get a lift back to Scone in the ambulance.

Katherine was back in town. Kellett had betrayed her and Kellett had to pay. At some stage Ken, who knew what she was capable of, had gone up to the Short Street house and taken away the gun, which was kept on the verandah. The family sent Shane, the little brother, to stay with her, but she told him not to go to sleep or she'd cut his throat. He figured they'd be better off back at their parents, so they went back to McAdam Street. He wasn't stupid enough to sleep there when his big sister was talking about picking up her knives.

When the Knights woke up the next morning Kath was

already gone. She had a plan. She was going to find some order in this chaos, some justice for the crime that had been committed against her. Somebody had to pay. She got up early and walked back to get her things ready. A cheque. A money box. Some bandages. Scissors. Knives. All the things that really matter.

That Tuesday morning Constable Mackell was sitting in the police house filling Sergeant Lyne in on the hysteria of the day before, but before he could complete the story he looked out the window and says, 'Crikey. There she goes now.'

Margaret MacBeth was a local teenager who worked with Kath at the meatworks and lived with her mum. They weren't friends. Margaret never liked her. That morning her mother, who also worked at the abattoir, woke her to say that Katherine was at the door, saying Melissa was sick and needed to be taken to the doctor. Kath then walked back across the highway to Short Street to get the baby ready. Marg, her siblings and mum got in the car and drove across the road to find Kath waiting on the corner in the purple top and trousers that she wore everywhere. Something was obviously not right. She seemed agitated and preoccupied, but Marg knew she was a weird one.

—What took ya so long?

Kath spotted the kids in the car and started muttering.

—There's too fucking many of ya, I'll have to get rid of some of ya.

The family could see she was acting very strangely, but were worried about the sick baby. Kath asked Margaret to come into the house and give her a hand with the bassinette. Margaret followed her in and waited while Kath appeared to be tucking the blankets in. Next thing she knew Kath had pulled a huge curved knife from the bassinette. Margaret backed off, tried to get away and stumbled like she was in some bloody nightmare where your legs don't work. Heart thumping like it was going to explode. Knees turned to jelly. She got out the front and fell under the lemon tree and Kath was on top of her. Nicked her cheek with the enormous knife. Margaret got away again but it was on for young and old. Kids were screaming and Margaret was bleeding.

She was saying it was no use yelling or screaming; she'd planned this and the neighbours weren't home. They weren't.

—Margaret, you know how much I like blood, don't ya. You know.

Margaret did know. She'd seen her at work nicking the arteries of animals. Kath said she was going to kill them all and showed them the knives and bandages and scissors and money boxes. Kath said she was going to cut them up and bandage them back together.

Margaret was a mess and the kids were freaking out. Cars were going by on the highway but they were trapped in this deserted dead-end street. Nobody could see them. Margaret's mother managed to calm Kath down, but she was still out of her mind. She wandered around the verandah. Kept going back to it, looking for something that should have been there. She wanted to take the car and drive to get Kellett, but they managed to negotiate. They'd drive her there. Margaret reckons they were at the house for an hour, talking and trying to calm her down. All the time Kath kept looking around the verandah. They didn't know what she was looking for.

At some stage Kath's brother and his wife arrived. He found his little sister in a right state and gave her a piece of his mind.

—Let 'em go, ya fucking mad bitch.

Kath told them to fuck off. They drove away saying they were going to get the minister. Maybe God could help her.

Margaret's mum said little Henry had asthma and was distressed; he needed to go home and lie down. Kath agreed to that and told him not to run as he took off. He wandered down to the end of Short Street, dashed across the highway and got the neighbours to call the police. Kath got in the car and told them she'd use the knife if they tried anything. They told her they needed petrol and so drove the 100 metres to the Caltex service station at the end of Short Street. Kath was happy with that; she wanted to cash a cheque. It was on the highway and Henry could see them from across the road. If only the police would come. Where were they?

At the service station the family made a break for it. Margaret, her mother and another sibling ran into the office and locked themselves in. They thought they'd be safe in there. But Katherine went berserk again. With one hand she grabbed a large metal blade off an agricultural slasher and started wielding it around. Her strength was incredible. Then she turned on old Ken Sullivan. Hoppy.

—You fixed Kellett's car for him, you cunt. You'll pay too.'

She grabbed his crutch and started to smash things with it. Kath was trying to get at the family through the window. Smashing the louvres.

—Youse tried to get away now I'm going to kill youse all. I'm gonna cut youse up.

Margaret was in shock. It was a horror movie and she couldn't get off-camera and back into her seat. The mad woman who nicked arteries for fun was only a few panes of glass away and sure as hell was going to kill them. Henry was watching from across the road. Where were the police? How could it take so long? The station was only a few hundred metres away. It was going on and on and they were nowhere to be seen. It seemed like half an hour before Lloyd Lyne and his partner arrived.

Kath dropped the slasher and grabbed one of the children by the front of his jumper. Boy in one hand, knife in the other. Even today the 73-year-old former sergeant remembers the fear on that boy's face.

He had on a football jumper—I don't remember the colours— and his little eyes were popping out. You hear about that when people are horrified and his were actually sticking out. The poor little bugger.

They convinced her to let the boy go.

When she let him go, he ran straight out of the station, across the road, through the gate and into his house and didn't come out again. He never looked back.

The two police came at her from either side, pushing her back with brooms. Sergeant Lyne talked her down. Then she expired. All the anger was gone. Her rage dissolved into despair again. She started to say that she wasn't going back to the hospital. They couldn't take her back there. She wouldn't go back to Tamworth. She wouldn't. She wouldn't. Kath said later she remembered the police threatening to shoot her. Melissa slept through the whole thing.

Kath was handcuffed and they decided that Tamworth might not be the answer after the previous day's experience. Sergeant Lyne had a nick on his arm that he thinks came from the knife but he says she didn't try to attack him. In Aberdeen today they say he was stabbed but it's not true. Again she was thrown to the psychiatrists. A doctor completed a Schedule 2 psychiatric admission form, which enabled the police to transfer her to Morisset Hospital on Lake Macquarie. Kath was kept in the lockup at the back of the station and Mrs Lyne fed her lunch while everything was organised. Then they left.

Back in Aberdeen the family nursed its wounds, physical
and psychological. They went to the police to press charges but
they were told it was pointless. They went to the Knights looking
for some sort of explanation and perhaps an apology. They
were told Kath was a mad bitch. Her twin, Joy, was interested in
the bit of the story where her sister had picked up a heavy piece
of steel that even the cops had trouble lifting. 'She's fucking
strong, isn't she?' Ken told them he'd taken the gun away and
that was what she was looking for on the verandah. Imagine if
she'd had a gun. Margaret thought she couldn't be chilled
more. Shane told them he'd tried to stay there the night
before but she'd threatened to cut his throat. The family figured she'd taken off at about 5.30 am. No apologies.

Kath was sedated and watched carefully. Morisset was a
large-scale old-style psychiatric institution built in 1909 and at
times held up to 1600 patients. It had a number of wings
including a high security section for the criminally insane and in
those days had an admissions ward. Even today disturbed men
and women catch the train to town and then make the long walk
out to the hospital gates to ask to be taken in, but the admissions
ward is now closed. They are turned away and wander back to
the station, the voices in their heads getting more urgent.

Kath told the staff that her husband had run off with
another girl who was pregnant and now he was spending all
his money on her. Said her parents didn't love her. Still sobbing and distressed, Katherine told the admissions nurse that
she had been depressed since her husband left and she'd
tried to hurt him, Melissa and herself. She said that once she
believed in God but now that she had been abandoned she no
longer did. She said she blamed Melissa for Kellett leaving
and wanted to kill her.

One doctor made a note during her stay that would prove
to be chillingly accurate.

This lady is of low intelligence—she can barely read or write. Her environmental background is poor—she is one of eight children who did badly at school and married at 17.5 years having had little to do with men prior to meeting her husband. Although she says she was not in love with her husband when they married she now does love him with the birth of their 3 month old baby.

The marriage seems to have been a very unstable one with sexual incompatibility and ... though it was a happy one until she became pregnant. The pregnancy was unplanned and she wanted it at first, as did her husband. After the birth of a baby girl her husband had shown his displeasure by calling it 'all the names he could lay his tongue to'.

On leaving the hospital he shipped her off to his mother's for a fortnight at Coffs Harbour, then to his brothers at Moree for a week. On returning home there were arguments and each threatened to leave the other.

At this time she says she felt that she hated the baby and wanted to kill her as she blamed the child for her husband's feelings towards her.

After seeing her doctor she was admitted to St Elmos Hospital at Tamworth where she stayed for a fortnight.

After returning home she was told by her twin sister that her husband was playing around with a 16-year-old girl and had gone to Sydney with her.

On hearing this news the patient went berserk at her home and was apprehended by Muswellbrook police and returned to St Elmos. She signed herself out however and on returning home proceeded to go berserk again, this time with a knife. She broke into premises to seek refuge from the police who eventually apprehended her.

She says now that the reason for her violent behaviour lay in the belief that she could get hold of her husband's mother and in that way get to her husband and obtain an explanation from him for his behaviour.

The girl has little insight into herself. She acts impulsively and violently when roused. She is both immature and intellectually [unstable] and seems to have little awareness of the consequences which might result from her irrational behaviour.

She has no real friends, has great difficulty with interpersonal relationships.

She says she feels that the relationship has ended and expresses many hostile feelings towards her husband who she says is 'spending all his money on the girl—he never spent any on me'.

There is probably little we can do for this girl but a cooling off period is probably required for the sake of all concerned.

He noted she was of limited intelligence and suffering a personality disorder. None of the doctors who examined her seemed willing to stick their neck out and say that Katherine was mad. None ever has.

*   *   *

Meanwhile, up the highway in Queensland, things weren't working out between Kellett and his new friend and she took off back to town. 'It was just companionship really, but as it was she was pregnant. Me and this girl never got on.' He decided to give it another go with Katherine; after all, they'd only recently bought the house and he was missing his daughter terribly. He rang her parents up to see if she would have him back. They told him she was locked up in the psychiatric ward and that they had Melissa. He was left with the distinct impression he wouldn't be invited to the Knights' for Christmas that year. David picked up his mother from

Coffs Harbour to help sort things out and then drove to Morisset.

They found Katherine heavily sedated in a high security part of the hospital. She seemed moved to see her mother-in-law and had some news for her. *I wanted to take the car and see ya because you are the only one that loved me, but I wanted to kill ya.*

Mrs Paulger thought it was the drugs talking. She remembers her daughter-in-law talking to a nurse about a man in the same ward.

—If he gets in me bed I'll kill him.

It struck her that despite the sedation, Katherine was alert enough about her sexual situation. Kath was always on guard about unwanted sexual advances and no amount of drugs would change that. Still, she was heavily sedated. 'She was like a zombie and it was a terrible place, the ward she was in had steel mesh and locked doors and there were males and females in there.'

Ken was sent a telegram by the hospital alerting him to a hearing before a magistrate about his daughter's continued confinement. In the end Mrs Paulger and Kellett fronted the magistrate at the hospital and Katherine was released into her mother-in-law's care—the woman she had been trying to kill when they brought her here.

Her discharge sheet added further confusion to the story about exactly where Katherine had been heading that Tuesday morning, but gives further insights into her state of mind at the time.

This young lady was brought to this hospital on a schedule 2 from Dr G. J. Young of Muswellbrook, escorted by Aberdeen Police. She had become violent and aggressive after hearing that her husband had deserted her. On one occasion she had taken an axe and was threatening people. She had been recently treated in Tamworth Hospital after expressing suicidal feelings and aggressive impulses which were directed at her three month old baby. The police escorted her back to the hospital at Tamworth. However, she was reluctant to stay and discharged herself the same evening.

On the following day she became disturbed once again. This time she was brandishing a knife at police. After damaging property in the town the police finally apprehended her.

On examination she was below normal intelligence and had poor insight as far as understanding the consequences of her actions. There had been numerous problems with her marriage and believed that her husband had deserted her. She was immature both in her manner and her attitude. She seemed generally concerned for the welfare of her baby but appeared to need guidance with infant's care.

Katherine settled down well after admission. On hearing of her admission here her husband and mother-in-law visited and expressed concern for her future. Her husband admitted there had been problems with the marriage but expressed the desire of reconciliation. Katherine was discharged into the care of her mother-in-law, Mrs F. Paulger . . .

Katherine was so relieved to be out, but even more happy to find that her husband had come back. She loved him as wholly that day as she had hated him two weeks earlier.

Kellett and his mother drove from the hospital out to Ken and Barbara's place in the early evening to pick up Melissa. The family were still living in McAdam Street and there seemed to be a lot of young adults and relatives around the house. Katherine went inside and fetched her daughter while the other two waited in the car. There was no way Dave was going in there. They'd kill him. The whole situation seemed menacing.

Suddenly Barbara Knight was at the driver's window with her hands around Kellett's throat trying to strangle him. It was like the wedding night all over again. There was a lot of screaming and yelling. Her brothers, smirking and laughing on the verandah, didn't move to intervene. Mrs Paulger, who wasn't in the best of health, was horrified. This was the streak Barbara told her had run through the female side of the family. 'She was choking my son to death and David just sat there staring ahead with his hands on the wheel. He didn't say a word, didn't even blink.'

Mrs Paulger ran to the house next-door hoping to get somebody to ring the police but nobody came to the door. She ran back, crying and pleading. Barbara was a powerful woman. By this time Katherine had emerged from the house. She knew how to handle her own family. Knights could take care of Knight business. She grabbed her mother by the shoulder, swung her around and knocked her to the ground with single punch to the head. *Git ya fuckin' hands off him. That's my man. We're going to work it out. He came back for me.*

Kellett says it knocked the old girl out. Katherine was a strong girl with big, man-sized hands and seemed to know how to throw a punch.

Kellett, his mother, Katherine and Melissa hit the road as fast as they could, leaving Barbara lying in the dirt. Mrs Paulger couldn't believe what she'd just seen. What sort of a family was that? What sort of a woman had her son married? She made them stop at the police station to make a report, in case the men tried to follow them up the road. As they drove they kept checking the rear view mirror, watching Aberdeen disappear into the hills. It was the second time Kellett had made such an escape.

Katherine and David were quiet on the drive back and remained close lipped on the events of the previous few months for the rest of their relationship. It was two decades before she asked him why he left, and while over the years he occasionally heard stories about a baby being put on the railway track, he dismissed them.. 'Kath used to love her kids. She was so protective of them she couldn't have. I heard about the car. Didn't she stab a copper?'

They proceeded to the NSW seaside of town of Coffs Harbour where Mrs Paulger was under strict instructions to make sure her daughter-in-law took her medication. Mrs Paulger began to notice odd things about the 20-year-old. She would lock herself away with the baby for long periods of time and it was a while before the older woman discovered what Kath was up to. 'She had a fixation with cleaning the girl. She was obsessively cleaning her vagina behind closed doors. She cleaned and cleaned and cleaned.'

One time Kath drew blood cleaning the girl's ear. Her behaviour became stranger. She had to be on her best behaviour around Mrs Paulger but would escape to Kellett's sister's place where she would let her guard down and be the real Kath, swearing and yelling and letting off steam. This cunt and that cunt and he's fuckin' this and fuckin' that and that fuckin' slut cunt. Hell she was angry.

After three weeks Kath and Kellett moved on. He had no intention of going back to Aberdeen where her brothers had sworn to kill him, so they moved up to Woodridge in Queensland to a flat in Pamela Crescent to see if they could make a new start of it. Kellett got a job driving trucks and later Kath got a job at an abattoir near Brisbane. She'd ride for hours every day on a motorbike to get to work.

Kath was apparently glad to have her man back

Even after we were separated sex was just mind boggling. It was a bit like the first time. Every time it was terrific, but then other

times it would be: 'You're not touching me, I don't know where
you've fuckin' bin.'

Her moods were unpredictable and her anger frightening. Mrs Paulger remembers telephone calls from Kath
where she would be screaming abuse about Kellett. Swearing,
yelling and accusing him of having affairs. Off her brain with
rage. The older woman stopped taking the calls; she was sick
with high blood pressure and it was the last thing she needed.
That little girl could melt the phone with her acid venom.

Barbara Knight, it seems, dusted herself off and accepted
the trio back into the fold. Kellett says she treated him well
when they went back to visit. It seemed she was used to getting
up out of the dirt and returning to the kitchen. Or the bed.
Despite her advancing years, it seems that Barbara's lot hadn't
changed much.

Her mother had bruises all over her face, black eyes. We'd go
down on holidays for a week or two, or long weekends and her
mother always put a big roast on for me and I'd say, 'What happened to ya?' and she'd say, 'That old cunt knocked me out
again for sex.' He'd knock her out. Knocked her out.

Life wasn't all crap for the reunited couple. David was
trying his best to keep her happy. In October a mate of his put
on a twenty-first birthday party for Kath at his place in
Woodridge. The party girl wore her favourite gold dress and
had the night of her life. It was celebration of Kath and she
loved it. She'd cut her hair and was looking great.

She was so perfect that night, her mum and dad were there and
my family and she was the perfect mother, wife, everything,
absolute magic, you couldn't fault her. Didn't swear or anything.

There's a touching picture of the pair kissing in the back-yard of their friend's home. Her hair is shorter, a little more sophisticated and they're wrapped in a Hollywood pash, clutching hands around a pink drink, her right hand grabbing the back of his neck. An above-ground pool, a Queensland backyard. Maybe things would get better. Then again her 'psychotic ways' were never far away.

Things turned ugly again one day, just after Kellett had been at the shop buying a newspaper. She went outside ready to go dirt bashing on her trail bike only to find it was gone. Riding the motorbike was her great passion. Her older brother Neville had a big road bike and the rest of the kids got into them after that. Sometimes they'd head off on trips together. Kath was a good rider. She was furious that it was gone. Someone was to blame. She came back up yelling and screaming and breaking things, smashing holes into the wall, accusing him of losing it. Kellett took refuge next door. He had walked to the shop.

It was up in Queensland that Katherine's love of her work knives took a further disturbing turn. She was already taking them with her wherever she went, travelling with them under the seat of the car. They were always within reach. In Woodridge she put hooks above the pillow and would hang them above the marital bed when they slept. The sword of Damocles suspended by the thin thread of her temper. She had two knives and a sharpening steel and they were razor sharp, you could shave the hair off your arms with them. And every night David could look up and see them. Hanging there.

Mrs Paulger remembers visiting the couple and asking Katherine why they were there. The young woman dropped her head and pouted like a petulant child.

'Just in case I need them. Or to kill somebody if I have to.'

The quiet little daughter-in-law had changed so much

from the meek little thing Mrs Paulger had first met. She told Kellett's mum she even slept with a knife in the bed. Poor Kellett was under terrible pressure. When she lost her temper, which was happening with increasing frequency, she took to throwing the knives and accusing him of all sorts of infidelities. She may or may not have been wrong, but the first separation had really shaken her and would haunt her for decades to come.

But two could play the infidelity game.

One night the phone rang in their Woodridge flat. The wife of Kath's union representative from the meatworks was on the line wanting to talk to her. Kellett remembers that she wouldn't take the call. It didn't seem that odd at the time. Kath had her moods. The next week Kellett decided to come home and have a sandwich for lunch. He couldn't park the truck in the crescent so left it at the top of the street and walked down. Kath was supposed to be at the abattoirs. When he got to their place he noticed two motorbikes underneath—she had replaced the stolen one. The truck driver figured she was up to no good and snuck upstairs, grabbing his .22 rifle on the way. He listened at the door and heard the unmistakable sounds of two people having sex in his bed. Gun in hand, he kicked the door open and caught his wife with the union rep. They had both taken sickies from work.

He says he made the man jump out of the window to the street below. The gun wasn't loaded but the bloke wasn't hanging around to find out. Katherine was crying and telling him to calm down, but Kellett was furious and stuffed her clothes into a bag before throwing it off the balcony, telling her to join her boyfriend. He told her he wanted her to go and that it was all over. 'She cried and was on her knees and I told her things had to change. No more psycho ways or you're out.'

She was on her best behaviour for the next few months. Kellett got some extended relief. She convinced him that they should have another baby to save the marriage.

The young family then moved on to Landsborough, a small town about the size of Aberdeen, 75 kilometres north of Brisbane on the Sunshine Coast. They stayed there for about three years. They bought a house and he worked hard, sometimes doing three jobs at once, but things were never really back on track. He'd been unfaithful, she'd been unfaithful and everybody had lost faith and face.

At Landsborough he used to play darts in a competition at the local club. If there was one thing that really sent Kath over the edge, apart from barking dogs and knickers on the outside of the line, it was her men staying out late. The competition was meant to finish at 10.30 pm, she rang at 10.10 pm.

—How long ya gunna be?

—Ten minutes.

—Get home right fuckin' now.

—I can't just walk out of the competition.

—Get fucking home!

Katherine could not cope with people being late. It made her so angry. It was another form of abandonment and she became frantic. She could never trust him again and kept thinking he was playing up. For his part, Kellett realised she was having a bad night and in one of those moods, but he kept playing and got home a little after 10.30 pm. Or at least he thought he did.

By the time he got there Kath had gone right over the edge. When he got home and walked in the door she hit him from behind with something heavy. He thinks it was an iron or a saucepan. In a daze he went to the neighbours before collapsing. He was bleeding from the nose, ears and back of the head and was rushed to Nambour Hospital. They kept him there for a week, doing X-rays to check for fractures and doing scans of his brain. He had big black eyes and a swathe of bandages that made him look like a car-crash victim.

He didn't know it at the time, but she'd also burned all his clothes in the bathroom. When he got out of hospital the walls were stained with smoke. The local cops wanted to charge her with attempted murder but Kellett didn't want to press charges. They had a young daughter with another on the way and, anyway, she was terribly contrite when he got out of hospital. Bought him all new clothes. He warned her that if she laid another hand on him, he'd pack her bags and send her back to her mum and dad.

Barbara came up to stay with them then and gave Kath terrible grief over what she'd done. The mother–daughter –victim relationship was confused to say the least. When Barbara hurt Kellett she was punched. When Katherine hurt Kellett she was reprimanded. It was like they were taking turns playing good cop, bad cop. Barbara stayed for a month or so.

In an effort to save money and possibly decrease the chances of further trouble, Kellett began to brew beer at home and one day a couple of his mates came back from the pub to knock a few off. It wasn't that long after he'd got out of hospital. Katherine was obsessively jealous and hated all his friends, referring to them as 'that cunt' or 'those cunts'. She never bothered with their names. Anybody she didn't know and many that she did were 'cunts' to Kath. The world was full of them. One of the blokes that walked down the driveway that evening was a Maori. All of Kellett's mates thought his missus was a right piece of work, but this day she really turned it on.

—Whose this black cunt ya've got with ya?
—He's a mate of mine. Shut ya mouth.

Kath never knew when to stop and anyway, she'd already

gone too far. The bloke was enraged. He charged at her and
everyone thought he was going to belt her. She backed off as
he approached, but he kept coming until they were toe to toe.
Face to face.

—If you ever call me that again, I'll drive me fist through
your fucking face.

Katherine took off and ran for the police, as she would
with increasing frequency over the years. She told them
Kellett had hired a Kiwi hit man to kill her. She wanted to
press charges. It blew over, like all of Katherine's storms. Poor
Kellett just cleaned up the mess and tried to keep his head in
one piece.

In March 1980 Natasha Maree Kellett was born in the
Nambour Hospital. Kath was now 24 and a mother of two.

Kellett says he never saw his wife mistreat the children,
although he heard she became worse over the years. Still, she
was a tough mother. He can remember stand-offs between
Melissa and her mother over eating chokos, a vegetable of
questionable taste. Kath would leave her at the table until
she'd eat them and Melissa would sit there long after her
mother had gone to bed. Then Kellett would intervene,
hiding the offending vegetable and telling his wife the tod-
dler had complied.

Mrs Paulger visited the couple several times and was
becoming increasingly concerned by her daughter-in-law's
demeanour. She witnessed repeated scenes where Katherine
became uncontrollable, enraged by the slightest incident; a
kettle that didn't have enough water in it would fly across the
room, coffee mugs would smash, every second person was a
cunt. The ones in between were worse. Kellett would do his
best to pacify her, calm her down. Apologise to his mum.

His sister remembers a more disturbing incident. One
day she heard terrible screams coming from the bathroom

where Kath was washing Melissa's hair. Kellett's sister ran in to find her rinsing the tortured child's hair with scalding hot water, fierce with determination. She pointed out to Kath that the water was burning the girl.

—Fuck off! Mind ya's own business!

Mrs Paulger found it hard to understand her daughter-in-law and cut herself off from her. The girl was impossible. A danger to herself and everybody around her, including her children and her husband. 'She used to scream her head off about everything and anything. I started to wonder why I had got her out of that hospital.'

In Katherine's mind she was always the victim. Her family repeat her version of the marriage and relationships in her life and tell you what violent men they all were. How her self-esteem was low and they treated her like shit. It's a family songbook and they all sing from it or get excommunicated. Still, Katherine's never accused Kellett of hitting her and he swears that he never did because he would never hit a woman. Especially one that towered over him like her. Still, she went for the cops more than once during their relationship.

In Landsborough she waved him goodbye one day as he headed off to work at a local windscreen place. Have fun. I'll see you when you get home. Kellett was a little bit pissed and when he drove the car out the driveway he hit the gate post. Oh well, nothing serious. He kept on his way. She'd been watching and something snapped. He couldn't get away with that. She went to the local cop who lived in the house opposite but he fobbed her off. She persisted and the police showed up at his workplace.

Kellett gave them a bit of lip, got a backhander for his trouble and a court appearance for driving under the influence. He lost his licence.

Later, in a similarly bloody minded act, she cost John

Price his superannuation and his job. She kissed Pricey goodbye the morning she did that too, like butter wouldn't melt in her mouth.

People who have been surrounded by alcohol as children often won't touch it themselves and while Katherine would have the occasional wine, a cask could last her a year, although later, when she met John Price she began to drink more. There's no doubt that Kellett drank a lot in his young days and so did all of her boyfriends over the ensuing years. *I pick the wrong ones. They were all drunk and violent.*

Alcohol is one thing, child abuse is another. Kath was obsessed by it. Without ever having read a separatist text she thought all men were potential rapists. The obsessive cleaning of the girls' vaginas indicates some trauma, probably from childhood and it's probably related to the violation by her brothers. Yet there was sex abuse at every turn. Or allegations of it. Partners, brothers and strangers. Perhaps it was just that she was the unluckiest woman in the world, because wherever she went, people were apparently trying to molest her or her children.

After the incident with the police she and Kellett separated. She moved down to a caravan in Dinmore, taking Melissa and Natasha with her, and found a job. She hadn't been there long when she rang Kellett.

—Git up here. Melissa's been raped.

He didn't have his licence thanks to Kath so he had to hitch, clutching a bunch of flowers all the way and worrying about what he had heard on the telephone. When he got there he started to piece together the story. There had been a terrible scene at the caravan park. The police had come and a bloke had been questioned and evicted. According to Kellett the man had only stopped to speak to Melissa and had never touched her. There were never any charges laid, but the man had to take off. Somehow there was an item in the local newspaper talking about the suspected rape.

Twenty years later Kellett's phone rang again, it was Melissa wanting to know more details about the rape. She'd just found the clipping in her mother's photo album alongside the clippings from incidents in her father's wild youth.

Why would you do that? The poor bloke never went to court. She hadn't been touched. What does that tell ya? You could put two profiles on Katherine and they'd both be opposite. She could be the most wonderful loving mother and wife—you could not wish for anyone better. And then ...

They got back together one more time after that. The flowers must have done the trick and she was on her best behaviour. Loving mother and housewife. Well, for a while at least.

Back in Landsborough Kellett woke one night and got the fright of his life, much like John Price 25 years later. The shock has never left him. He had worked a string of jobs and by this time was driving furniture trucks. That evening he went to bed, the knives hanging over his head, ready to leave in the truck at 5 am the next day, but in the middle of the night he woke, aware of a weight on his chest. Kath was sitting on top of him, pinning his arms down, and digging one of the knives into his throat near the jugular. Sharp as a razor. She only had to move it a few centimetres and it would have sliced right through the artery. The bitch was as calm as could be. *Is it true that truck drivers have a woman in every fucking town? Is it? ... You see how easy it is, Kellett? I could do ya in right here.*

Kellett didn't need to be told, he knew he was a muscle twitch away from bleeding like the stuck pigs she worked with every day.

I had to talk fast, I can tell you, I was sweating and shaking. I couldn't even push her off. She had one arm across my chest and the knife into my neck. I thought I was gone. I was shit scared. It was the most horrific memory I have.

Years later Kath would deny this ever happened but there seems little reason to doubt Kellett. He lived through that one, but life was becoming increasingly uncomfortable as she began to attack him more often, flying off the handle and swinging at his head. Always at his head. It was at just the right height and she could really knock you about. Punch like a man.

The marriage was ending, she was growing more distant but there was a final strange twist for Kellett in the horror ride that was his marriage to Katherine.

He returned one night from a three-day job in the truck up at Kingaroy in Queensland and noticed something odd about the house. The curtains were missing. Strange, she must be washing them. He went in the door and reached for the light switch. Nothing. The bulb must have gone. He used his cigarette lighter but the little flame failed to illuminate anything. There was just a vacant darkness. He couldn't even make out the furniture.

She'd done a runner.

While he'd been away she had hired an open truck and had the place cleaned out. Melissa, Natasha and their mother were gone and they'd taken everything in sight. Even his power tools were gone from the shed. But she hadn't been a total bitch, leaving behind an old couch of his sister's, two cups, two saucers, two plates and some old Tupperware containers for his lunch.

Two?

Maybe it was a message.

Katherine had become sure her husband was having an

affair with a 17-year-old neighbour—a girl they both knew and that he would tease about being the only virgin in town. Kath had found a bra when making the bed and accused him of sleeping with the girl. Kellett swears he wasn't. Katherine said it wasn't her bra, it was too small for her.

It was hers. It was Kath's bra. The girl next-door was 13 stone and Kath was 10. It was too small for her. It was hers . . . I did end up with the sheila next-door but that was two years after me divorce and it only lasted 12 months.

Kellett says that once he got over the shock of finding his tormentor was gone he went out and got pissed to celebrate. After living in the empty house for a while he tried to make contact to see if the girls were all right.

I rang her parents up and they wouldn't tell me where she was, they just said she's down here. Her brothers reckoned they were going to kill me because of what I'd done to her. Charlie and Shane. Charlie's mellowed over the years.

Kellett and Kath's elder brother had had a falling out at her parents over the home brew during a visit to Kath's parents in Aberdeen. They'd been sitting up at the table drinking and Barbara Knight told them to put their bottles away when they went to bed. According to Charlie, Kellett told him to leave them, that he'd do it, but Charlie copped a blast the next morning from his mum because they were still there. In anger he went out and smashed the bottles in the bin. This, according to the elder Knight boy, enraged Kellett who wanted them to put more home brew in. Charlie remains angry about the incident. Things can get pretty petty sometimes. The Knights were like that.

There'd been a few family punch-ups at the Knights' in Kellett's presence. He reckons it was 'hillbilly central', people drinking and smoking pot and carrying on like idiots. One night he said something to Patrick, who was a union rep, about an industrial dispute in town. Suddenly the eldest Knight leapt across the dinner table and began to choke Kellett.

Katherine says that all of her brothers drank and smoked marijuana and that she tried smoking it on a handful of occasions.

After Kath left him Kellett never found a reason to visit Aberdeen again. He was happy to have survived. 'I just had no interest in the place.'

Melissa Knight's second statement to the police after the murder of John Price referred to her mother's relationship with her father.

From knowing my mother, I can say that her major hang-up during her life which constantly upset her was that my father was being constantly unfaithful. From talking with Mum I believe that her belief in this was the reason that she suffered a low self-esteem in her life. This compounded with being brought up in an exceptionally violent atmosphere seeing her father bash her mother unconscious just for sex. In those days my grandfather was a very violent person which created violence in the family.

8

She's back
Mid-1990s

—Am I going to be safe?

—As safe as ya've ever fuckin' bin.

The nightmare had returned. David Kellett thought he'd escaped with his life, but almost two decades later Katherine Knight—she changed back to her maiden name after the divorce—was standing at the door of his home in Queensland. Insisting they go for a drive.

—I want to talk to ya about something.

She was agitated. She had arrived without warning, the two youngest kids from two relationships since in tow. She told Kellett the kids would stay in the house while she took him in the car. He wasn't keen on the idea. In fact, he was shitting himself. Had she come back to settle the score once and for all?

He got in the car reluctantly and they drove off, pulling up on a back road. She turned off the motor and twisted around in the seat to face him. For Kellett this was almost as frightening as the time he woke up with the knife at his throat. He started to wonder if she had the knives under the seat. Shit, what had he done?

—David . . .

She had never called him David before. It was always
Kellett.

Katherine wanted to know why he'd left her twenty years
earlier, why he'd abandoned her with young Melissa. She was
almost shaking with emotion. It was the first time she'd ever
asked. He says he told her that he'd been unhappy. That he
was married to her and not her mother and that her psychotic
ways, the yelling and the screaming and the swearing and the
smashing, had been too much. He said that he thought she
needed professional help before she hurt someone. He told
her his friends had names, it wasn't right to call people cunt.

—All men are cunts and you're no exception.

—Yeah. Yeah.

Then she was calm again. Like a burden had been lifted
from her shoulders. She said she'd never loved another man
like she loved him. She told him that he was the one who
ruined her faith in men. And then she leant across the car and
gave him a kiss on the cheek.

—C'mon. I'll buy ya a beer.

Kellett said that he had some in the fridge and they
should get back in case somebody dropped around and
found two strange children in his house.

It was a curious coda to a relationship he had done his
best to forget. He felt sorry for her, dragging those two kids
around and trying to find out why she was so fucked in the
head. Letting that bother her for twenty years without
breathing a word.

When they'd got divorced she got the kids and the houses
in Landsborough and Aberdeen. Over the years she used the
girls as emotional pawns in her battle with Kellett. He never
saw Melissa between the ages of 6 and 16 and even the presents and flowers he sent when she turned 13 never arrived.

Kellett and his new wife would make plans to take the kids on holidays and at the last minute Kath would change her mind or invent a way to stuff things up. Kids were handy for Kath. Handy for negotiating and tormenting their fathers with. The kids were full of terrible stories about their fathers and the other men Kath lured home. Melissa in particular.

—Mum reckons ya need ya dick cut off, Dad.

Years later in Aberdeen Melissa had come home from school and told Mum she fancied a certain boy of the same age. Kath said it probably wasn't the best idea to get involved. He was her half-brother.

Kath was in the area when Kellett moved house in Queensland. She came over and helped him pack. It still gives his new wife the creeps thinking about it. Sometimes she picks up a piece of crockery and thinks that Kath has touched it. Her husband's first wife always spooked her. When she had to do an overnight trip to pick up Melissa and Natasha she'd sleep with a chair up against the door, worried she'd be attacked. She had an irrational fear that future events indicate was a little intuitive, that Kath would use a knife.

Once Kath came up to visit with John Price. He and Kellett went to the club together to have a few beers and it was like some bashed wives support group. They both spilled their guts over a few schooners.

He told me then he wanted to get out of it but he doesn't know how. She could manipulate ya, you know. Like she'd go off the deep end and start smashing things and then she'd start to cry and, you know, and apologise and say sorry and then take you to bed and that made everything better to her; by taking you to bed made everything better.

9

The investigation begins
March 2000

Bob Wells had flown up the road to Aberdeen full of beans, but coming back the New England highway that night he was starting to fade. It had been a long, trying day. Alone in the car, he became aware of a foul odour clinging to his clothes from the crime scene. He wound down the window and pressed on, eager for some comfort and sanity.

Bob Wells is a copper's son, and as such, the last thing he was going to do was join the force. After a year in a clerical job he realised the old man was right—in those days the super, sickpay and holidays for police were well in front of any civilian job. He did the medicals and interview in 1978 and pulled on the uniform for the first time in April 1979.

Wellsy was a country cop's son and was destined to be a country cop. He is a nice bloke with no airs, who has no trouble getting on with people. He is the sort of copper you want fronting up when there is trouble, not too young, officious or aloof. The force can wear you down though. The job's a frustrating political game these days and the working copper is a pawn of governments and talkback radio.

Management seems only to be interested in saving money and face. Then there's all the trauma that is just part of a copper's day-to-day life. The murders, the distraught parents, the car crashes, the abuse, the fights, the constant exposure to humanity's ugly underbelly. If you spend too long in the kitchen the smell gets in your clothes.

Bob has had a few tough times in the bush. He's had a lot of dysfunctional towns out in the west. Places where the residents beat each other senseless every welfare day. Then, on the way to the lockup they'd vomit in your van. Sometimes it has got serious. One January in Moree, with the temperature pushing the high 40s, he was bailed up by a bloke with two butcher's knives. Wells was off-duty and didn't have his gun. Later, when they'd nabbed the man he looked at Bob and hissed, 'I could've fucked you today, copper.' Wells knew how true that was.

There have been plenty of other times like that. In Bourke they celebrated Christmas by rioting and the cops would have to face off angry mobs of drunk fellas throwing rocks and bottles and anything they could get their hands on. They had perfected the art of tossing the missiles high into the night so the cops couldn't see them coming back down until it was too late. At times the emotional strain of the job is worse than the physical violence. In Moree a cranky doctor insisted he witness the autopsy of a little girl the same age as his own youngest. 'I sat there and all I could see was my little girl's face as he cut up this poor kid. It's the worst thing I've ever done.' There's been a few ugly car crashes too. Nursing teenagers as they gurgled and expired on a country road. Breaking the news to their parents.

He used to figure it was all part of the job. You did it, you had a few drinks, tried to forget and move on, but after attending John Price's house in March 2000 those things started to play on his mind. For Wells the investigation was like a journey into a cave. Sometimes it felt like he'd never see daylight again. Every time he closed his eyes he saw the defiled remains of John Price. As the head detective he would live and breathe the case for months on end. It filled every waking thought, pervaded his dreams and fouled his subconscious, dredging up nightmares past and fears unspoken.

This was a huge job and when the homicide detectives drove back down the highway to Sydney he was basically left alone to run a murder investigation. Wells is an experienced cop and from that first morning in March he realised that Knight was probably going to try for some medical or psychiatric defence, but as every day passed and another piece of the story fell into place he knew she couldn't get off that easily. Deep down he was certain that this 45-year-old grandmother was a killer who knew what she was doing and had been working towards it all her life.

In the heat of that Aberdeen morning he'd got the ball rolling. There were search warrants to organise, statements to take and leave to be cancelled. The police found Knight's two kids safe and well at Natasha Kellett's and got her to make a statement. Knight's wild-eyed second daughter was a good starting place. Mick Prentice got her statement on paper at about 3 pm. She gave them a little background about her life: being born in Nambour, moving back to her grandparents when Mum split from Dad, a housing commission home in Aberdeen and the string of blokes that filled the gap—every one of them violent towards her poor suffering mother. Natasha had a baby daughter, who she was struggling to raise by herself. She was starting to understand some of her mother's pain.

I can remember feeling very helpless when Mum was being abused because I was so young and scared and I couldn't help

her ... Mum spoke to me about her problems when she was
young. She told me that she had been molested by her brother
when she was growing up. I was 15 at this time.

Natasha left home at that age and moved to Queensland,
before moving back in with her mum. She got her own commission house in Muswellbrook just two months before all
this went down. She clearly wanted the cops to have some sympathy for Kath but couldn't keep herself from telling them
about a feeling she'd had the previous night when Kath came
around for dinner.

Mum seemed really quiet and placid and usually she is more
bubbly and happy. It seemed as though Mum was thinking
about a thousand things at the one time ...
    When Mum was leaving I sensed that Mum was unstable
within herself. I said, 'I hope you're not going to kill Pricey and
yourself.'
    Mum said, 'Oh no no no.' Mum was very calm and quiet
when she said this.
    I said, 'I love you, Mum'.
    She said, 'I love you, Natasha'.
    Mum then offered me a cigarette and drove away in her car,
a red Toyota van.

It was great stuff and Mick Prentice knew it. It got better too.

I said these words to Mum about her killing Pricey and herself
because there had been an occasion in the past when we'd had
a conversation about this. This conversation took place within
the last sixteen months and Mum was driving me to Newcastle at
the time. Mum and I were talking about her being abused by
Pricey and the stressed [sic] that it caused her. It was after Mum
and Pricey had split up for a little while and then they'd get back

together. During that conversation, Mum said to me something
like, 'I told him that if he took me back this time, it was to the
death.' This didn't surprise me because I knew the anger and
hurt that she felt by being abused throughout her life.

Mum also said to me something like, 'If I kill Pricey, I'll kill
myself after it'.

. . . About 9.30 am this morning my cousin Tracy came to
my house and said to me, 'Your mum's killed Pricey'.

I said, 'Has she?'

Natasha Kellett signed the bottom of the brief six-page
statement with an artless signature that dropped her mum in
it big time. Her evidence pointed clearly to intent and that
goes a long way towards getting a murder charge up over
manslaughter and makes it difficult to suggest temporary
insanity. Kath knew it too, because later when her second
daughter visited her in prison she told her she could murder
her before the prison wardens made it across the yard.

Joy Hinder also came down to the station late that
Wednesday. Kath's twin gave her occupation as housewife.
She lived up the road from Pricey in St Andrews Street. A solid
red-faced woman with grey hair, she wasn't in much of a mood
to be talking to the police. She'd been in Newcastle with Val
Roughan that day taking her dad, Ken Knight, to the doctors.
Barry Roughan, Joy's half-brother, had called with the news.
He said she reacted hysterically. When she got back she was
tired but the police insisted on an interview. She told the cops
a little bit about Kath being locked up in Morisset Psychiatric
Hospital in 1976, about Kellett and the other blokes. 'All the
men that Kath had been with were drinkers and it was when
they were drunk that Kath would get assaulted.'

She said that Pricey and Kath had a lot of fights.

They just seemed to blue all the time and then they would be friends. Kath told me, when we were walking, that the morning after the blue on Sunday that Pricey had got up the next morning to go to work and he had kissed her goodbye. That was just the way they were.

I have told both Pricey and Kath to just let it go, go your separate ways, but they just got back together.

She signed the statement in the presence of John Alderson.

In the meantime Wells was running back and forward from the house to the station. He was at St Andrews Street when the forensic boys went through. Andrew Dellosta had to get a fingerprint from Price's thumb—there was a bit of skin left. Wells watched as they put the pot with Price's head in it in a plastic bag and tied it up for the trip to the morgue. It was a filthy place and disgusting work. The scientific officers wore booties and gloves and made sure they got plenty of fresh air.

Back at the station, Wells got a phone call from a woman claiming to be Melissa Kellett, the daughter of Katherine Knight. She said Natasha had called her and said Mum had killed John Price. 'Is this some sick first of the month fucking joke?' The detective was guarded: as far as he knew it could be anyone on the phone. Told her Katherine Knight was in hospital being treated and she should come in to give a statement when she got to town. Melissa lives in Queensland.

The other police had fanned out from St Andrews Street, canvassing the neighbourhood and getting statements from the group collected outside the home that morning. A few doors down from Price's they found Lisa Logan, who told them about the sighting of Knight in the middle of the night. That was to prove important later, but at this stage didn't fit anywhere. Why had she taken her car home in the middle of the night? It didn't make sense.

Barry Roughan had been called in when the police set off the alarm while searching Kath's place for the kids. He is on the video they make later that day as they collect evidence. When they're finished they ask him if he's satisfied with what's happened and he says politely that he just wished it had been under different circumstances. At first he figured that Kath and Price had been fighting and she killed him. He had heard enough of his half-sister's stories about Price not to have time for him. Anyway, he didn't like Pricey after he pissed on Roughan's bathroom floor one night when drunk. One of the cops at the house told the half-brother some of the detail of what his sister had done. Roughan was horrified. Maybe it hadn't been as simple as he thought.

In the statement he gave John Alderson at Muswellbrook Police Station he told how Kath dropped in late the night before while he was watching 'Third Watch' on TV, a new police show. He told how Kath, he, his wife, Val, and Kath's twin Joy would walk most mornings and how close the women were. That night Kath and Val had compared notes. Kath had just left her grandchild and Val's had just been born.

I have no recollection at all of what Kath was wearing that night. All I can remember is that she was by herself. Kathy did wear pretty short clothes when she went out, I can't remember that she was wearing anything like that. I wasn't really taking much notice, I was watching the TV show.

When Kath arrived my wife let Kath in. I had general conversation with Kath as she came in and she appeared to be in good spirits ...

He recalls that Kath left the house around 10.30 pm, just before 'Third Watch' finished. He told them a little about her background.

Kath has had a few [other] relationships. These blokes have always been drunks and Kath would get assaulted. Pricey, even though I would have considered him a drunk too, appeared to be better than the others at first but as he got to know Kath, and she would tell me that he assaulted her too.

He told the police how he'd helped Kath move out of Price's place two years earlier after she caused him to lose his job and that she'd soon moved back in. He mentioned the incident the previous Sunday, when police had been called to her house.

Price's workmates Peter Cairnes and Geoff Bowditch came down to Muswellbrook and told the police how Pricey had told them about Kath stabbing him and how scared he was. In this situation it was handy that Price wasn't hanging on to a life support system because the rules of evidence would have precluded these stories as hearsay. As it was, Pricey was dead and the gloves were off. Their stories made things a lot hotter for Knight. Pricey's neighbour Keegan told them more about the weekend incident and how he'd had a beer with the little bloke a few hours before he was murdered and how worried he'd been that morning before they knew what had happened.

That day there was a procession of people into police stations at Muswellbrook, Scone and Aberdeen, and things were looking pretty bad for Katherine Knight. With all this ammunition piling up, Bob Wells wanted to have a go at questioning her while things were fresh. A cop is always keen to step up and have a crack at their suspect, but in this case it wasn't so easy and that was frustrating.

I wanted to get in there and get stuck into her but the doctor didn't want us to interview her and while I was itching to have a

go, I wanted to get it right. She had been sedated and I didn't
want anyone to say we'd taken advantage of her.

Later that night Johnathon Price came to the Scone
Police Station wanting to know the full details of what had
happened to his father. It was the moment the police had
been dreading. Wells and Ford figured he better be told now,
rather than let him find out from town gossip and Ford got
the job because they knew each other.

It was pretty hard. He knew his father had been murdered, but
he didn't know the full extent of what happened. He knew he'd
been stabbed but he didn't know how many times and he didn't
know anything about the other stuff.

Ford reckons telling his mate the details of his father's
murder was one of the toughest things he's had to do. When
he'd finished he walked down to the Golden Fleece Hotel,
where his girlfriend worked. By that stage the stories were
already getting around Scone. He proceeded to debrief in the
age-old manner of cops around the world. One schooner at a
time.

After talking with his colleague, Wells jumped in the car
and drove back down the highway to Singleton where he
knocked off, satisfied at least that his crook was in custody and
that he had made good ground. He then drove another hour
down the road to Newcastle, getting in late. He put his clothes
straight into the washing machine and then tried to rinse the
smell away from his clammy skin. Wells was rattled and woke
up his wife Cath who had been a policewoman herself to tell
her what had happened. Talked on and on about it. He was
pumped up and couldn't sleep well as he went over and over
what he'd seen, what he'd learned and what he'd have to do.

There were a million things going through Wells' mind, but the one he kept coming back to was just how on earth any human being could do that to another person. He'd never encountered such gross inhumanity and he'd encountered plenty.

He woke in the morning with a belting headache, his guts in a knot about the job ahead.

Wells spoke to a few of Pricey's friends on the phone and then had a word with the other cops. He was still keen to have a go at Knight but the doctors reckoned she wasn't up to it; at least not if they wanted to be safe.

There was a truckload of forensic evidence and that was a problem in itself. Crime scene police were back the next day and had collected 106 exhibits, many of which needed DNA testing for blood samples. But it wasn't that simple. The powers that be had decided all local area commands (LAC) now had to pay for the services of the analytical laboratories, which had, until quite recently, been free. Before the laboratory would even look at anything they wanted a letter of authority from the LAC agreeing that the costs would be met. The bill was going to be $20000 for the 106 exhibits. After a lot of negotiating the testing was limited to 28 exhibits at a cost of $5600 to the local force. It was just another example of how the bean counters and politicians were making the job harder for the copper trying to catch a crook. Another pain in the arse and another round of memo writing, phone calls, requests and bureaucracy.

Wells called Detective Sergeant Cynthia Donovan of the Child Protection Investigative Team at Tamworth to interview Knight's youngest children, and she arrived with Wendy Wilson, the assistant manager at the Muswellbrook Department of Community Services. Getting a statement from kids is a highly specialised skill.

Wells also rang Phil Lloyd, a senior sergeant at Newcastle and prosecutor. He wanted to know how best to proceed with the questioning of Knight if and when he could get near her.

For the second night in a row Wells didn't sleep well. To make matters worse that headache had set in and it just wouldn't go away, no matter how much codeine he gobbled. He never got headaches but this one was making up for all the ones he had never had. It was a bastard running here and there, trying to keep on top of all those things and the whole time your head was sounding like a bloody techno record. Boom. Boom. Boom.

He didn't recognise it at the time, but this was his body saying to hell with this. He was stressed by the whole deal. He was running on adrenalin but it wasn't a good feeling. He was anxious and spooked. Everybody was feeling the stress of the situation in one way or another, but few of them realised it at the time. Wells' boss lined up psychiatric counselling, but Bob was going a million miles an hour and couldn't stop. Didn't need it anyway. He was a copper. A bloke.

> Mate. I'm trying to get a crook in the book, I want to find out what's going on. Fuck going up to Aberdeen RSL Club because they're going to debrief everybody. I didn't have time for that shit. That was just the way I felt at the time. I probably should have; then again, there was no attempt to debrief me after that either. You know what I mean? I'm not trying to blame anybody, but there was so much work to do.

Friday morning he transferred a prisoner up to Maitland with Mick Prentice and stuck his head in to see another psychiatric doctor at the hospital who reckoned Knight would be up to an interview at 8 am Saturday. The next day.

The investigation was moving along pretty well. They were

making some progress, and then one of the biggest break-throughs just walked in the door that Friday when Natasha fronted up to the station with a home video for the police to watch. Mick Prentice and Bob stuck the tape in the machine, pushed the play button and sat there with their mouths open. There was Knight saying how she hoped to see her children again. The tape was made only six hours before the murder. The police knew this was a genuine smoking gun. You didn't have to be Sigmund Freud to read between the lines and see that this was some sort of last will and testament.

Wells drove home again, had a couple more pain killers and hit the sack with that same thumping techno beat playing in his head as he tossed and turned, thinking about the inter-view the next morning. What should he ask? What would she say? He was at the hospital at 8 am with Mick Prentice to make sure everything was in place. He was checking out the room when he saw a familiar bloke in a suit walking past.

—Shit! Mick, she's got herself a barrister.

It was Peter Thraves. Somebody had got onto Brett Wiggins, a local solicitor and he had brought in Thraves to help out. The beat in Wells' head got suddenly faster. He wasn't expecting her to get a lawyer. Maybe they weren't going to get a squeak out of her.

Thraves told Wells that Knight had no recollection of what happened on the night of the murder and that although she was prepared to do a brief interview she didn't want to know anything about what happened in the house. The bar-rister said they'd get about ten or fifteen minutes and that Wiggins would sit in on the interview and stop it if the ques-tions went too far.

Shit. Shit. Shit. Wells thought he had it all ready to go. He had a letter from the doctor saying she was fit to be inter-viewed and now there was a bloody barrister there to upset the apple cart. He excused himself and went out to a back room where he phoned Phil Lloyd again. The pair agreed just to lead her gently up to the crime and see what happened from there. There wasn't a lot else that could be done.

He took a deep breath and walked into the room ready to wrestle with the woman who had committed the worst crime he'd ever encountered. Even a cop gets the wind up them about something like this. This woman was plain bloody evil as far as he was concerned and now he had to have a nice little chat with her and find out what she was willing to say without ever mentioning the murder. He was wound up like a thousand day clock, ready to confront the monster behind the door.

10

Katherine's police interview
1-4 March 2000

Katherine Knight had been taken from the crime scene to Muswellbrook Hospital where she arrived at 9.30 am Wednesday morning suffering from the effects of a mild overdose. She was transferred to the Newcastle Mater Misericordiae at 1.15 pm under police escort. The next morning she was alert enough to tell the doctors what pills she had taken (blood pressure and mild antihistamines). She said she wanted to sleep and not wake up. She still wanted to die. Later that day she was transferred to the Maitland Hospital secure psychiatric unit where she was alert but claimed no memory of the previous days. She arrived after lunch with her eyes still closed, but gradually opened them as she received a stream of visitors.

Jason Roughan, her nephew, arrived with a bunch of flowers. He loved Kath and was worried about her. She had taken him in when his parents had thrown him out of home. He came with his girlfriend but they wouldn't let him in. He was turned away, but left the flowers and a number for her to call.

The next day Knight's case was taken up by Dr Joanne

Barrett, a part-time law student. Aware that the patient was
going to be interviewed by the police she took it upon herself
to make sure she got a lawyer. That morning Kath's two half-
brothers, Patrick and Neville, visited and left a phone number
for a solicitor but he couldn't be contacted as it was show day
in town. Somebody eventually contacted local lawyer Brett
Wiggins and he agreed to drop in.

Joy and Melissa went to the hospital, Melissa having made
the trip down from Queensland after finding out that this
really wasn't some sick first-of-the-month joke. The family, as
was their want, had a vigorous argument outside the room.
Melissa was angry with both of her uncles. There were further
troubles at Aberdeen when Patrick and Neville let themselves
into Katherine's house to pick up some clothes for her. Barry
Roughan arrived and told them to get out. At the same time
Chillingworth arrived to get things for his son. Roughan
flagged down a passing police car.

Kath was worried that her youngest daughter was with her
father, David Saunders and his new wife. She arranged with
Melissa to get an AVO taken out on the girl's behalf against
her father. It alleged sexual abuse. Katherine's ability to cause
trouble for others was not inhibited by the fact she was locked
up in a psychiatric hospital facing possible murder charges.

Wiggins visited and agreed to be there when the police
interviewed her the following day.

Both sides were ready.

*   *   *

And here she is, an unremarkable woman, sitting on a chair at
a table in a small featureless hospital room. The monster of
Aberdeen, the woman who slaughtered John Price is just so
ordinary. Could be a librarian. Wells hadn't expected horns

but this 45-year-old mother of four and grandmother is disturbingly mundane. You wouldn't look twice if she walked past you in a supermarket. She's tall, with long, greying red hair, glasses and a straight back.

Detective Victor Ford, Mick Prentice, two other detectives and the custody officer have come along for the ride. The atmosphere in the room is tense and awkward. Silences echo off the clinical decor. The pressure is on Wells and Ford, who will conduct the interview, to come out with a good result.

She is seated in front of a large whiteboard, her arms folded, her glasses case on the table and her solicitor, Brett Wiggins, at her side. There's a nurse there also. They do their introductions for the video camera, then custody officer Senior Constable Barry Miles asks her a few preliminary questions to see if she is fit to be interviewed. He asks if she has read a document setting out her rights.

—I can't read . . . I can read a little, but not enough to save meself.

He asks if she is an Aboriginal or Torres Strait Islander. Knight replies that there is some link five generations back, according to her eldest brother.

—But, we don't use it.

They start the formal interview at 10.29 am and she folds her hands on the table. Wells explains that the interview is being recorded and may be used later in evidence. It kicks off with all the formalities: how she'll get a tape and that she hasn't been pressured or promised anything. It's not until question 44 that the detective approaches the crime.

—Okay. As I've told you, Kathy, I'm investigating the death of John Price, known as Pricey to a lot of people in Aberdeen on or about Wednesday, the 1st of March, this year. I have reason to believe that you may be the person responsible. Is there anything you can tell me about the matter?

Knight shakes her head.

—I don't know anything on it.

—Can you recall, recall the last thing that you do remember?

She begins to fidget, moving her hand from her glasses to her neck. You don't need to be a body language expert to see she is uncomfortable with the question and will attempt to avoid answering it truthfully.

—The last thing I remember was going out for tea with me daughter and the kids. Coming home.

—Okay. Could, could you give me a time, I've been told that that was Tuesday, the 29th of February, this year. Can you tell me anything about that?

—No, then I don't know anything about the next day then.

Wells asked her again what she remembered about Tuesday.

—I had to go to Muswellbrook for the test, to show the doctor the bruises on me breast, and I asked me daughter would she like to go to tea, 'cause she up . . . upset over her little girl's father.

—Right.

—So, we went out for tea and we, I was watching a video and it was too late to take the kids home to bed so they spent the night at Tasha's, and I just went home to [pause] Pricey's.

She says she drove her red Toyota Lite Ace and that Pricey was her defacto and fiancé, that she met him six and a half years ago through her little girl's father, David Saunders, and then one night asked him to dance—she can't remember the year—but the date was October 8.

—Your de facto relationship commenced virtually from about that time?

—No, not quite.

—Okay.

—No. He lived at his house and I lived at mine.

—And you, did you move between those residences from time to time?

—Yeah. He, he was being pretty nasty to me at one stage, and Tasha was having hassles at home, and I went to Brisbane to the alcoholic side of things [*sic*]. The only way I could get into it was saying I was an alcoholic, to get help for meself and for Tasha, and Pricey come up there with me that time.

—What ...

—And when I come back he wouldn't let me live down in me own house. I had to go up there and live with him.

Following Knight's answers is a bit of a wild ride, but Wells hangs in and then asks her to explain the type of relationship she has had.

—I really can't. His wife wanted me to go with him and he come round. He was nice to my children, he was nice to me, and before I went up to live with him, as I said, I went to Brisbane for help meself and my daughter, he'd be, he had sex with me and called me some other woman's name ... He was just being nasty all the time to me or the children ... Pricey would hit me.

—Was there any time that you may have hit Pricey?

—The last time I put me arms up to stop him from choking me and he had me by the breast and all I could think of was the pain in my breast.

—When was that occasion?

—Not too long ago, 'cause I still got the bruise there ... he called the police in ... He was rubbishing me having different fathers for my children again, and I just said to him, 'Hang on,' I said, 'You said last night at a party that your parents were married and they're, and they weren't', and he just went off his brain and said, 'Don't say anything about my mother.' And then he attacked me.

Knight claims confusion about the incident because the

pain in her breast is 'just too agonising to see or think of any-think'. Wells asks about how often she drinks.

—Every now and then ... I like Cadbury's liqueur, Baileys, I don't get that very often, or I'll have a beer ... I used to drink rum a long time ago. Pricey got me to taste that and I like it, but it's not something I drink now ... I can build up a lot of [sigh] what do you call it, I can handle a lot without it, but when I've got it in me I explode quicker. I let, like, you could, you can say things to me and say it and say it and say it and say it, when I haven't got alcohol in me. When I got alcohol in me I come back and say something back to you. You know what I mean?

Wells starts to chip away at her about how much she remembers, testing her alleged memory loss. He asks her what was the last thing she recalls on the night of the murder.

—The last time I recall was ... I went inside and watched a bit of TV.

—Right. Was Pricey there?

—Mmm ...

He backs off for a few questions, before approaching again. It's a delicate matter, any wrong move could get the lawyer's back up and they'd be finished. Wells is trying to pull teeth in the quietest way possible.

—Can you recall what the, what the video was that you were watching?

—No, it was 'Star Trek' ... I only seen a little bit of it 'cause I went to bed meself.

—Okay. So, you remember going to bed?

—Mmm.

—Okay. Was Pricey in bed when you went to bed?

—Mmm.

—And can you recall ...?

—He had to have been.

—Do you recall that he was there or not?

—I don't even remember meself, so... I just remember watching a bit of 'Star Trek' ... I don't remember anything, so, I would have had to have gone to sleep.

—So, you can't. Can you tell me the next thing that you remember after that?

—Them telling me that I'm in the Mater Hospital.

—Do you recall being brought from the Mater here to Maitland?

—I've got a faint recollection of sitting in a, well, lying in an ambulance.

She remembers visits from her sister Joy, her daughter Melissa, her sister-in-law, Val Roughan, and also from her half-brothers Patrick and Neville in the past days. Wells had asked some 223 questions to get to this point and lets Victor Ford take over for a while. Ford takes her straight back to the events of Sunday and the AVO that was served on the Monday evening by the police.

—So, did you have, after the police left, did you [and] Pricey have a discussion about this order?

—Everything was fine between me and Pricey, even before they brought the order in.

—Mmm.

—There was no problems between me and Pricey.

—You realise that what the order is is for you not to sort of see each other or approach each other. That's what part of the order is.

—I can't read very well.

Wells came back to ask a few more questions, the policeman trying to find out if Knight was aware that Price wanted her to leave the house. A matter of motive.

—Was there any discussion from Pricey that he wanted you to leave the house and end the relationship?

—He has said that several times over the whole lot of our relationship.

—Was there any prospect recently that that was going to occur?

—No.

—Is it that Pricey didn't want you to leave or that you didn't want to end the relationship?

—No. Pricey tells me he loves me, and he's sorry and things like that.

—And?

—He wanted me in the relationship with him. He just fires off every now and then.

—And can you tell me what causes him to fire off?

—That he sometimes goes off because of his job.

—All right.

—Other times he's—him losing his job in the mines. If there's a bit of dust on the floor, you know, something's dropped on the floor, he'd go off.

—In the days leading up to Tuesday, the 29th, do you recall any incident where Pricey was asleep in the bed and it was the early hours of the morning and he woke up [to] find you standing at the end of the bed?

—No.

—That, which caused him to jump up out of bed startled.

—No.

Another memory lapse. Wells moves onto past domestics, asking if she can recall the police ever being called.

—One was when I was drunk. But I never got to see the police on that one. So, what went on was really between the police and John there.

—All right. Do you recall any of that at all?

—Not with the police there. Not with the argument up to

it. Pricey was trying to tell Rosemary that Johnathon had sex with my daughter up the arse.

There's a little confusion about who is who, but it's established that Johnathon is Price's son, Rosemary is his daughter and Knight is referring to her daughter Melissa.

—And I told him he was a liar, that it was he [*sic*] jerked himself off with washing up detergent at her, and she was petrified. She rung me up. I went to Pricey about it. This was in the early stages of our going together.

—Is there any other . . .?

Knight starts to ramble from one topic to another with allegations of different children and husbands and sexual abuse. The cops don't seem too interested in pursuing this line and probably find it hard to keep up with her as she jumps about. The interview is suspended at 11.11 am, forty minutes in, as the audio tape needs changing. Everyone seems happy to have a breather. It's hard work getting anything out of her while not pushing her so far that Wiggins will call them off. They've logged up nearly 300 questions but haven't made great progress. They change tapes and Bob Wells starts again.

—I've been told that there was one incident earlier, sorry, later last year on, in or around August, 1999, that you caused a minor stab wound to Pricey's right chest.

—Yeah. That's right.

—Okay. Can you tell me the circumstances of the incident?

She tells them some convoluted story over a four-way argument between Price, his youngest daughter, his ex-wife and her, and how she accused his kids of interfering with hers.

—And he's turned around and said my kids deserved to be raped by his children. And it could have been a fork, a spoon or anything in my hand—it was a knife that you cut

your meal with and I aimed it at him and it got him. He was
leaning closer than what I thought. And . . .

—Were, were you . . .?

—My eyesight was bad at that time, I've only had new
glasses since then.

—All right. Are you aware of where you actually . . . where
the wound was?

—It was up on the shoulder.

—Do, are you aware of what shoulder it was?

—Not any more.

—Can you tell me your recollection of when that was?

—Nope. I went to the solicitor on it and I went to the
police and told them about it.

—What solicitor did you go to?

—Noonan, is it? Mmm. In Muswellbrook.

—And what police did you go to?

—Scone.

—And can you tell me if there was any police action or
further inquiries made in relation to that?

—No. There was none.

—Do you know if there was a record ever made of it?

—Well, they said that they were going to, because I told
them Pricey would most probably come in and report it. So, I
don't know.

—Are you aware of, aware if Pricey came in and reported it?

—No.

—Is there any other occasion where you've assaulted or
caused any injuries to Pricey?

—No.

Wells goes back to Tuesday night. She doesn't remember
what she wore to bed. He asks her to draw a plan of the house,
to see where it will lead, but she and Wiggins decide she
won't, so he moves on to a bit of her history and then revisits

her version of the alleged incident between her daughter Melissa and Price's son Johnathon.

—He took her once on his motorbike ... and he jerked himself off in front of her and petrified her and she rung me up to come there. She didn't want to press charges so I had to leave it. I told John about it and he just said he's just taking notice of his silly mates.

—So, she told ... You didn't go to the police about it at all?

—No.

—And you spoke to John Junior about it?

—I spoke to, no, I never spoke to John Junior till he, about 12 months ago on it, when he yelled it out in the pub.

—What do you mean by that?

—Well, he yelled it out in the pub that he rooted Melissa up the arse, and I said, 'You're nothing but a liar. You did not' ... I was very angry about him doing things like that to my daughter. But my daughter did not want charges laid, so I had to leave it.

Knight went on to claim, without foundation, that not only had Price's son abused her daughter, but his youngest daughter had interfered with her two youngest and that her girl's father had also interfered with her daughter.

—Has there been any other incidents where you've had a confrontation with a person with a knife?

—Yes.

—Are you able to ...?

—I asked this lady to take me to Coffs Harbour to my mother-in-law's place to stay.

—Do you know who that person was?

—Molly Perry.

—Can you supply me with the circumstances surrounding that incident?

—Prenatal, from having the baby.

—Post-natal?

—Yeah. Whatever it is . . . She was very sick [Melissa]. I got her daughter to go over and get her, I signed a cheque from, at the garage. I was arrested and put in Morisset.

—And did, the incident with the knife, do you actually remember what it was about? The . . . What you did with the knife?

—Nope.

—And do you recount . . . Recall to me what year that was or how long ago?

—No. My 23-year-old daughter was only just a baby. They said I swung her around by her legs, I don't remember none of that.

The two police start to grill her further about her movements before the murder, what she was wearing and why the children stayed at Natasha's. She says she hadn't planned for them to.

—The recording of the, the video on that Tuesday at Tasha's, do you know how long that recording went for?

—Not very long . . .

—And at one point there you look at the camera and say, 'I love my children'.

—Ye-es.

—'I love my children and I hope so see them again.'

—Well, I say things like that . . .

—Okay. It . . . any significance in that?

—No. It was just being cheeky on the camera with my children.

—At one time I think you say to your daughter . . . something about a pram, an antique pram or something.

—Yeah. That's her little pram.

—And can you elaborate on that bit of the video tape?

—Well, her father promised her her push-bike two Christmases back.

—All right.

—And I was just letting her know that [Natasha's daughter] wasn't getting the pram; it's her.

The detectives ask her if she will provide a copy of her handwriting, but she refuses. She also says she can't say who Pricey's friends are, only that he goes to the pub every day and that she goes with him on Fridays and some weekends. She then agrees that she knows Geoffrey Bowditch, Anthony Keegan and Jon Collison. She says he doesn't have any enemies she knows of.

Knight then claims that her youngest son ended up hating Pricey because he would grab the boy on his 'dickie', a practice that made the older man laugh but upset her and the boy. Another log to keep the sexual abuse fires burning. Knight also displays a degree of knowledge about the interview process when pressed about Price's cars, asking Wiggins if the police are allowed to repeat questions. She claims no knowledge of how her car came to be back at her house.

The interview is petering out.

—Are you aware, did anybody come to the house while you were watching 'Star Trek' that evening?

—Not that I'm recollecting.

—Okay. Do, do you recall if there was any other person there besides yourself and Pricey?

—No.

That's 504 questions and almost one hour of interview time and the police realise they are not going to get any more so they wind it up. Wells has one last thing to say to Knight.

—Kathy, on Monday 6th of March—that's next Monday, Kathy—I will be arranging for a court hearing here at the hospital. It will be at this hearing, after I've made other inquiries, that you will be charged with the murder of John Price.

Knight looks at him sideways.

—I don't even know he's dead yet.

She isn't letting go of this act for a minute, but Wells has got a little more out of her than he thought he would. She's indicated that there is a bit of violence from Price and other men to her and now he's got to find the husbands and get their stories.

He rings a few of the senior police and briefs them about the interview, then heads off to see Phil Lloyd at Kalipa Bay on Lake Macquarie. His head is still thumping and he's excited, shaking, on a dirty adrenalin high. He's wondering if he could have got more from the interview. Where should he go next? How is he going to handle all the work? This is the biggest job he's ever done. He knows he has to try for a murder charge but that raises the investigative bar so high. Crooks will almost always cop a plea for manslaughter when you've got them cold and the prosecutor's office is usually happy to accept it and tie things up neatly and cheaply. To Wells this is a murder, a calculated murder; the worst he's ever seen. He doesn't want her taking a plea.

As he drives on he suddenly remembers that they've forgotten to ask her about Natasha's story of her saying she was going to kill Price. Fuck it. How could that happen? Things are going faster and faster. Fuck. Fuck. Fuck. How could you be so fucking stupid? Confronting Knight has brought back all the horrors from that house, the skin and the head and the butchered body. He can't get over what she did to Price, what the poor bastard went through. In his time he's seen dozens of terrible car accidents, train deaths, even a body crushed in a wool press. He could accept the damage done to somebody in an accident but this was done by the woman he was just sitting with. He's almost hyperventilating, freaking out and he can't keep driving. He pulls the car over near the Ryehope cemetery and puts his head in his hands. He's disturbed the bats deep in the cave and they're beating their wings against his face. He feels bloody awful. Exhausted but unable to slow down. After a while his heart gives up trying to bash through his ribs and he gets some composure back. He feels like shit but crawls around to Lloyd's where the prosecutor assures him they can ask a supplementary question on Monday. Lloyd senses something is wrong and puts his arm around Wells as the detective goes to leave. He asks if he is okay.

—Of course I am. I'm fine, mate.

—Just take it easy.

Wells has to get off to Singleton early the next morning so he heads home. It's already after 6 pm and on the drive back he starts to get into a state again. His head's still throbbing like a bastard and his heart's banging away so much it's hard to catch breath. At home he gropes towards the bedroom, unable to talk to Cath or the kids. He breaks down. He is sobbing and rocking back and forth on the bed like a distraught child. Cath walks in, she thinks something terrible must have happened. He tells her that it's the murder investigation that's getting on top of him.

—I can't handle this ... I can't get over what she did ... How could somebody do that to somebody else?

Bob's two young daughters look in and see Dad in this terrible state, Mum trying to comfort him. Cath wants him to go to the doctor's but he says he'll be fine. That night she wakes and finds him screaming and running around the house.

—Where are the girls. Cath ... Are the girls alive? I've got to find them.

He has no recollection in the morning. It is the classic hypervigilance associated with post-traumatic stress disorder. Another night he dreams he is being wheeled into an operating theatre. He looks up as they are about to put the oxygen mask on his face and Katherine Knight is staring down at him. He is paralysed by fear.

The next day he takes it easy, fires up the barbecue and the family have their traditional Sunday affair. Wells tries to keep up appearances but he's still feeling pretty awful. To make matters worse, the stress has caused his gout to flare up. He finds himself hobbling around for the next few weeks with one shoe on and another nearby. It's all he needs. It's a hereditary disorder that he can usually keep in check with pills, but this time they're not doing the trick.

Over the weekend Knight has been taking it easy in the hospital. They've had her on one-to-one nursing worried that she might react badly to the interview but she is fine. She is sleeping when the family visit later in the day.

On Monday Bob Wells hits the ground running again. There's going to be a formal charging of Knight at lunchtime at the hospital and he prepares a statement of facts for the magistrate. He types out that supplementary question for her in capital letters.

YOUR DAUGHTER, NATASHA MAREE KELLETT, HAS MADE A STATEMENT TO POLICE. AMONGST OTHER THINGS, NATASHA HAS SAID THAT ON AN OCCASION AFTER YOU AND PRICEY GOT BACK TOGETHER AFTER A SPLIT-UP, THAT YOU SAID SOMETHING LIKE, 'IF I KILL PRICEY, I'LL KILL MYSELF AFTER IT.'

QUESTION:—WOULD YOU CARE TO COMMENT ABOUT THAT? YOU ARE NOT OBLIGED TO COMMENT UNLESS YOU WISH TO DO SO. ANY COMMENT MADE BY YOU WILL BE SUBMITTED AS PART OF THE BRIEF OF EVIDENCE AGAINST YOU. DO YOU UNDERSTAND THAT?

He types out the word ANSWER and leaves a space for her to respond.

When it's presented she gives a three-word reply: 'I don't know.' Lloyd writes it in the space left by Wells. She signs it.

Up at the hospital Wells and Lloyd talk with the barrister Thraves and the prosecutor writes out a document by hand that will give them consent to take blood samples and medical records. They formerly charge her before a magistrate at 1.30 pm in the same room that she was interviewed in two days earlier. The magistrate orders a psychiatric assessment to be completed before she appears in court again.

Then a strange thing happens. Knight is refused bail and released from the hospital into the custody of the police. Bob Wells and Phil Lloyd wait while she gets her stuff ready then she gets into the back of their car and they drive her to Maitland Police Station. Knight sits in the back seat with two suitcases at her feet and talks with the prosecutor about the fishing at Glenbawn Dam as they head down the highway.

On arrival at Maitland things get stranger. Ross Dellosta, the forensic officer, has taken a footprint from the kitchen floor and wants to see if it matches hers. They've never done this before and end up putting a piece of A4 paper on the floor of the police station. Two police reluctantly support Knight while they ink up her foot and then she places it down on the paper. One remembers cringing as she leant on him. He'd seen what she'd done with those hands.

They lock her in a cell and Wells goes upstairs to see how Dellosta is getting on. The fingerprint expert is battling similar demons to Wells, although neither of them quite understand it at this stage. Dellosta stumbled on the Strathfield Shopping Centre massacre in 1991, when Wade Frankum ran amok with a knife and gun, killing six people and himself. It was a horrific murder. His first victim was a school girl he killed with a machete. Things like that knock you around. You never really recover. Dellosta made two trips to 84 St Andrews Street: once while the body was there and once the day after, dusting for prints on knives and light switches and walls. He found Knight's bloody print pattern on a laundry door, an empty coffee mug and one filled with solidified human flat. Seeing the woman who did those terrible things to Price seems to upset the 51-year-old detective. When Wells walks in Dellosta looks panicked. Ashen-faced.

—It's not her footprint! It's not a match!

—Jesus fucking Christ. What do you mean?

—It's not hers.

Wells can't believe it. It's a bloody nightmare. He walks down the stairs again with the world crashing down around his ears. Was someone else there? Did she have an accomplice? Did somebody else murder him? It's just the sort of bullshit a good defence lawyer can use to muddy the waters. Handled properly it can create doubt and destroy the police case.

He goes into Lloyd and tells him the news but as he is talking Dellosta comes bounding down the stairs. It's all right. Everything is okay. He made a mistake. It is her footprint. Soon after this Dellosta stops working and takes sick leave. He has never been back since. The experience with Katherine Knight was the last straw. He can't even see his best mates who were on the case because they remind him of that crime. A few of the police involved have found it hard to see each other since. It unsettles them. There's never just one victim in a murder.

Lloyd and Wells then put Knight in the car and drive down to Newcastle, tailed by a highway patrol car just in case. They hand her over to the corrective services who take her into custody while papers are prepared for her transfer to Sydney.

Knowing she is soon to be locked up is some relief for Wells. The bird is in the cage and she has been charged. That night Katherine Knight spends the first of many nights in

Mulawa prison, Sydney. Still Bob has a bad sleep. His head pounding so bad it feels like AC/DC are playing under the pillow. More nightmares. The next morning he has an appointment with a forensic pathologist.

11

Katherine and Dave Saunders
1983–90

Dave Saunders, panel beater and defacto of Katherine Knight, is dead. Kath's killed him because he left her. She's broken the news to their two-year-old daughter but the little one doesn't believe it. She is sure he will come back. He's just gone away, after all, he's gone away before and come back. He could walk through the door at any time.

The finality of death is a difficult concept for any of us to grasp, let alone one so young, and one day while out driving she becomes particularly adamant that her father is alive.

—That's Daddy there, Mummy. There's Daddy. He's not dead. It's Daddy . . . DADDY! DADDY!

The excitement in her eyes is something else. She wants it so bad she really can see him. And, sure enough, like Lazarus, David Saunders is back from the dead, walking among the good people of the Hunter Valley as if nothing had ever happened.

Nothing had happened. Saunders wasn't dead. Never had been. Katherine had announced his premature demise to his baby daughter because he had had the audacity to leave her. It was a last attempt at payback; a desperate twist of the knife.

The main street of Aberdeen looking north, 2002. Katherine Knight's house is marked.

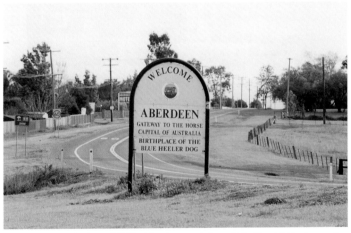

Aberdeen road sign, 2002. The town claims it is the birthplace of the Blue Heeler, but Muswellbrook erected a statue of the dog, asserting ownership of the breed.

A view of the derelict Aberdeen abattoir looking west toward the town, 2001.

Katherine Knight and David Kellett on their
wedding day, 1974.

Katherine Knight in more
recent years.

John Price and Katherine Knight. She is wearing a cap supplied by the mining company from which she had him sacked.

John Price.

John Price's house, 84 St Andrews St, Aberdeen, 2002.

Katherine Knight's house on the main street in Aberdeen, 2001. The windows were boarded up after the crime to stop vandalism.

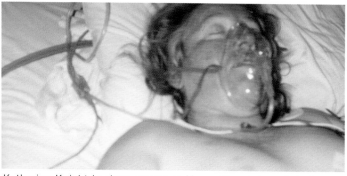

Katherine Knight is given oxygen at Muswellbrook Hospital after being apprehended at the murder scene.

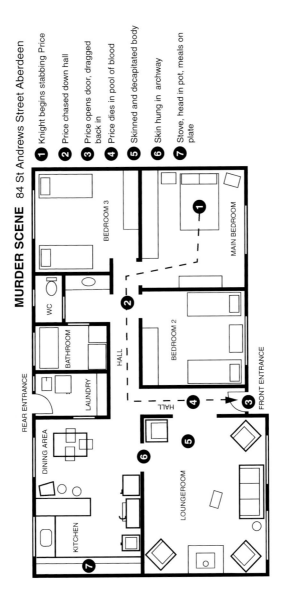

MURDER SCENE 84 St Andrews Street Aberdeen

1. Knight begins stabbing Price
2. Price chased down hall
3. Price opens door, dragged back in
4. Price dies in pool of blood
5. Skinned and decapitated body
6. Skin hung in archway
7. Stove, head in pot, meals on plate

BEDROOM 3

MAIN BEDROOM

WC

BATHROOM

LAUNDRY

HALL

BEDROOM 2

FRONT ENTRANCE

REAR ENTRANCE

DINING AREA

KITCHEN

LOUNGEROOM

HALL

Floor plan of John Price's house showing where the stages of his murder took place.

Bob Wells outside Aberdeen police station during the trial, 2001.

Some people insist on the last word but she insists on inflicting the last wound.

That day, however, the game was up. With the two-year-old carrying on in the back, Kath reluctantly turned the car around and let the pair reunite, leaving Natasha on hand to supervise. For some reason she never trusted Dave. It was just like that bastard to come back and haunt her.

*   *   *

Katherine's world got a whole lot tougher after she bailed out on Kellett. The stress of raising two children in a world where your only real support was a dysfunctional family unit took its toll. The following years were spent hopping between meat-works, caravan parks, tough towns and violent relationships. Everything had seemed so nice there for a while. She and Kellett had a little house with a lemon tree out the front, a little baby, and then he left with that teenager and everything was spoiled. Later, even Katherine, with her terror of aban-donment, could see that it was time to move on. It showed a degree of maturity she didn't have when they married. Calling the removalists while he was away driving the truck demonstrated a considerable strength of will. Maybe she was finding her feet.

Kath initially sent Melissa and Natasha back to her mum and dad's at Aberdeen, where Ken had bought a small farm block on Rouchel Road near Glenbawn Dam with a payout he got from hurting himself at work. The new place had been subdivided from one of the larger properties after the turn-off to the dam. An idyllic rural setting at the foothills of the mountains that was far enough from town to afford some privacy but close enough not to be inconvenient. Kath stayed on at the meatworks in Dinmore and for a short while at

Beaudesert. She drove down to see the kids as often as she could.

When she first brought the girls down she was worried she might be pregnant. It would be an absolute disaster if she was knocked up so soon after having Natasha. Especially now she was single. It turned out she wasn't pregnant, so she went back to work. In the meantime the girls got a crash course in being a Knight. Melissa remembers the interlude at Nan and Pops with some of the same wide-eyed horror that her mother displays when she recalls her youth. Melissa saw Pop hitting Nan, Pop hitting Mum and Pop abusing them if they got out of line. Ken seemed to suffer from a lot of frustrations. Barbara used to say that Katherine and her father were too much alike, but in reality Kath had got her nature from both parents and, if anything, more from Mum than Dad. For her part, Melissa, who was old enough to be aware of what was going on around her, was starting to see life through Mum's eyes. If the girls didn't have the nature, they were getting a taste of the grass-roots nurture.

Eventually Kath moved back to Aberdeen and got a job at the meatworks. Eight years after she'd driven away, leaving her mother lying bruised in the dirt and the whole town still talking about the baby on the railway tracks, she was back at the slaughterhouse where it had all begun. To hell with them and what they thought.

Ken and Barbara must have had some idea of what she was going through; they'd been through the same thing when they had left town back in the 1950s. Katherine liked to pretend nothing had ever happened and if she saw any of the family she had bailed up at the service station she looked through them as if they were complete strangers.

Back at home things took up where they had left off. Ken was still Ken and Kath was still Kath. Kath's medical records include a note on 4 September 1984 that says 'Father allegedly hitting pt (patient) with fist last night'. The records show Kath had a bruise over her left breast. She was sent off for X-rays but there were no broken ribs. She would say years later that Ken had assaulted her in 1983, but it could have been the same incident—beatings are like Christmases: they all start to merge into one over the years.

Kath had photographs she showed Saunders of bruises she said were caused by her dad. She also says he hit Natasha when she was four, which would have been around the same time. There is no record that it was a serious incident, but it wouldn't have had to be much to become part of the rich, sometimes fantastic weave of Kath and her children's victimhood. With her return, father and daughter recommenced their life-long war and soon stopped speaking to each other—a stand-off that lasted a couple of years and would be repeated many times over the next twenty years.

Things were always a little odd at the family home and Barbara became sick around this period. Neville Roughan, who was going through his religious phase and was running a nearby youth centre, gathered the family all around her in a recliner rocker and they laid on hands in some form of Christian healing ceremony.

Katherine started having back and shoulder problems at work. Like many other members of her family, she found herself suffering a possibly lucrative work-related injury. She had two weeks off in 1984 after falling down the stairs. In January 1985 she was off again with a back injury. A month later she was off again. Kath had originally hurt it up in Queensland in a car accident in 1979 and then in a motorbike accident the year after. In February 1985, after she'd already been placed on light duties because of shoulder and back pain, a tub of meat fell from the line and caught the hook in her belt violently wrenching her back. She was hospitalised for three days.

These were restless years and the trio of Kath and her two daughters moved around a lot. Melissa remembers moving with her mother into a house in Wells Gully. It's an out of the way spot on a road that winds out of Muswellbrook. Pretty but isolated. 'Mum had met a man while we were living at Wells Gully. This man had exposed himself to us, so Mum left him immediately.' It was becoming a familiar story.

Melissa remembers having to do a lot of the domestic work because Mum was incapacitated with her back injury. Barbara Knight moved in with them for a while, but things were a little hard for the women. There was an incident with a dog dying under the house after taking a bait. Melissa and Mum climbed under to get it out. There was a bushfire too. The women decided to move back into town to a house on the east side of the railway tracks, near where John Price would later build. Katherine then found a Commission house at 104 Segenhoe Street. A man moved in for a while. Melissa has been told about him too. 'He didn't hit us but Mum said he had sexual intentions towards us kids, so she left him.'

Another man. Another potential molester. It was becoming a pattern. The divorce from Kellett came through in 1986 but Kath still wasn't feeling the best and had been seeing the doctor and getting prescriptions for her nerves when David Saunders stepped into the ring.

Dave, or Saundo, as his mates call him, is another hard drinking Valley boy. He's a rev head, a former speedway driver who is either in the pub or under the bonnet of a car. He has a friend in every bar and a terrible capacity for the grog. A rough diamond with a puppy-dog look and a soft side that reveals itself, appropriately, in his child-like passion for dogs. A good bloke, maybe a little hopeless. Dave was working down the valley at the mines when they first met, although he was a panel beater by trade.

At the time he had a mate called Kelvin Dunn who he'd drop in to have a drink with at the Aberdeen Bowling Club on the way home from work. One time they ended up playing cards with this outgoing redhead called Kath Knight. It turned into a long night and they had so much fun they re-convened the next night and the next, before he worked up the courage to ask her out. Kath, Dave, and another couple, Terry and Dawn, headed to the local Chinese restaurant. Everyone had a good time and Saunders could see that this woman was interested.

The new girl proved to be pretty handy in the sack too. Not many inhibitions on that front. Saunders, an inveterate pants man, looked like he was onto a good thing. He found out she had two kids, but he had three of his own and a former wife, so there was a bit of a balance there. It also turned out he knew her kids and her brother. Like Kellett before him, he'd had a session or two with Charlie and one time got pissed out at Ken and Barbara's and ended up sleeping the night on a couch outside. Melissa and Natasha were staying with their grandparents at the time.

Dave remembers Barbara was not that engaging but once he showed an interest in her daughter she asked him, 'What sort of fella are ya?' To which he replied, 'A pretty fair one.' And that was that. It must have been some sort of vetting process. Ken had bought an old combustion stove and Saunders installed it for him. He fixed up Ken's Chevrolet Luv too. The perfect son-in-law.

Saunders and his dingo pup moved down from Scone to 104 Segenhoe Street with Kath and the kids and for a while there things were just dandy. He was working long shifts at the mines and putting in equally long sessions at various pubs. He was in great demand as his panel beater's eye made him one of the area's better pool players. It didn't take long until this started to annoy Kath. Saunders was mates with every second person in the valley and had a lot of socialising to do.

Saunders is one of those blokes who hates being alone, maybe hates being home and he is way too fond of the grog, even by his own reckoning. A lot of the time Kath left Melissa in charge of the kids while she accompanied him from one pool table to another, one pub after another.

She was feeling pretty good about herself again. The new bloke wasn't a bad catch—miners earn a lot of money—and she was back in her own town. Then, in December 1986, not long after the couple moved in together, they got a phone call telling them to get around to her parents' place straight away. Her mother had collapsed and was very sick. They raced around to Rouchel Road and found an ambulance there with Barbara in the back. Kath climbed inside to be with her but she was too late. Barbara was dead. It was terribly traumatic for Kath—her mum was not a pretty sight.

> She had all of this stuff coming out of her mouth and it stunk . . .
> I couldn't understand why she died and left me. I don't know
> why God took her and left me in pain. I hated her for dying too.

Kath was devastated. And angry. She came out of the ambulance and launched into her father. Shouting that he had killed her. Him and his violence. It had to be somebody's fault. Things got ugly and fraught. It was a terrible scene, all the yelling and swearing and distress. Death is hard for any of us to accept, but for somebody like Kath it was doubly confusing and frightening. The family went up to the hospital that night to view Barbara, but nobody had prepared the body. She was still an awful sight, lying in a hospital blanket, contorted as if still in pain, her tongue poking out obscenely. Everybody was shocked by what they saw. Mum didn't seem at peace.

The following day Kath became so upset Dave took her to Scone hospital. She was sedated and sent home. The death of her mother left her vulnerable and alone. A frightened child without protection. She had been abandoned again and it felt like she was dropping into a dark hole. She loved her mum. Loves her. Wants to be with her. Despite the beatings, her mother had been her protector at home. The one who made it a bit safer. It was Barbara who picked up her skirts and trudged off to the local school when Kath was being belted by the teachers. She was the source of all her daughter's knowledge about the world and men.

For the whole family, but Kath particularly, Barbara's passing spelt a terrible finality. Now there was never any chance of having the love they craved. Joy was equally upset, as were Barbara's sisters. In Katherine's mind somebody had to be at fault. The circle of blame grew. Sometimes Kath says that she had just told her mother about Ken hitting Natasha and other times that she had just told her about the sexual abuse from her brothers. She seems to see some connection between the knowledge and the terrible death and feels guilt over this. She lost her faith in God. At times she just craved to be with her mother. Hated her for going, but wanted to follow. There were thoughts of suicide. She even seemed to reject her own children. If she'd been abandoned they could be too. Times like these are dangerous for the dependants of somebody who is terrified of independence. When Kellett had left her she blamed Melissa and seemed to want to take it out on her. This time her father Ken seemed to wear most of the blame.

Saunders says that in the midst of her turmoil Kath was left to organise the wake. He felt like the family had abandoned Kath, but Barry Roughan says he doesn't think it was like this. He says Joy was the apple of her mother's eye and Kath was not the sort to organise things, which isn't to say she didn't see it differently in her mind. Another brother says it is more likely that Kath did the work; she was the connecting point for the dysfunctional group. Roughan says that his half-sister was affected by the death for a long time to come.

The funeral was held in the little church in Aberdeen and was a hysterical affair. Barbara's sisters were distraught and at least one threw herself on the coffin. Neville did a reading and battled through a eulogy. Barbara was cremated and her ashes were spread in the mountains outside town as she had wished.

And then she was completely gone: no grave, no memorial, just a few possessions, a number of which Kath kept and surrounded herself with. The death of Mum triggered another downward spiral in Katherine and her new relationship. Another plank collapsed.

After a brief honeymoon period—two months at best—life started getting pretty uncomfortable for Saunders. Kath was paranoid, she couldn't be out with him all the time and when he wasn't there on time she would start to go crazy. Uncontrollably angry. Minor separations like this were another form of abandonment and every minute was distressing. She started accusing him of sleeping with other women. Yelled and screamed. In his roamings there were plenty of women friends, but Kath's real problem was with a woman called Glenda 'Gert' Reichel, another local girl who had had a relationship with Dave and cared for him a lot.

A month after Barbara's death Saunders took off. All the abuse and accusation had got too much for him and he decided to find a bit of peace. He shifted back to Scone to his old place in Liverpool Street in January. But Kath had other ideas. He wasn't getting off that easily.

The very day he moved out she went looking for him. She had worked herself up into a state. Her anger was volcanic. He'd been out having a couple of beers with Jon Collison—the same man who would drive out to find Pricey fourteen years later—in Guernsey Street, and decided to leave his car there and walk back to Liverpool Street. Kath drove up and he wasn't home. She saw his car and decided to take it out on that. Saundo loved his cars. When he got home later, Kath arrived at the door. She seemed pretty calm and wanted to talk about the relationship, wanted him to come back to Aberdeen. So he jumped in her car and headed back there. On the way he clicked that something had happened to his car and demanded she drive him back to it. Sure enough, he found the windscreen wipers, the aerial and the inside damaged. He was furious. They headed back again to Segenhoe Street and things got really heated, but she wasn't taking a backward step. She accused him of sleeping with Glenda. And then some.

—You're fucking that bitch. You're fucking her and you've got me pregnant!

It was a bombshell and then the volcano really erupted. She was at him, calling him all the names under the sun, pushing him, screaming and abusing him. His head was spinning. She was out of control. It was the first time things had got physical and Saunders says he pushed her away to protect himself as she started to throw big heavy punches at his head. Kath got more incensed and was yelling loud enough for the whole valley to hear.

—You kicked me in the stomach! You kicked me!

She was hysterical, absolutely out of control, and next thing they were in the kitchen. She ran to the drawer and grabbed one of the knives. Saunders was sure she was going to stab him, but instead she ran out the back door. He didn't follow her out immediately, but when he did she was holding his dingo pup in her arms. Something seemed odd and then he realised there was blood everywhere: on her, the dog and the knife. He looked more closely and could see a gaping wound across the dog's throat. It was already dead. There was blood everywhere. She had calmed down, but was even more frightening because now she seemed to be in control.

Saunders was terrified and ran for his life, taking refuge at a mate's home. Somebody rang the police. When they arrived at 104 Segenhoe Street nobody was there. Kath had done a runner too. Saunders wandered back from the neighbours and the police asked him where his girlfriend was. He didn't know. They looked inside and the place was like an abattoir. There was blood all over the kitchen floor. Where had the blood come from? He showed them the dead dingo. They seemed reluctant to believe him but eventually moved on.

According to her daughter Melissa, her mother showed up at her sister Joy's house after she had cut the dingo's throat. She was carrying a shotgun in her hand, saying she had killed Dave. On going back to the house they found blood everywhere and no sign of Saunders. Just the dead dog.

Saunders drove back to Scone around midnight and noticed Ken's Chevvy Luv parked at the Scone hospital. He didn't know what it was about, but was shitting himself that she had spun some line and the cops might come back to arrest him. Sure enough, Kath was inside the hospital reporting that she had been attacked. She said her boyfriend had kicked her in the stomach and punched her and that she was pregnant. Apart from a slightly swollen lip and a small bump on the back of her head she had no other physical manifestations of the attack. The only kick in the guts Katherine had taken was when David left. She complained of general body soreness and was given an aspirin and told to come back and see the doctor in the morning. Unsatisfied, she went around to another doctor a few hours later. This time she had lacerations on her lip and forehead and a bruise on the arm. She said her thigh and hip were sore and she felt giddy.

Kath had probably left the hospital and hurt herself before seeing the next doctor. There was no limit to what she was willing to do to square up with Saunders for leaving her. In her mind it was totally justified. It turned out she wasn't pregnant either.

Showing the same sympathy he would to a confused pup, Saunders went back to her. He was a man of infinite sympathy and somehow he found a way to love her. Being pissed a lot helped too, but she was back on her best behaviour and when she was well behaved she was a wonderful person, caring and full of loving energy. However, the incident set a pattern for the rest of their relationship.

Meeting Saunders had proven to be good for Kath's finances. She stopped work because of her back. He ended up giving her $300 a week for housekeeping and Katherine loved money. Sometimes the money wasn't enough. Saunders remembers one week she said she'd lost it and he gave her $300 more. Later he was in the roof and found a machine for transferring Super8 movie to video that cost about $300. She was greedy and pawing like that. She loved easy money and he was a good source of it. All the miners were.

Things with Katherine were never smooth for long and soon it was on again. Glenda Reichel remembers her storming into the Belmore Hotel one afternoon searching for Saunders, who was talking to her. You could hear the ground shake as Kath bowled into the pub and confronted the pair. Calling him all the names under the sun. It was one of life's shitty little coincidences according to Glenda and Dave, but Kath wasn't wearing that bullshit.

—You want her or me? If it's me, you follow me out of this fucking pub right now.

Glenda watched as poor old Dave whispered an apology, shrugged his shoulders and followed.

Like a mongrel dog.

The effect of Barbara's death on Katherine was demonstrated further a few months after she killed the dingo. Saunders and Kath were returning from Wingen when they stopped at Scone to pick up Wayne Partridge, better known as Shakey. Driving back to Aberdeen, Kath got herself into a state again, although nobody can remember why. She had been agitated all day. Distracted. The boys had been drinking a fair bit and everyone was a bit cranky. Just another pissy day with a moody girlfriend. There were roadworks near what the locals call Water Tower Hill, and it was around here she got so worked up that she opened the door and tried to jump out while they were driving. Shakey grabbed her and managed to keep her inside until Dave stopped the car. She eventually calmed down and they drove slowly on to Aberdeen, dropping Shakey off at the caravan park before heading home.

When they got to Segenhoe Street, Kath went into the house while Dave stayed outside talking to the neighbour Kelvin Dunn. Then Natasha ran out crying.

—Help, Mummy's on the floor! Mummy's fallen down!

Saunders found her on the floor with an empty bottle beside her and pills scattered around the floor. Dave was pissed and panicked. He got Kelvin to drive up to Scone Hospital while he tried to keep her awake. They stumbled into the emergency department and on cue Kath collapsed unconscious. The doctors wanted to know what sort of pills she'd taken and Saunders got in the car and drove full pelt all the way back to Aberdeen. He can't remember now what had happened to Kelvin. He was in no condition to drive. He rang the name of the pills through and then they asked how many she had taken. With a bit of guidance he did the sums and they got a fair idea. She was pretty crook though and was admitted to hospital with suspected inhalation pneumonia. It was 10 May 1987, Mother's Day, and the first Kath had spent without Barbara. The date seemed significant. As the years passed, family members became wary around Kath near the anniversary of her mother's death. She would get stressed, depressed and moody.

That year the family rallied and began to visit the troubled twin. She told her dad Ken she wanted to go home and finish it all. She didn't want the kids, she just wanted to be with her mum. It was Melissa's birthday but Kath still thought it was Mother's Day. A girl at school told Melissa her mother didn't love her; that was why she tried to commit suicide and was in hospital for her birthday.

Kath was counselled by Reverend Ian Johnson from the Aberdeen Presbyterian church and his assistant counsellor Neville Knight, Kath's half-brother. Neville visited Saunders while his sister was in hospital. He said that she was blaming his drinking for all the violence and that he had better lay off her. Sanders told Neville he had never hit his sister and she was the one who was violent. The brother seemed to accept this and asked if he would go and visit her in hospital. Saunders said he would and in an act of faith agreed to give up the grog.

There was a miraculous change in Kath after Dave dropped in. She reverted from suicidal to ecstatic and she was released from hospital soon after, but the doctors were wary of her instability and made sure she had no drugs at home, briefing Saunders on the dangers and even contacting the local pharmacy to make sure she didn't get her hands on any. Katherine's moods could always turn on a pin.

She was referred to a psychiatrist and remained unstable on release from the hospital. Later she asked Saunders to take her to a psychiatric hospital near Wollongong where, he recalls, she stayed for two weeks before he brought her back to Aberdeen.

They stayed together. How could he abandon her when she was such a pathetic mess? After six months he decided to drink again. He had stayed sober all that time and nothing had improved. She would still launch into him at will, having what he called her little fits. He concluded his drinking didn't affect her moods but it certainly helped him put up with them.

Later that year she was back at her local doctor's complaining of back pain. Dave can recall that she was trying to bluff compensation out of the meatworks and would lift wardrobes, hoping to exacerbate the injury before seeing a doctor. After 1986 she never worked again. It was a big change in her life, she'd been wielding her knives on and off for nearly fifteen years and now the days were a little more empty. Katherine was always keen to move, to do something. She didn't like being still much.

After she got out of the psychiatric hospital, Kath finally got pregnant to Dave. She had difficulties with morning sickness early in the term and was admitted to hospital at least three times in November, although by her last visit the doctors suggested that the extent of her illness was exaggerated and suspected depression was the real cause.

Dave and Kath's daughter was born in June 1988. She had her mum's colouring and she was given Barbara as a middle name as a mark of respect to the Nan she never knew. Now there were four girls.

Around this time, Saunders borrowed money and bought a dilapidated old weatherboard shop at 50 MacQueen Street on the main road at the north end of Aberdeen. He began doing it up and it became his refuge during their arguments. He needed it; life became absolutely miserable after the birth of the baby as Kath couldn't stand its crying, but when the child was six months old they all moved in there. The place was single-fronted, adjoined by an identical building and shared a lane with a shop on the Muswellbrook side. There were only a few windows and a low wooden awning over the footpath, so it was pretty dark. It was a great spot for Saunders as it was only a short swerve across the highway to the pub, but as a house it left a lot to be desired. It looked like it hadn't been painted for years. When the trucks went by on the highway the whole place shook and dirt would fall down from the wooden ceiling. Later Kath developed a cough and asthma and thought the dust might have been the cause. The subterranean rumble caused by heavy vehicles was profound and it appeared the place was built on some sort of hollow. One day when Dave was digging in the back the crow bar broke through a crust and just sank. Only the really big trucks shook the house, but they gave it a big shake.

The new place must have brought back memories for Ken too. There is a small park opposite where the Knight family home once stood. Ken and his brothers were raised here, next to the old open-air picture show. In this part of the world you move a lot but never get very far from the family ghosts and Kath was comfortable at home with the ghosts. She began to hang old bits of farm machinery, cross saws, scythes and old mowers from the exposed beams. She nailed tin plates on the walls and started to decorate them with skins, skulls, horns and stuffed animals. She loved prints of Indian chiefs and American eagles. Feathers arranged to catch dreams. Mail order mysticism. And she began to arrange pictures of relatives, alive and dead, creating a casual shrine. Later she described it as her 'dream home', but it is a long way from most people's suburban dream. Crowded, dark, dusty and noisy, but over the years Kath found some spiritual comfort surrounded by these inanimate objects.

It was around this time that her back injury paid a dividend. Just like Dad and her brothers, she got a compensation payout for her work-related injuries. She used the money from this and the sale of the Landsborough property to pay off the house and in Saunders' mind this seemed to coincide with another bad turn in their relationship. Kath was going to the doctor's a lot because of her back and 'nerves'. Saunders was awake to what he calls her 'fits'. She could swing from love to hate in an instant. He remembers sitting in the back seat while she, Ken and he drove back from playing cards at the workers club in Muswellbrook. The next thing he knew the car was stopped and she told him to get out and walk. He never knew why. Just as he could never tell when it was coming. Fits. Psycho ways. The family streak.

Saunders says that you couldn't leave Kath if she didn't want you to. He tried many times and she stalked him. Showing up wherever he was, like the times she came to Scone to get him. If he was at a mate's place she'd arrive. He'd go to the pub, she'd be there. Waiting for a weak moment. He had plenty of those. He'd never met anybody as wild in bed as her and somehow he kept falling for it.

In 1989 she did some unpaid work at the bowling club as part of an employment project, but her back became sore after standing for a short period so she never went back. Around this time they have a big breakup and he left for ten weeks before she wooed him back again. Life was a protracted nightmare by this stage, littered with arguments, police, doctors and AVOs for Dave—whenever there was an explosion she would ring the police and accuse him of beating her.

If he thought that the early incidents were an aberration he was to be proven painfully wrong. Saunders found himself trapped in a violent relationship, unable to escape. He says that while he was the one accused of the brutality, the truth was he was the victim. There are a number of witnesses to their increasing number of fights who confirm this. Kath's cousin, Brian Conlon, would often drink with Dave and he remembers a Saturday when they went fishing at Glenbawn Dam with Melissa, Natasha and Charlie's daughter, Tracy. It wasn't long after their little girl was born.

Dave wanted to give Kath a bit of a break from the kids and let them have a swim. Late in the afternoon they got back to town but before going home Dave got them to wait in the carpark while he saw a mate at the RSL. It had been a long day away from a beer tap. He got distracted inside and despite a number of hurry-ups from an anxious Conlon, didn't come out for a while. Dave says it was only two beers. In the end it made no difference as they were late for dinner. When they got back to 50 MacQueen Street Kath was ironing and in a state. Her fury has been building and building. That strange mix of panic and vindictiveness. Melissa says the men told her to not say where they'd been. The moment they get inside she told Kath they were waiting outside the pub for Dave for ages. Kath didn't need excuses and grabbed him by one arm as he entered the front door and had him off balance. She had the iron and began to swing it at his head. He had a six-pack under one arm and she was swinging him around and around. It was farcical. Saunders was yelling for Conlon to grab the beers each time he went past. In the end they went flying and broke. She smashed the hot iron into his head.

Melissa remembers that Mum tipped a pot of peas on his head.

Conlon says his cousin just started screaming at his mate the moment they walked in.

> David had a go back at Kathy, shaking her and telling her to wake up to herself as she was well and truly fired up. She was yelling and screaming and definitely out of control.
> She had the iron in her hand and hit David in the head. David stumbled a bit and ran out the door to the back yard.

Now the cousin was in the firing line and he was terrified. She seemed superhumanly strong when she got like this.

> Kathy turned on me and grabbed me by the arm, I tried to tell her that I had nothing to do with David going to the club. She would not listen at the time as she was wild. She then flung me like a match stick and I hit the ground.

It shows you just how strong she could be, that physical strength that scared men. Conlon picked himself up and ran for his life, finding Dave out the front under the shop awning. Both were too frightened to go back in the house. The cousin spent the night at the Commercial Hotel before high-tailing it back to Sydney. Dave licked his wounds in his car. He was burned and bleeding. A bloody, sorry sight. To this day the blokes in the pub give a little snigger into their beer when the subject of the steam hole burns to his face are raised. The poor bastard really copped it.

One of Saunders' work mates and friends, Ron Wilton, used to car pool with him at this time and describes Saunders as a decent and gentle bloke. The Monday after the iron incident he came by to pick up his friend at 50 MacQueen Street but saw him further up the road and drove up to get him. Saunders climbed into the car. Wilton took one look at him and was stunned by the mess his mate was in. Saundo looked like he had done twelve rounds with Mike Tyson.

—Shit, Saunders. What the bloody hell happened to you? You look like you've been in World War Three. Fuck, mate!

Saunders was in no mood to talk about the terrible state of his head.

—Yeah, yeah ... C'mon, let's go.

They pulled up at the service station and Dave went inside to buy his lunch. He came back with a pack of orange slice biscuits. Wilton called him a silly prick. He'd lend him money if he needed it. 'I'd give him whatever I had in my pocket, he's that sort of bloke and he'd do the same for you.'

Saunders grunted and told him to keep driving.

That night coming home from work, Dave was ready to talk about it. He began in his usual elliptical fashion.

—You ever been ironed out?

—What?

—Have you ever been ironed out?

Saunders went on to tell the story about Saturday night and how he had been sleeping in the car ever since, too frightened to return. Wilton, like a few of his mates, wondered why he kept going back. After all she'd cut his dog's throat, stabbed him, ironed him out ... surely a bloke knows when he's had enough. Saunders told him, and anyone else who asked, that he'd been fucked in Asia and fucked all around Australia, but none of them had ever been as good as Kath. Of course there's being fucked and being fucked. She had him sorted on both scores.

Dave's mates, like Kellett's before him, were suspicious of Kath, or Big Red as they called her. Some were just plain frightened. She was like a guard dog around him and didn't like them coming close. As far as she was concerned they kept him out drinking and led him into trouble.

Her carousing cousin, Brian Conlon, got caught up in their domestics more than once. He recalls one time pulling Saunders away from Kath and being knocked down, cutting his leg on the heater for his trouble. Saunders was not a tough guy and Conlon came back and knocked him out. When Saunders came to he called the police and the warring trio filled in the time by arguing about who should leave the house. It was all pretty pissy and pathetic.

The attacks on Saunders became so regular that Wilton and the car pool guys began taking bets on what sort of injury he would have that day. One day they picked up Dave and he had a cut to his stomach from where she had stabbed him with scissors. Kath and he were arguing in the morning when she turned on him with the scissors. Again he left the house and found refuge at a mate's place. The cut was bleeding and Dave wanted the guy to stitch it up for him. This was giving a new definition to domestic violence and the boys in the car pool thought it was pretty funny, but even this hard drinking group of miners had an uneasy feeling about Big Red and her temper. Ron Wilton told Wells that Saunders was a gentle guy.

David and I worked together at Hunter Valley Number One Coal Mine during the 1980s. During this time we travelled together in a car crew to and from work with a number of other men. During the time that I have known David I would describe him as being a quiet, honest, passive man.

As well as working with David, I socialised together with him. David would drink beer, but I never saw him aggressive towards anyone with alcohol in him. I never saw David involved in fights or other arguments at the local hotel or club.

Another member of the car pool, Dave Fittock, remembers

numerous incidents when they'd pick him up in the morning and there'd be bruises and cuts to the little bloke's face. Fittock recalls Saunders with stitches in his hand, facial injuries, broken ribs and on and on. The coal miner says all the violence was one-way. He knew Dave well as his mate was married to his aunty for twenty years before meeting Kath and there had never been any problems there. They had three kids and the nephew wasn't aware of any violence in the relationship, which was different to what was going on now. 'I saw that there was a lot of violence. This violence was not by David towards Kathy, but by Kathy towards David.'

Saunders reckons the broken ribs weren't from her but from a mate of her brother's who got him in a pub one night. It was only a matter of degrees of separation. Wilton, like most people, was scared of Kath. Years later he told the police of his method for detecting her moods.

Although I knew David well, I did not know Kathy all that well. I would see them out together at the Bowling Club, but I never witnessed any physical violence between them. There was one thing that I could tell about Kathy and that was when she was unhappy, her complexion would change. She would become red in the face and her facial expression would change.

You could tell from this expression that she was not happy and when I saw it I would not approach her or David.

Katherine had developed an ability to involve a bloke's mother in her dramas. On one occasion Saunders had gone up to play bowls at the local club and was wearing his late father's bowling clothes. When he got home she had the shits again and had locked him out. After a while he got in and she flew at his head. 'She took plenty of bark off me face, she could throw a punch. Kath was bloody strong.'

Then she was on the phone to his mother, telling her that her son was a cunt and he'd been beating her. Saunders' mum came down and saw the state of her boy's face. She took him away to fix him up. While they were gone Kath took to his clothes, chopping them all up. Every single item, leaving him only what he was wearing. Dave's dad had served in the war and had a special limited edition book produced by his regiment. Kath destroyed that too.

There were so many beatings Saunders found himself lying to hide what was going on. One day his injuries were so bad he told people he'd rolled the car on the weekend.

There are two sides to every story and Kath's time with Dave Saunders went down in the annals of Knight family history as one where she was abused and beaten by a drunken maniac. That was the way that she told it, anyway.

Saunders carries the scars from too much drinking and hard living, but has a gentleness that would appear to back his claims that he never hit Kath.

> If I was to do something wrong I'd admit it. If I fucked up in the pub or something I'd be up there first thing in the morning apologising to everyone. Not that I've ever had to, but I would. I never hurt Kath. She was the one doing all the damage.

He is the sort of bloke who apologises at the drop of a hat and appears genuine and honest. His first wife had no complaints. Nor his second. Yet when Detectives Wells and Ford interviewed Knight she painted a different picture of her relationship with Saunders, including predictable allegations of child abuse, which have never been substantiated and are almost certainly untrue. Ford asked her what she had done about the sex abuse allegations.

—I spoke to the woman he was living with to keep her eye on him.

—And who was that?

—Glenda Reichel.

—. . . Do you know when you spoke to Glenda Reichel about him?

—No. 'Cause she was gunna punch my head in there one day at the pub.

—This relationship with Dave Saunders. How did that end?

—With him punching me.

—Was it just a lot of violence in that relationship?

—There was on his part. I just kept calling the police every time he hit me.

—All right. Was there ever a, an incident with Dave Saunders' dog?

—Yes.

—Can you tell me about that incident?

—He laid his steel cap boots into me one day when I told him I was pregnant. I went out and cut his dog's throat.

—Did it go any further or did you, did you see . . .?

—I ended up having my nerves treated, but at that stage I had just lost mother through ballooned arteries and I touched her and the smell that come away from her was something terrible.

—When you cut the dog's throat, did the dog, was the dog dead?

—It was a clean cut, they said.

If Kath drove like she answered questions she'd clip trees on both sides of the road. Pleased to hear it was a clean cut, Wells continued questioning her on the incident about the dog.

—Did you say anything to David at the time you did that?

—He said to me to kill him and I threw the knife away and picked up a frying pan and hit him over the head with it.

—Did, do you recall saying anything to him, though, about it?

—The dog, he seen it.

Knight told psychiatrist Dr Robert Delaforce that she believed for two months that Saunders had killed the dog and later learned it had been her. She expressed some regret, which was highly unusual.

—It was very cruel, vicious . . . It's all still vague. I've shut it out.

Knight told her next partner that Saunders was violent so she cut his dog's throat. That was that. She told her neighbour, Gerrie Edwards, a woman who bought the shop next door in MacQueen Street in 1995, about the dog business.

Katherine spoke to me about one of her ex-partners. I can't remember exactly what was said but it was similar to: 'He hurt me and I hit him over the head with a frypan and slit his dog's throat.' When Katherine told me this I became wary of her and she scared me . . . Basically I kept to myself because over the time that I had known Katherine I found her to be weird, in that she justified her actions for things she had done by saying 'they deserved it'. I got the impression that as long as Katherine believed that her actions were right, it didn't matter what society thought.

John Price's daughter, Rosemary Biddle, asked her about the dog and Kath said, 'It fucking bit me and I slit its throat. I have nothing against animals.' Rosemary doesn't buy the story. 'That's crap, 'cause we'd be in her van going down to get bread and milk and if she saw a cat or a dog, she'd swerve to hit it.'

Such stories cause psychiatrists to shudder. John Travers, one of the men convicted of raping and killing Sydney nurse Anita Cobby, would slit sheep's throats as a party trick. Travers had also been employed at the local abattoir. Gregory Allan

Brown, the man who burned down the Kings Cross Back-packers, enjoyed dropping live chooks into an incinerator and listening to the panicked flapping of their wings as they died. Cruelty to animals is always a disturbing trait and Katherine Knight certainly exhibited that: the nicking of arteries at the abattoir, the dingo, the strays on the road. On a more passive scale she filled her house with trophies from dead animals, skins, skulls, horns and the like. She said they were beautiful and weren't dead to her.

Knight told the psychiatrist Dr Robert Delaforce that she had called the police five to ten times as a result of Saunders' violence, that she had photos and videos of injuries inflicted by him, that he had damaged walls in the house and thrown a bassinette onto the baby but the police wouldn't charge him. She claims he mentally abused her children.

Melissa and Natasha were going to school in Aberdeen when he came into their lives. They called him Dave. He cannot recall any animosity with Kath's kids but they backed their mother's story when the police asked. Melissa Kellett paints a bleak picture of the time.

From day one the abuse was there. He would drink and pick on Mum. Then he would pick on us kids and Mum would step in to defend us and cop it worse. He got Mum's esteem down very low with his abuse and he used to ash on her. He would never bath. I remember he would leave dirty undies lying around with extremities [sic] in them. There were several times where he beat her beyond recognition and it got worse and worse.

There was one time when he kicked her down, kicked her in the stomach to make sure she wasn't pregnant. I'm not sure which order this happened; whether she killed the dog or tried to overdose, but Mum took a lot of pills to try and kill herself again. I remember all through growing up she was suicidal and

162	**BLOOD STAIN**

taking pills to kill herself. When she went for help all the doctors would give her pills for her nerves. He continued to flog into her. When she attempted to take her life my little sister Natasha found her.

Around this time she cut Dave Saunders' dingo or half-dingo's throat. She doesn't remember doing that. She had went to Aunty Joy's place with two shotguns in her hands. She doesn't remember this. She was unsure if she had killed Saunders. She didn't know it was a dog she had killed. Uncle John and Mum went back to the house in Segenhoe Street and walked through. The house was covered in blood and they were unsure where Saunders was. The police were phoned. Mum then admitted herself into Tamworth psychiatric ward to get help. She didn't remember the dog. About this time Mum found out that Natasha was being molested by the neighbour.

We were given to our grandparents again and Mum was in there for about three weeks. After she came out of hospital there was never any follow-up. She was out about a week when she went back to Dave Saunders. I can't remember her being counselled, only medicated.

Shortly after that, [Saunders' daughter] was born to Mum and she bought the house in MacQueen Street, Aberdeen. Mum had been able to buy this house from a compensation work payout and the sale of land in Aberdeen and the sale of the house in Landsborough. Dave was also there with us. The beatings on Mum got worse. One time he took us up to the club near the post office. He had us sitting in the car for hours, When he got back he told us not to tell Mum where he had been. He was really flogging Mum for the next three years. He would beat up on Mum and beat the kids. I remember him pinning her down to the lounge and choking her, but Mum had her hands free and was able to scratch and kick back. I recall her being thrown through the walls. There were massive holes left and splits in the wood.

During this she was hospitalised several times. There was a lot of violence. He would rip out the phone and nobody would help us, the neighbours or the police. She was with Dave for five to six years. He would beat up on us kids when we stepped in to help Mum or phone for help or ask the next-door neighbours for help.

Mum and Dave's relationship finished in 1992 and there was peaceness [*sic*] in the family.

Melissa's recollections tally vaguely with real events, although her allegations of violence by Saunders would seem at best to be highly exaggerated and at worst to be total fabrications promoted by her mother. Melissa said later she has memories of running up the street in her pyjamas because the phone was ripped out of the wall during the fighting. She says the neighbours wouldn't answer her knocks at the door and she ran to the police who wouldn't attend because her mother never pressed charges.

'Mum could fight back, but she always came off second best.'

Natasha Kellett also backs her sister's and mother's version of events during the Saunders' years, although without as much detailed recall.

I can remember seeing my mother being bashed by David. On one occasion, David threw Mum through a wall in the lounge room of the house and also pushed her head through a wall in the master bedroom. These walls had to be repaired when Mum renovated the house about three years ago. Mum and David used to argue a lot, especially when David had been drinking beer. David used to abuse Mum physically and mentally while they were together ...

Kath's sister Joy tells the same story.

There was a lot of domestic stuff in this relationship too and as a result of this arguing Kath cut David Saunders' dog's throat. David and her were having a blue when she done this . . . There was always blues and then they just split up because Kath was being bashed by David.

Except, of course, you don't just split up with Katherine Knight and perhaps it is in the detail of Saunders' exit that we see who really was the victim here. Dave snuck away. He was shitting himself at the time and fled into the night like a bashed wife.

On 3 May 1990, just before midnight, Kath had called the ambulance to the old house and told them she had been beaten by her defacto. She said she had been punched in the stomach and the face and had stomach pains. She said she might be pregnant as she had said the first time they fought. They took her to the Scott Memorial Hospital where she was found to have a slight reddening to the face and neck but no bruising. The doctors thought she might be putting it on, but she said she had ringing in her ears and so she was kept overnight and discharged first thing. Ken picked her up. She wasn't pregnant.

Saunders moved out with Brian Parsons but that still didn't give him enough space. The trouble continued. Kath couldn't sleep when he was gone and she began to stalk him.

The problem was with Katherine that she always threw me out and then harassed me to return. In the end I couldn't take it any more. Every time I went back she would just become violent again and we would argue.

Saunders decided to take radical action. He took long service leave from the mine and told Kath he had to go and do some work for a bloke in Tottenham, but he was actually in Newcastle in hiding with no intention of returning to Aberdeen. He told his best mate the truth and nobody else, and stayed out of town for three months.

'I just figured I was going to keep on copping it, I didn't think it would end up as bad as Pricey did, but I had to get out. It was the only way I could get out of it.'

Saunders said it broke his heart to leave his daughter behind. It was then that Kath told the kid he was dead. Despite all the violence and grief, Saunders still burns a small candle for Kath.

I feel sorry for Kathy because she's a better person that what she's been. I mean you don't freak out and do stupid things, that's why I think that [killing Pricey] was premeditated but what she did after that wasn't premeditated. She just went with it. She had to get out of her problem.

At other times he seethes about what she did to his mate Price. Can't bring himself to say her name. 'It never showed any remorse. Pricey was one of the nicest blokes you'd ever meet and it killed him and it didn't seem to give a fuck.'

On returning from the dead, Saunders began to get some access to his daughter, but the situation was fraught with difficulties and ghosts of violence past. Around 1999 his dog had puppies which were about six weeks old. His daughter saw them during an access visit and wanted one. Dave drove her back to her mum's place at MacQueen Street with one of the pups in her shirt pocket.

—Can I keep it, Mum?
—Go on, Kath, let her have it.
—If you leave that here I'll cut its throat.
Just like that.

12

Autopsy

2000

It is not often a corpse's head arrives in a saucepan, but when John Price's remains were delivered to the Newcastle Department of Forensic Medicine the packaging spoke volumes about the bizarre nature of his death.

Six days after Price's death, Bob Wells drove up to visit Dr Tim Lyons, the forensic pathologist at Newcastle just to touch base and clear up a few little details.

The British-trained doctor is the forensic pathologist for the Hunter region and holds an appointment to the Royal Australian Airforce Specialist Reserves as a wing commander with a special interest in aviation pathology. Plane crashes. Lyons is generally not too fussed about whether you use the term 'corpse' or 'body', but admits that when an airplane makes an unscheduled landing he finds the term 'human remains' more appropriate.

He hasn't always worked with the dead. In a previous career he worked with the dying as an orthopaedic and trauma surgeon in the United Kingdom. At one stage he found himself at the Groot Schuur Hospital in Capetown, South Africa. The place where Dr Christiaan Barnard com-

pleted the first heart transplant in 1967, and one of the
busiest trauma units in the world. Its emergency ward sees
more gunshot wounds than most. The doctor then trained in
anatomical pathology in the UK, before moving into forensic
pathology and taking up a post in Australia.

Lyons arrived in Tasmania in August 1994, eighteen
months before a friendless blonde youth by the name of
Martin Bryant walked into the Broad Arrow Cafe at the Port
Arthur convict site. By the time Bryant finished shooting, 35
bodies lay scattered around the grounds. The case load for
Lyons was so large he had to get help from the mainland just
to deal with all the bodies.

Lyons is accustomed to the human form in all manner of
disarray and with Port Arthur he experienced it in mind
numbing multiples, but John Price's murder stands out in his
mind as the most bizarre he has ever encountered. He was in
Sydney the day John Price's body was discovered and hitched
a lift up with the police. Arriving in the afternoon, he examined the scene with Neil Raymond, Peter Muscio, Ross
Dellosta and Geoff Maurer, who was shooting a video. He
wrote up a report a few weeks later.

The house is a single storey brick build construction. Entry from
the street leads into a small cork tiled hallway to the left of which
is a lounge area. Access through sliding doors. Through the
small doorway and to the back of the house on the left is a
kitchen and eating area of [*sic*] which is a corridor which leads
to 2 bedrooms facing onto the front of the house, a 3rd bedroom facing to the rear of the house and a bathroom and toilet
area.

A decapitated and skinned body is situated, lying diagonally
through the space from the small entrance hallway into the
lounge. The body is lying prone, left leg crossed over the right.

There has been complete removal of skin apart from small
amounts of skin on both hands and feet and around the left side
of the chest. On the anterior aspect of the chest on the left hand
side at approximately the level of 5th and 6th ribs there
appeared to be two obvious wounds. There is extensive bleeding
and smearing of blood over the entire cork tiled hallway and
blood is smeared on the hallway wall.

To the right of the body there is extensive blood staining of
the carpet and a brown plastic handled carving knife with a
blade measuring 170 mm. On a . . .

The forensics were one more headache for Wells. Early
on, there had been talk of treating the corpse as two bodies,
as a match between the head and torso was made impossible
by the cooking process. This meant that they were running
around trying to match dental records. The last dentist Price
had seen was in Gunedah and he was dead, and there were no
records. In the end the scientists managed to match the two
pieces and that made Wells' job a lot simpler.

Lyons typed up an autopsy report for the court. Under
the heading External Examination, he noted:

This is a headless body which is human in origin and weighs
70 kg and measured 167 cm. Rigor mortis is present. The head
has been removed at the shoulder approximately through the
level of C3/C4. There has been virtually complete removal of the
skin apart from a small amount of flesh remaining on the dorsal
and palmar aspects of the hands and feet, anterior left chest area,
right shoulder and fragments of skin on the arms and legs.

The head is separate and was received in a large pot with
vegetables—both were well cooked. The head and neck were
devoid of flesh. Eyes had coagulated and the cartilaginous parts
of the ears and nose were attached to the skin.

The skin was received in virtually one piece and had been removed by making the following incisions:

– across the shoulder down the front of the body to the pubic hair line

   – around the pubic area and down the front of the legs

   – down the posterior aspects of the arms

   – across the top of the head

   – penis, scrotum/testes, ears and nose were included with this specimen.

Separate pieces of 'cooked meat' appeared to be gluteus maximus muscle from the right buttock area.

In order to allow orientation of the pattern of injuries the body was reconstructed.

Lyons had conducted the autopsy in the presence of two assistants, Peter Ducey and Douglas Gillespie, a few days before Wells came up. The crime scene detective, Peter Muscio, sat in on the surreal session and added the grisly play to his store of images from the murder.

The two assistants had the terrible task of rebuilding Price. They placed the head on the neck, slipped the body's skin back on like it was a jumpsuit and then stitched it all back together again. It was an experience beyond description, even for morgue workers. John Price re-emerged in death. If you had put sunglasses on him to cover the damage to the eyes from cooking he would have looked like an ordinary corpse. Except for the stab wounds. All 37 of them (only 37 could be counted. There may have been more to the neck that were disguised when the head was severed).

To measure the stab wounds properly the forensic pathologists stitched them back together. Price had been stabbed four times in the chest, four times in the stomach, nineteen times in the back and ten times in the buttocks, upper legs

and lower back. The wounds are recorded individually in a
language clinical enough to almost bleed them dry. Almost.

> There are a number of incised stab wounds to the chest and
> abdominal cavity. These are as follows:
>
> Wound 1 is situated in the left side of the chest. It passes
> through skin, subcutaneous tissue, pectoralis muscle, enters the
> chest through the 5th intercostal space, passes through the lat-
> eral side of the lower lobe and exits through the 7th intercostal
> space into adjacent soft tissues of the left lateral side of the body.
> This wound appears to be at least 16–18 cm in length.
>
> Wound 2 is situated in the left side of the chest. It passes
> through skin, subcutaneous tissue and enters the chest through
> the 6th intercostal space passing through the anterior border of
> the diaphragm, the free edge of the left lobe of the liver and
> passes in through the anterior border of the middle of the
> stomach. This wound appears to be at least 15–17 cms in length.

In layman's language, she stabbed him in the left-hand
side of the chest, near the nipple, passing through the fifth
and sixth ribs, by the top of the heart and down through the
lung before the knife exited between the seventh and eighth
ribs. Wound two came in a bit lower and down into the guts.

When Katherine Knight was finished John Price had stab
wounds into his left lung, diaphragm, stomach in two places,
spleen, liver, aorta, descending colon, or bowel, and kidney.

Lyons listed the cause of death as: 'Multiple internal injuries
secondary to multiple stab wounds. There has also been
almost complete post mortem skinning and decapitation.'

There is one chilling line towards the end of the pathologist's report.

'There are no obvious defence wounds.'

How on earth could a man be stabbed four times in the

chest without defending himself? Had he been asleep? Was
he already dead or expiring by the time she finished him off?
Lyons made no findings as to the sequence.

There is another point of conjecture about the pattern of
wounds to the upper torso. One doctor suggested that the
deep stab wounds to the left of Price's chest might have had
something to do with Knight's experience at an abattoirs. In
an animal such wounds would have pierced the heart but
because a human is broader they managed to miss.

Bob Wells probably didn't need to be reminded of what
had happened to Price, but after the conference with Lyons
he limped off to the carpark further determined to make sure
he gathered enough evidence to convict Katherine Knight. If
she was fit enough to stand trial. The detective was already
hearing that she would try for some form of insanity plea,
which could mean there would never be a day in court.
However, until he knew one way or another, Wells had to continue putting together a brief for the prosecutions.

He got the detectives in Muswellbrook to chase up some
statements to relieve a bit of the pressure, but nothing was getting rid of the headache that had been dogging him for a
week now. On the Thursday, Wells and Detective Muscio took
some of the select exhibits down to Sydney. They dropped the
tape of the interview with Knight off to the transcription
service and then headed to the document examination section, where they hoped to get handwriting checks done to
match the notes found at the scene with samples of Knight's
handwriting. They were told it would take months, that the
section was understaffed and there were more important jobs
in front of them. The analysis was not completed in time for
the trial.

There was also a minor controversy raging over an article
that appeared in the *Scone Advocate* that day spelling out the

full details of the crime. The story was printed all over the front page and was accurate in describing what had happened inside the Aberdeen house. Earlier articles in the *Newcastle Herald* had reported that Price had been decapitated, but stopped there. The publication caused a lot of grief. The Price family wrote to the paper complaining; ABC's 'Media Watch' pontificated about the bad taste of it all and in the process repeated the offending details. Veteran commentator Phillip Adams wrote a column for the national newspaper, the *Weekend Australian*, about the rights and wrongs of the issue. Adams lives in Gundy near Scone. He had heard talk of the crime around town.

'Here was a story that had been passed on and on and on. To retell the story allowed people to release a tension, an opportunity to reduce their own anxiety by sharing it.' He wrote that it was a crime that would have appalled Edgar Allan Poe and 'humbled the imaginings of a Stephen King', suggesting it had become as instantly mythologised as Azaria Chamberlain's tragic death.

The story was becoming big news and it wasn't long before it had reached the international media as well. Mentions of Katherine Knight began to appear in bizarre corners of cyber space and most European newspapers.

The local superintendent, however, was not happy when the story appeared in the *Scone Advocate* and an informal investigation was launched as the bosses wanted to know who had told the paper. It blew over when it was pointed out the details had spread like wildfire. Some of the attending police dropped into the Golden Fleece Hotel in Scone after being at the scene that day and were amazed to hear the whole pub talking in detail about what had happened. Still, Wells had to deal with that too. From then on all the police were gagged. The crime scene videos were numbered (there are three) and guarded carefully so that no other officers could see them (partly because the police force was concerned about the impact seeing it would have on other police).

Wells was firing on all cylinders. Attempting to source psychiatric records from Tamworth and Morriset, chasing down family and friends, fielding flak for the cost of the investigation. His head was pounding constantly; he was nervy, agitated and he just couldn't relax. Couldn't take a deep breath.

On the weekend he finally took his wife's advice and went to the family doctor, who referred him to a psychiatrist. On top of the physical symptoms, the emotional episodes and nightmares had not let up.

The psychiatrist, who specialised in working with emergency service officers, diagnosed post-traumatic stress disorder. The symptoms of this include re-living the horror through nightmares or flashbacks, increased arousal, irritability, sleeplessness, distress and impairment of function. Another aspect of post-traumatic stress is avoidance of exposure to reminders of the event. Some of the attending police found they couldn't even speak with their mates who were at the scene because they reminded them too much of the horror. There were days in this period where Wells could not function at all. He took two weeks off. He avoided taking the prescribed medication, but he could not avoid the case. Not for a minute.

He flew to Brisbane to interview David Kellett. When he laid eyes on the little bloke he noted that Price, Saunders and now this one were all much shorter than Knight. Back down in the valley he found Saunders' mates were keen to help. Wells was amazed to discover that these tough talking miners were frightened.

They were just hard working coal miners with good families who were just very lovely people and they were saying, 'Mate, you've got to get this mad bitch for me', because they were shitting themselves.

The whole town was shitting itself that she would never get convicted, that one day she'd be released, go back to town.

They were terrified of her—still are—and they kept saying things like 'Bobby, you've got to do this.' I felt all along like I was taking on a responsibility—they were good blokes, genuine, nothing special about them, always cooperated at difficult times, lovely people, but they always used to finish with: 'Get this fucking bitch, Bobby. We don't want her out'.

It was like: we're two rubbers all, Bobby, and you're playing the fifth set of the Davis Cup and you've got to win it for us, you know.

I felt like I was their last hope.

Saunders told me about how she used to flog him and about the dog and cutting up his clothes and his other injuries and I said, 'Now, let's get down to the nitty gritty. Either she's telling bullshit or you're telling bullshit. If we're going to get this sheila I need corroboration.' That's when he gave me names of the blokes from the car pool and one said to me: 'We used to laugh when we'd pick him up in the car. We'd wonder which piece was missin'. He'd have a whack in the ear or two black eyes ...' Things were coming together for me and I started to realise I was on the right track with the investigation.

In April, Wells finally got posted back to Newcastle and started a job with the Target Action Group, but he had to finish the brief he started at Singleton. That was the deal with the boss up there. He'd had a falling out with her over the transfer and a few other issues and felt he was being punished by having to keep working on the brief alone, but at least he wasn't driving a couple of hours to work every day.

I was really getting crook at this stage and I mean really crook, I was looking to get as much done as I could, but there were new names popping up all the time. I started to deal with Ray Price and these sorts of people. Ray was the brother. It was a real problem dealing with Ray and Bob [another brother]. They were violent people and just plain difficult. Ray wouldn't sign statements and they were giving me the run around.

Wells was fascinated by the pieces of jigsaw that were falling into place. Meeting the former boyfriends and husbands was an eye opener. Kellett was a nice bloke. Up in Queensland, Chillingworth had left the room in the middle of his story about a fight in the car and come back with a twisted up pair of steel-rimmed glasses. A souvenir of the good times.

While getting his brief together, Wells heard about a woman called Elaine Gill who lived out of town in one of the cabins out at Glenbawn Dam, outside of Aberdeen. He was told she might have some relevant information. He figured it was worth a look and drove out there to find a skinny woman already well into the drink at 11.30 am. She'd been seeing Charlie Knight and said that Kath had spoken about killing Price in the past.

She wasn't going to be much of a witness so Wells got Victor Ford to go down and get a statement out of Charlie who lived at Muswellbrook.

Charlie Knight's an invalid pensioner in his late 40s with a moustache and few chooks in the backyard. He saves his money for birthdays so he can put in a big one at the RSL, feeding the pokies from early in the morning until his daughter picks him up when it's all gone. Charlie reckons his sister is a stupid bitch and the stress of the murder means he can't sleep unless he gets on the piss. He liked Pricey and he was fairly frank with Ford.

In the past ten years I have not been real close with Kathy. Kathy would have probably come to visit me only about twenty times in the past ten years.

Over the past few years Kathy has said to me that she was going to kill Pricey if he kept going the way he was. On these occasions she wouldn't say why. She always appeared unhappy and I would tell her just to leave him. She has said to me that she was going to kill John several times. It could be three, four, five, six times.

About three to five weeks before Price was killed, Kathy came to my home in Muswellbrook. Kathy appeared really depressed and said to me, 'I'm going to kill Pricey and the two kids too.' By the kids, I knew she was referring to her two small children ... I said to her, 'Wake up to yourself. The kids have done nothing to you.' I was angry at her as this was getting beyond a joke and I yelled to her, 'Don't come back till you wake up to yourself.' Kathy then left my house. I then just slammed the door. I have not seen Kathy since.

I can recall a time before this. It was about five months ago. I was at home with my cousin Brian Conlon. Also there was my daughter Tracy and her boyfriend Jason Wilson. Kathy arrived with her daughter Natasha and her baby. I remember being in the kitchen at the kitchen table. We were all having a beer and during the conversation Kathy said, 'I'm going to kill Pricey and I'm going to get away with it.' She also said, 'I'll get away with it 'cause I'll make out I'm mad.'

While Charlie is in the best position to judge which two kids his sister meant to kill with Price, later events indicate she might well have meant two of Price's children. Wells was waiting for Ford to fax up Charlie's statement and was over the moon when he saw it. Not only did it shore up the suggestions of intent, it also went some way to taking the wind out of any insanity defence. Two months later, Charlie changed his statement. He decided his sister may have said she would pretend to be mad in the second instance and not the first.

> She said this to me on a few occasions. She told me she was going to kill John but she said it so often I did not believe it. I thought of it as being like the boy who cried wolf.

Wells chased down the other people who were at the kitchen table that day. He caught up with Jason Wilson, Charlie's daughter's 20-year-old boyfriend.

> I was living with my defacto, Tracy Knight, at Flat 3/60 Brentwood Avenue, Muswellbrook. At the time Tracy was pregnant with our daughter. We went to visit Tracy's father, Charlie Knight, at his house. We were there a while when Tracy's aunty, Kathy Knight, came to visit. Also there was Tracy's cousin Natasha and her daughter [Kath's daughter and granddaughter].
>
> After a while I was in the loungeroom watching a video when I heard Kathy Knight talking. I was not really listening but I heard her say something like she wanted to kill or 'I'm going to kill him'; words similar to that. I do not know who she was talking about but I just heard her say it.
>
> I stayed in the loungeroom watching the video and did not go out and listen to what they were talking about.

As you would. What could be interesting about somebody's plans for murder? Tracy gave a statement at the same time. She and Jason had shifted to a new address in Muswellbrook and were both out of work.

> I remember that we were sitting around the dining table talking and Dad was having a beer. We were talking about all sorts of

things when Aunty Kathy started talking about her defacto husband, John Price, who was known as Pricey to everyone. Aunty
Kathy was complaining about Pricey and I remember her saying
words similar to: 'I'm going to kill him and I'll get away with it
because they'll think I'm mad.'

She was complaining about something, like if she could not
have Pricey no one else could. After Aunty Kathy started talking
like this I sort of switched off. I didn't need to listen to Aunty
Kathy and her problems with Pricey.

Tracy Knight recalled a little vignette from the Kath
Knight school of charm.

My father and my Aunty Kathy were not particularly close and
Aunty Kathy did not visit my father that often. She would mainly
visit when she would drop Natasha off to visit me. Not long after
this, Aunty Kathy and I had a falling out over her having a go at
Jason and me for driving Natasha's daughter around in our car
without a car seat.

I told her to get out of my house and she started saying to
me that my father was not my real father. This is the sort of
person that Aunty Kathy is. She can become very vindictive with
people when they have a falling out.

Issues of other people's paternity pop up time and again
with Katherine Knight. It was an obsession and a weapon.

Wells was racing to get everything ready for a committal
hearing in August. The deadline had him sweating even
further.

I was ratshit. I wasn't functioning, I wasn't sleeping, I was dragging my sorry arse to work, trying to start this new job, blue-ing
with people over the cost of the investigation, blue-ing about my

pay from the previous job and I needed some time off before the committal and that meant I had to work harder.

I was seeing the psychiatrist regularly. He was trying to get me to take medication but I'm not a medication person.

Katherine and John Chillingworth
1990–94

David Saunders has vanished, but Katherine knows he's got to come back for a drink at some stage. This afternoon she is waiting patiently at the Willow Tree Hotel. A crocodile at the watering hole. The pub, on the main street of Scone, is one of Saunders' regular haunts. He's in hiding, but she'll find him. She always does.

When Saunders did a runner Katherine was left alone to chart a course through the chaos of her own life. Time hadn't healed any of the childhood trauma and the scars flowered into a violent and distrustful resentment of the men in her life: her father, her brothers, her first husband and Saunders. She didn't need any radical feminist texts to come to the conclusion that all men were bastards and potential rapists. It was the world she was born to and the world she continues to perceive, regardless of the reality of the situation. Her mother knew these things and waits for her in a better place where there'll be no violence or sex. Still, she wouldn't have minded Saunders coming back. She hates separation, couldn't sleep well when he was gone. In many ways Kath is a recidivist.

That afternoon at the pub, another victim happened by

and she moved in, just for the hell of it. A girl had to eat.

John Chillingworth is tall, ruggedly handsome, recently single and often drunk. The sort of guy who would never walk past a pub. Like all of Kath's men, he has a fierce passion for grog and cigarettes, and it seemed only appropriate that they meet in the pub. They were both on the rebound—he was finishing up a long-term relationship in Newcastle and had been down there earlier that day sorting things out. Johnny had moved back to Scone to be with his mum. He didn't drive, so he'd caught the train back up the valley, enjoying a few beers along the way. He'd got to Scone at lunchtime and with a few under the belt he headed to the Willow Tree to keep up the momentum. There's nothing worse than coming down in the afternoon. Chillingworth kept drinking for the next hour or four and noticed a couple of sheilas checking him out. One, 'a red-headed piece', as he puts it, came up to him. Nice arse.

He was flattered by the cheeky approach and, although he didn't realise it, had first met her ten or fifteen years earlier. At a pub lost in time. Chillingworth worked at the abattoir as a butcher. He was a Valley boy who had been living in Newcastle in a relationship for the previous fifteen years before moving back.

John and Kath got talking and decided to head down to the Commercial Hotel in Aberdeen where he had a few more before going over the road to her place. She was a pretty easy going girl and good company for a drinker. She even drove him back up the road to his mum's when they were finished.

A few weeks later Chillingworth was putting in another early afternoon session at the Commercial and planning to hitch home, but he got a bit of courage up and popped over to visit Kath in the old shop and they took up where they'd left off. Two adults swinging out of one relationship into another. Kath was a handy bird to know, her place wasn't far from the abattoir. She was happy to knock you up some dinner, take you to bed, get you some breakfast before work and then maybe drop you home to Mum's a little later. She was a good time gal. She spun a comfortable web, filled the trap with warm honey. If Kath had learned anything from Kellett and Saunders, it was that a man can be manipulated easily once you find the right way to get a hook in.

Chillingworth's family are locals and they knew the Knights for long enough to be less than keen to see John hanging out with Kath. His uncle and Dad have known that mob from Aberdeen for 60 years and both let him know they thought there was a streak of madness in them and he'd be best to keep his pants up and move on. But it was too late. Later than Chillingworth thought.

The couple had a great old time for a few weeks. She can fall in love as quickly as she falls out of it and so can he. And then Kath started to feel a little queasy. A little emotional. She was pregnant. Chillingworth was more than a little surprised. It was all so quick. There'd never been any hint of conception during the fifteen years of his previous relationship and this new girl was knocked up in a little over a month. He was happy though. The thought of being a father swelled his chest.

Kath's youngest, Saunders' daughter, was only two years old; Natasha was 10 and Melissa 14. Another would be handy for her, in that at least it would be an anchor to the new dad and guarantee her another income stream, although she made no demands that he move in to the house that Saunders bought. Probably because she could get the single mother's pension without a man around. She was already pulling in maintenance from Kellett and Saunders and before Chillingworth had even processed the news, she had gone and registered him with the authorities as the father of the unborn child, explaining to him that it was his and he had to be made financially responsible. Kath has always had a highly developed sense of other people's responsibilities.

Hormonal changes can mellow a woman, but not Kath. She gets pretty stressed and argumentative. Chillingworth's habit of arriving home from the pub full of drink, like every other man she'd ever shared a bed with, started to grate and then the fights began in earnest. There were not so many lifts to Scone any more and he was back to hitching. Almost from the moment she told him she was pregnant, Kath began to tell him the child wasn't his. It was a particularly cruel form of psychological torment. She might have had a baby in her womb, but it was a fish hook in his gut and she was holding the line, playing him in and out at will. However, Kath did seem to have some honest concerns over who the child's father was. Her dates were confused.

One day Chillingworth arrived at the house and she told him she had got back together with Saunders over the weekend and they were going to try and make a go of it again. Chillingworth was devastated and begged for another chance. He got it, but Kath had the upper hand now and wasn't relinquishing the power. She would play the paternity issue time and time again. She also started to tell him about how many men she'd been with and this was a new torment to Chillingworth, who believed that half the men he worked with at the abattoir had been with her or knew she was easy. For his part, Saunders denies that he and Kath ever got back together, so it appears that story was another attempt to punish Chillingworth.

Still, the intensity of their arguments began to increase and Katherine would often resort to a trick she had found worked with Kellett and Saunders—if you can't play the man then play his mother. It was strange, she was always nice to the older woman, but whenever there was a fight Knight would denounce her partner's mother in the vilest language possible. John's mother was called a whore and his siblings were bastards. It really hurt him to hear his mum described like this and Kath knew it. For her part, Mrs Chillingworth thought Kath kept a filthy house and often asked her son how he could stay in such a slum, but she was polite to this strange woman her son had taken up with. You have to wonder if Kath saw these men and the strong bonds they had with their loving mothers and resented what they had because she had never had it herself.

News about the paternity issue started to get around town and found its way up to Scone where Chillingworth's mum heard about it. His family were asking him what he was going to do. What could he do? Chillingworth was confused. He didn't know what the truth was. He even drove down to his doctor in Newcastle to see if DNA testing could be done. Every day up to the birth he lived with the doubts. The baby was induced a few weeks early because Kath was suffering from hypertension or blood pressure problems. She gave birth to a boy on 3 March 1991. John Chillingworth was over the moon and by this stage believed the boy was his. Maybe he was too far over the moon because on at least one occasion when he called, Kath told him not to come to the hospital because he was pissed.

Despite the arguments with Chillingworth, Kath was happy to have another child. It was a boy. She had always wanted a boy. She was looking forward to playing soldiers. Even after the birth, Chillingworth was not asked to move into the house at Aberdeen. Kath didn't want to lose her welfare cheques. Anyway, it was her place and she didn't have to share it. She owned it without any man. He wasn't too fussed about it as generally he would stay between two and four nights a week and it suited him.

I was living up the road. We were just going together and rootin'
I s'pose you could say. I would stay over there at night, go to work
in the morning and she would cook me breakfast. It suited me.
I got very deeply involved even before the boy was born. I
thought it was love.

Kath was never a clean woman and the house in those
days was a pigsty. It was really not much more than a roughly
converted shop space and the place was scattered with clothes
and suchlike. She hated cleaning and if Melissa or Natasha
didn't clean up, nobody did. However, Kath continued to decorate the walls. It was an old saddlery and it seemed
appropriate that she chose old saddles and farm gear to hang
around the place, but it wasn't just decorative to her. She
would talk to Chillingworth of the dead uncle, Oscar, the
rodeo rider, who was now, according to Kath, some sort of an
angel. The walls became a shrine to him and other things that
had crossed from life to death. There was a crystal cabinet in
which Kath had preserved mementos of her mum. Nobody
was allowed near that stuff. It was sacred to the memory of
Barbara.

The little house was developing the aura of a mausoleum
and she liked that, liked the feeling of the relatives in these
inanimate forms. Maybe it was because they couldn't hurt
her. She could talk to them at will and, perhaps even more
importantly, nobody else could demand the attention of her
mother. Kath had her all to herself. She often spoke of being
together with Mum again, how she would be happy to live into
her 50s like Barbara did, and then just step off to the world of
the dead. Barb and her happy ever after, away from men and
their sex and drinking and children and their endless
demands. Dead and free.

Chillingworth never held a licence for very long in those
days but decided that he had better get Kath a decent car, now

that they had four kids to drag around. Four weeks after the
boy was born he took her down to Newcastle and bought a
Mitsubishi L300 van for about $6000. Down in his old
stomping ground he got on the grog with a relative and gave
it a serious nudge. Kath's youngest brother, Shane, had come
down with them to drive the van back and he took it all the
way out to her dad's place at Rouchel Road, while she and
Chillingworth made their own way back to Aberdeen in her
old car with the baby in the back. Kath was cranky that he was
drinking and around Muswellbrook she said she was taking
him home to Scone, which started a round of bickering. He
wanted to stay at her place at Aberdeen and she wouldn't have
a bar of it. The thought that he was being shunted off after
just paying $6000 for a new car that was sitting at her dad's got
him worked up. As they drove through Aberdeen words
turned to blows. Chillingworth says he can't remember who
threw the first punch, but at one stage she grabbed his glasses
and screwed them up. She whacked him in the mouth. He
gave her a backhander or two and it was on.

—You cunt. I'm taking you to the fucking cops.

—Ya wouldn't be game.

—Just fucking watch.

Chillingworth was a prisoner in the front seat and sat
there as Kath drove up to the police station and ran in. Too
pissed to care, he stayed there. The next thing he knew, a cop
had come out and told him to get out of the car because he
was being charged with assault.

—You've got to be fucking joking.

Like Kath, the cop wasn't calling anyone's bluff and took
Chillingworth inside the station, but even this wasn't enough
to make him pull his head in. The drunk abattoir worker
mouthed off at the cop and found himself thrown up against
a wall, his arm twisted behind his back. That stopped the chat

for a second or two. The copper was pissed off and twisting so hard big John thought his arm was about to break off at the shoulder.

—Don't break me fucking arm, you smart cunt!

Wrong thing to say. The cop twisted it harder and the pain was excruciating. After that, he gave the bloke the statement he wanted and got locked up in the cell for a few hours until he had sobered up. When they let him out he found that Kath had taken out an AVO and he wasn't allowed to go near her or call. He headed back to the Willow Tree and got on the piss again.

Meanwhile, Kath had made her way up to the Scone hospital, saying she had been punched three times on the cheek and chin. There was some swelling and bruising and they gave her an ice pack to treat it. Melissa says her mother made a video tape of the injuries and her face was swollen 'beyond recognition'. She had to take a day off school to care for her. 'She had a bruise like a golf ball on her cheek. He was a brutal man.'

The next day Chillingworth tried to call and she wouldn't speak to him. He kept at it and finally got her on the phone. She'd organised a christening for the boy the following weekend and he wanted to come but he wasn't allowed to because of the court order. Anyway, she wouldn't let him. Chillingworth didn't handle it well, but he needn't have panicked too much; they were back together by the end of the week.

John thought it had all settled down, but he was at her place a day or two later when Ken and Shane arrived to do a bit of their blood's bidding. The brother looked like a nasty piece of work and he talked the talk. 'If you ever touch me sister again I'll break every bone in ya fucking body.' The old man seems to be of the same mind and Chillingworth thought it could get ugly. He used to work with Ken at the abattoir, where he got the impression that Kath's Dad was a quiet, peaceful man. He has since learned that things are different in the bosom of the family. Ken started to mouth off. 'You never hit women. Never ever hit my daughter or . . .'

The hypocrisy launched Kath into gear and suddenly she was laying into her dad, telling him what a violent bastard he had been to her mum and how John had said sorry and they were going to make a go of it. This really got Ken going. He told them they could get fucked and he wanted nothing more to do with them. Bolstered by the support from Kath, John told the old man that he could take it out on him, but he didn't need to be angry with his daughter. It got heated again and Ken called him a useless cunt.

It wasn't finished there.

Ken was a regular at the local club on a Friday night, where the sausage sizzle, raffles and darts were about the biggest draw card in town. Everybody would go, kids included. That Friday, he and Chillingworth crossed paths after a few beers and after a few words punches were thrown. Neither landed with much impact but Chillingworth still regrets the incident. From then on, Ken and Shane avoided Chillingworth. If the old man brought eggs around and he was there he wouldn't come in. It didn't have a big impact on Kath though; she was always fighting with her father and around this period they stopped talking for a couple of years.

Two weeks after the birth Kath booked in to be sterilised. Her haste seems almost indecent, but possibly she was content to have a boy child to go with the three girls. Either way, she was going to make sure this was the last one. At 35, with four kids to three fathers, Kath was hanging up her uterus.

A few months after Chillingworth bought the van, Kath went

through an intersection and got hit by another car. The L300 rolled and was a write-off. She wasn't hurt. Around the same time she sold the block of land for about $25 000, which helped her pay off the house and left her enough to buy another van.

While Kath had been violent with Saunders and Kellett, she was more circumspect around the new bloke. He was bigger than her for a start; not that she couldn't handle herself. She was as strong as any woman Chillingworth had ever met. She'd go collecting wood with him, bring along her own chainsaw. When they needed top soil for the yard she matched him shovel load for shovel load. That said, to hurt this one she had to be more cunning.

On one of many nights of beer and words, Chillingworth says he threw his hand back and accidentally hit Melissa in the mouth. The kid says he deliberately punched her. The next morning he woke up to find the bottom plate of his false teeth smashed to pieces in the bathroom. It couldn't have fallen, he knew that, and he figured it must have been Melissa. It cost $600 to replace and it wasn't until much later that Kath confessed to the destruction of his teeth.

—You hit my kids I'll get even with you somehow. Hurt them and I'll hurt you.

She'd tell him how she squared up with Saunders by slashing the dog's throat. It was a simple incident. He hurt her, she killed the dingo. No remorse needed. She still got shitty thinking about the last relationship; it played on her mind that he had gotten away so easily and sometimes she would talk about smashing the windows of his ute when it was parked at the pub, but Chillingworth counselled against it. One time, however, Saunders came around to pick up some things from the shed, and Kath and her new partner ganged up on him, telling him he couldn't take them. Eventually they called the police, who thought some of the stuff had been pinched from the mines, but it hadn't. Just another shitty incident. Things were always complicated.

Chillingworth says Kath was a good mother to a degree. While she may have been denied love or encouragement as a child, she did her best to give her own kids what she could. It wasn't much, but it was more than she had got. She had a quest to protect her daughters from abuse, at times to the point of hypervigilance. Of course she had no qualms about disciplining them, resorting to kettle cords when all the wooden spoons were broken. Melissa says you learned never to cross her and to do as you were told. That way your life was relatively easy. She was strict with the girls and while Melissa was the apple of her eye and the one who was going to succeed in life and get away with anything, Natasha never seemed to be able to do anything right. When the second daughter was around 12 years old Kath and John had a couple of friends visiting from Ipswich. While the adults were talking, Natasha gave her mother a bit of cheek. Wrong move. Without blinking, Kath punched her full in the mouth, splitting the child's lip open and then told her to get out of the house before returning to the conversation with the visitors as if nothing had happened.

'Mum had a heart of gold; you just didn't cross her.' That's what Melissa says.

Katherine clearly loved the two youngest and indulged the boy with toy guns, soldiers outfits and shoot 'em up videos. He wanted to be in the army when he grew up. She was even closer to the girl, but at times seemed to resent having to mind them. Melissa told relatives she left home because she got sick of being a live-in child minder. Natasha then found herself with a new job.

Kath got tied up with one of the local churches during

those years and became a keen student of the Bible, going to weekly classes, rediscovering a faith in God she professed to lose after Barbara's death. She was following in the footsteps of her brother Neville, who had been some sort of lay preacher. The kids too were sent off to Sunday School. Then she started on sewing classes at the local TAFE. She became passionate about the sessions and wouldn't miss them for anything. They were the highlight of her life and stayed that way for the next decade.

She began to design her own clothes and they were appallingly tasteless. Kath loved to show off her body and would wear skirts that barely fell below the panty line. Patrons of the 1992 Scone Horse Carnival were treated to a revealingly short American Indian style dress with tassles and great big boots. She looked cheap, to say the least, but Chillingworth was in love and couldn't see it. Behind Kath's back the people of Aberdeen were fascinated with her clothing choices. She could often be seen in gaudy jumpsuits, terrifyingly short skirts, backless tops without bras and other provocative items. It was a town joke, but one you made sure she never heard.

Kath suffered a lot of skin problems over these years and had a number of small cancers removed. She suffered from a reddening of her face that resembled rosacea but the doctors struggled to treat it. It gave her a frightening, angry expression that only exacerbated the impact when she lost her temper.

Chillingworth gave up drinking after his son was born, but nothing changed. By late 1993 Kath and he were fighting regularly and things just seemed to be getting worse. Melissa had moved out of home around this time. Despite her mother's desire that she be an air hostess, she had run off to Muswellbrook when she was barely 16 and set herself up in a caravan.

Melissa has some pretty startling memories of the Chillingworth years, as she did of her mother's experiences with all men.

Mum [then] met John Chillingworth when I was about 13 or 14, but he never lived with us. He stayed at the house a lot but Mum would never let him move in. She didn't let him move in because of how nasty he was. He lived in Scone with his mother and when he beat on Mum she got him out of the house so he couldn't hurt us kids. He was particularly cruel to [Saunders' daughter] and myself. Mum was hospitalised by him several times. He put her through fibro walls. I think with him Mum really tried to protect us from him. There was one night there when he started on her and she got him in the car and was driving him to Scone when he punched her continuously to the left side of her face. I could not recognise her as her face was split and bruised.

I remember him pinning her down on the lounge and strangled [*sic*] her. She ended up severely bruised. I think the only reason she survived that was she passed out. He picked up Natasha and threw her into the wall. She had her arms up and broke the impact to the wall. She was about 10 at the time. He was a football fanatic and one time [Saunders' daughter] skipped past him, watching TV. He tripped her and she fell and skinned her little face. She was about two years old. Mum would go cranky at him, but he would simply backhand her. I think what hurt Mum the most is that she couldn't protect us either from physical abuse or sexual.

There was another occasion Mum had gone out and we were left with him. [Saunders' daughter] was in her bedroom, picking up toys and making a noise. He walked into her room and there was a loud smack. I couldn't hear her cry, then I heard her take a gasping breath as if she had stopped breathing. I walked in and

saw her crying and her entire face was the print of a hand mark.
When Mum came home we told Mum and she upped him. He
blamed us that we had picked on [his son]. John Chillingworth
didn't drink. He was just nasty and would beat up on Mum and
us kids. She was with him for about two to three years.

Natasha had her own memories.

I remember seeing John hit Mum and also my sister Melissa. I can
remember John hit Melissa in the face with the jug chord. John
was aggressive towards me and the other children and also
towards Mum. John also used to abuse Mum physically and mentally. I can remember feeling very helpless when Mum was being
abused because I was so young and scared and I couldn't help her.

Chillingworth's relationship with Knight was chaotic, dysfunctional and there was definitely some violence, but
hospital records fail to reveal anything to back up Melissa's or
Natasha's colourful account, apart from the bruises to
Katherine's face after the fight in the car. The former defacto
admits he hit her then, but says that was the only time. He says
he has never physically disciplined the children.

I only ever hit Kathy once during the time I was with her. It is not
my nature to hit women. Kathy is the only woman I have ever hit.
I have been married once before I met Kathy and I have since
remarried. I have never hit either of my other wives . . . I hit her in
the car and she had me charged. There were no other times that
I hit her or caused an injury to her. In saying that, there was never
any times where Kathy hit or injured me apart from the incident
in the car and the time she broke my teeth. We had a lot of verbal
arguments almost constantly, but I was never threatened by Kathy
with violence. She would always get back at me in other ways.

He says that in an instant she would turn into a screaming monster. She agreed that their relationship was bipolar in an interview with the psychiatrist Dr Delaforce. 'When I hated him I hated him. When I loved him I loved him'. She told the doctor that he only hit her the once but he was *nasty* to the children.

It was all getting Chillingworth down and he wanted to get out of town, move up to Ipswich where their friends lived and buy a place. In 1991, with Kath's help, he gave up drinking, got his licence back, and now it seemed a good time to make a new start. Kath wasn't so sure. In late 1993 he took a week off from the meatworks to have a bit of a look around and got a bit distracted, staying an extra couple of days. The meatworks sent a telegram to his home address saying he had to be back within 24 hours or he'd be sacked. By the time he got the message it was too late. It seemed to be fate.

He came back to Aberdeen and Kath agreed to move up with him and see what it was like, but already she had something else on her mind. One October night in the pub a curly headed little bloke had asked her to dance. He was full of happy-go-lucky energy, outgoing and relaxed. Chillingworth was aware she was taking in some sewing from this hard-drinking miner, but didn't think too much of it. Kath was always doing favours for people. She had a good heart if you went looking for it.

Chillingworth found a place at the Woombye Caravan Park on the Sunshine Coast, just south of Nambour and he was happy. They were going to start a new life. Kath still wasn't totally convinced but agreed to come up for six weeks to see what it was like. She was only up there ten days at best when Chillingworth came home and found her in the van with another bloke from the park. She was hardly wearing anything and it was pretty obvious what was going on, although she tried to deny it.

—We weren't doing nuthin' and anyway, I don't want to live with you any more. You're a jealous cunt and I'm pissing off in the morning.

That night she told him to sleep with the kids. He got into bed and put his arm around her and she went berserk. Said she'd ring the police. Chillingworth retreated and waited for it all to blow over. The next morning she packed the car and headed off. He figured she was bluffing and waited a while before heading around to their friends Phyllis and Ray's house to get her. She had been there, just as he had assumed, and had said she was going into town to buy some wool and would be back in an hour. Their friends said she seemed pretty upset and might not want to see him.

He waited one hour. They said she wouldn't have just gone without saying goodbye to them. Another hour passed and he decided to go looking for her. He started on the highway towards Aberdeen which was an eight- or nine-hour drive away.

> I was worried, concerned, pissed off—all emotions mixed into one. I thought she would come to her senses, not thinking that this was serious. What happened was nothing. I was thinking why would she carry on like that? It was only a blue, a bit of jealousy on my part. Nothing to worry about.

Chillingworth stopped at a service station in Wallangarra on the border and asked the bloke if he'd seen a woman come through in a red Lite Ace van with a couple of kids.

—She's got red hair and is wearing a pink jumpsuit. You'd have to remember her.

The bloke did. He said she'd been through a few hours before and was in a real hurry. Chillingworth had thought that maybe she had seen his car at the house in Ipswich and

taken off, but by the sounds of it she had headed for
Aberdeen the moment she said she was going for some wool.
Kath had a bit of cunning about her.

The chase was on. John had an 1983 Falcon XE V8 and he
floored it all the way to Tamworth, where he had to stop and get
more petrol at about midnight. She had been through there at
about 10 pm and also stopped. He'd made up about fifteen
minutes on her in six hours. In his desperate state he jumped
back into the car, thinking he could still catch her before
Scone which was only two hours down the track at the most.

> I belted straight through Scone and here's her van parked out-
> side her place. She never said goodbye to Ray and Phyllis, never
> said goodbye, kiss my arse or nothin'.

He noticed another car, a little green one, also parked
outside her place but didn't think much of it. He jumped out
and checked her car. The tyres were cold. She'd beaten him
home by a long way. Defeated, he went back up the highway to
his mum's place at Scone, but couldn't sleep. Chillingworth
was starting to unravel. Later he reckoned he must have been
having a nervous breakdown. Kath should have recognised
some of herself in the frantic way he was reacting to the separation. Right at that point Chillingworth just felt like
somebody was shitting on him and he didn't know why or
what to do. At 7 am he rang Kath and Joy was already there.
She was pretty clear about the situation.

—Kath aint gonna talk to ya, she says to tell ya it's finished.
Don't ring no more.

Chillingworth kept ringing and ringing. When he wasn't
trying to get her on the phone he was cruising past the house
in the Falcon. A couple of times he knocked on the door but
she didn't answer.

He went back up to Ipswich to fix things up and ended up staying for a week. It was Christmas and he was so uptight he couldn't eat. His guts felt like he'd swallowed barbed wire. There was something in there. Christmas is a bastard of a time to be abandoned and you couldn't pick a worse place to reflect on your grief than a caravan park in a strange state. On Christmas Day it really got to him. There is a shop on the other side of the four-lane Bruce Highway and he figured if he got some bananas he might be able to eat something. If God wanted him to. With his head down and no regard for the traffic he set off for the other side of the road. It was a passive form of Russian roulette. Nobody ran him over so he bought a few bananas and tried again. He made it back to the caravan park. Maybe the roads were empty because everybody was at home opening presents and having turkey with their dumpling wives and two by two families. He felt so bloody sorry for himself.

Women, Kath excepted, have a capacity to respond to trauma or crisis with stillness; a man generally needs to do something. Anything. Drink. Fuck. Fight. Flee. Anything. If you are moving you are a more difficult target for the tip-truck of grief that's waiting to pour its load. Somehow John was staying off the grog and he wasn't of a mind to find comfort or violence with somebody else, so he kept moving.

Two days after Christmas Chillingworth loaded all his gear back onto the blue trailer and headed back to Aberdeen, pulling up outside her house in the early afternoon. She said to put the car around the back and come in for a coffee. He thought it might be a good sign. Maybe she had come back round and was tired of the torture. He unhooked the trailer, but inside she told him there was no future for them. It killed him to hear this. She had his son, he'd given up the grog for her, lost his job in an attempt to find a new start away from all the shit and strife of Aberdeen life. He'd even parked the trailer in the backyard. And she still wanted out.

Then she really let him have it.

—I'm seeing someone else.

—So soon?

—Yeah. So soon.

—Well, that doesn't fucking surprise me, Kath, 'cause you split up with Dave on a Friday and got with me on a fucking Saturday in the pub and I bet you got with this fella in the pub too.

She said it was the club, actually. He wanted to know who it was. She said, 'You know him but I won't tell ya because you'll only go and beat him up.' The news didn't bring Chillingworth any piece of mind; if anything he started to get crazier. With no one to fight he hooked the trailer back up and drove up to his mum's place at Scone, where he unhooked it and in his distracted state let it roll down into the back of the car, smashing the back of it. It made him angrier but in an irrational way. He loves his cars and has always kept them immaculate. He didn't care that it was dinged; it was just another little thing to piss him off.

His mother has been watching all this and told him he needed to pull himself together. They exchanged words, Chillingworth telling her there was absolutely nothing wrong with him and he would get Kath back. All the time his guts were churning and his mind was racing up and down a highway between Kath and nowhere. Pissed off with his mum and the world, he hooked the trailer back up and said he was going back to Queensland. His mother could do nothing but watch and worry. He stayed two more days up there before coming back down the highway, arriving back at Scone on New Years Eve. He unhooked the trailer again and headed off down the road where a mate waved him over and told him that Kath was knocking around with John Price.

—That ratbag? You must be joking.

He wasn't. It was insult on top of injury. He'd got off the grog for her and she'd taken up with a pisspot. The next day he headed off towards Price's place at St Andrews Street, where he started banging on the front door. Only then did he note the little green car that had been hanging around Kath's for so long. Pricey arrives at the door in his underpants and said she was in the bedroom. It was mid afternoon New Years Day. In John Price's room he finds his two-year-old son on the floor and his mother naked in bed, the airconditioner going. He was insane with rage.

—Thanks a fucking lot, you fucking whore.

She got dressed and started to call him every name under the sun. She really got stuck in and then she said she'd had enough of his jealous bullshit and he was never going to see his boy again. She was going to change his name and make sure it happened. He stormed out to the car and she followed him saying she was going to get the cops. He knew he hadn't done anything and said so, but it was never going to stop Kath.

In the car Chillingworth began to cry. He got up to Scone and broke down in front of his mum and told her what had happened. Then it was back into the car, Mum begging him to stop, and back to Queensland again. Don't ask him why, he hasn't got a clue, he just had to do something. Anything. At Willow Tree, which is about 120 kilometres up the highway, Chillingworth stopped to call his mum and apologise, and she said the police had been there. The old lady was distraught. Chillingworth rang the police and they told him there had been a complaint; if he kept going towards Queensland then they'd let it go. Suited him.

And that was it. It was all over. Kath was gone and she wasn't coming back.

In the end Chillingworth left the state. She made it almost

impossible for him to see the boy and he couldn't stay in town knowing that he'd lost his missus to a bloke like Price.

At the time he didn't know how lucky he was.

She was a good party girl and fun to be around, but I didn't like the violence and temper. She'd call my mum all the filthy names under the sun because she knew my mum was special to me. All this garbage; it used to hurt. I used to try and brush that aside.

I always believe Kath has two sides. Most women get cranky and its over in five minutes. Kath has this hatred deep inside her and she'll get even. If ever she got out she'd probably get even with me and Dave Saunders and Kellett. We'd be the first on the hit list.

When she left me, she wanted to keep twisting the knife: 'Fuck the child. You don't have anything to do with it.' The mental anguish that woman can put a man through could be enough to kill ya and I know because I've been there and she's done the same to Saunders—to Dave Kellett. I know she treated Saunders like shit. She told his daughter her father's dead.

When Pricey wanted her out she couldn't handle it and she couldn't do any more to him. She'd already got him the sack from the mines, she couldn't get him the sack from his new job. She couldn't do any more to him.

—Can you understand what she did?

—I can understand it.

—Why did she do it?

—Hatred. Pure, gutless hatred and the desire for revenge: 'If I can't have ya, no other bastard's gonna have ya' ... She mustn't have known that she was going to cut him up, but I think she stabbed him and decided to go the whole hog.

—Would she enjoy that?

—Yeah. I think so now.

John saw her in prison six months after the crime and couldn't believe how calm she was. She seemed at peace for the first time in her life. His mother died in 2002 and Katherine rang him to say how sorry she was. She was crying.

14

Katherine and John Price
1990–2000

In July 1989 Soviet pilot Colonel Skurigin took off in his MiG-23 fighter from the Kolobzreg airbase in North Poland. Not long into the flight the afterburner appeared to fail and the plane began to lose altitude. With his aircraft just 100 metres above sea level the pilot ejected to safety. However, the plane did not crash. In fact it righted itself and began to fly towards the west, the autopilot steering it across northern Poland towards Germany. It passed into and through East Germany and then into West Germany, where a pair of American F-15s shadowed it, ready to shoot it down if it became necessary. It wasn't. The unguided missile kept flying and the French authorities were alerted to the fact the aircraft was heading in their direction. In north-west Belgium, an 18-year-old man was going about his business at home oblivious to the drama in the skies. He heard a strange noise. It was the MiG-23. After flying over millions of people in four countries, Colonel Skurigin's plane came crashing through the roof and killed the teenager. As if he had been chosen.

Perhaps John Charles Thomas Price was chosen. Katherine Knight had flown over David Kellett, John Saunders, John

Chillingworth, the men of her family and numerous anonymous others before climbing into her van and heading to Price's home on the night of 29 February 2000.

Had Barbara Knight, her mother, foreseen it all those years before when she told John's wife Colleen Price to be careful around her daughter? Colleen, who professes some psychic ability, says she was twice warned about the demonic nature of Katherine Knight. Once by Kath's mother and once by a strange force. An intuition. Around 1997 Colleen parked the car outside St Andrews Street. She had come to pick up her youngest who had spent the weekend with her dad. Colleen didn't have any problems with Kath, but she had no intention of going inside the house. She'd just keep her distance, even though Pricey would often invite her in. It was no place for an ex-wife.

This day Kath came out with something on her mind.

—I heard that Pricey used to hit you.

—What?

Kath repeated it. Said that she heard from some bloke Colleen had driven home from the club that Colleen had said to him she'd copped a belting from Pricey in the old days.

—For a start, Kath, I've never given a bloke a lift home from a club because this town is too bloody small, and if he said that Pricey hit me, tell him to come and say it to my face because it is just wrong.

Kath backed off.

—Oh, no, I just heard that.

Colleen remembers that Kath then put her hand on the driver's side door next to hers as they spoke.

I had this flash. I just knew she was going to do something bad.

I went around and spoke to John and I said, 'Listen to me, I'm going to tell you something and I want you to look me in the eye and listen.' I said, 'She's going to do something to you, she's going to do something bad to you,' and I said, 'I don't know to what extent, but it's going to be something bad. Now listen to what I say.' And he said, 'Nah, Col, she's okay. She's right, Col. Don't worry about it.' I made him look me in the eye. This was three years before she did it.

Three months before it happened I went to a psychic in town and she said, 'Be there for your girls.' Rosemary [Colleen's daughter] was driving to Sydney that day, so I got her sister to ring her and tell her not to go. She [the psychic] didn't mention Pricey. I misunderstood what she was saying.

Colleen Jones was a 16-year-old tomboy living in Wee Waa with her aunt and uncle when she met John Price outside the local cafe in the early 1970s, about the same time that Katherine Knight and David Kellett first got together. Price was barely 17 and was working on the big earth moving bulldozers over at Cudgewoi. He was a knockabout little guy with curly hair and a cheeky manner. A zest for life. He rode a 750cc motorbike that his parents had driven to Gunnedah to pick up. It fell off the truck on the way back to town, but still went all right and he loved riding. They fell in love.

John came from a rough background. The Price family were boxing in the same class as the Knights when it came to dysfunction. There were four boys and two girls and there were enough fights among this lot to start up their own championship division. John was the happy-go-lucky one; he didn't seem to fit in with the rest of them. He hated all that shit and just wanted to have a bit of peace and quiet. 'Just be happy,' he'd slur. 'Just be fuckin' happy, ya silly cunt.'

Sometimes being happy wasn't that easy. He loved his mother, Cynthia, dearly, and was devastated when she became the innocent victim of an argument between his father and his brother. Bob had become enraged with his dad and grabbed a shotgun, apparently firing off a shot to express his displeasure. At that moment Cynthia happened to walk around the corner and was hit behind the ear. She was killed and Bob was jailed. The Prices are vague about the exact details and whisper that it might not have happened exactly that way, but Bob was the one who did the time. John Price was devastated and never got over the tragedy.

Paul Farrell, the Aberdeen Hotel publican, can remember him getting weepy one day when talk turned to mothers.

> I asked him what's wrong and he said he'd give anything to bring his mum into the pub and have a beer with her and show her his life. I asked him what happened to her and he said his brother shot her, but he didn't mean to. He said he was trying to shoot his father but missed.
>
> If you mentioned his mum he'd burst into tears on the spot. He was a champion bloke and a softie. Just loved his mum.

Pricey didn't get much education and never learned to read or write properly, but he was driving earth moving equipment before most people had learned to ride a bike. Oversized trucks, cars and motorbikes were his life and his entree card to some of the great sand dumps and mines of Australia. Hard places populated by hard men and hard women. Frontier people. A restless mob who shifted the earth around and shifted around on the earth.

Pricey came across as a tough sort of bloke. He had an enormous appetite for ciggies and beer and a voice that could scrape the mortar from a brick, rasping and guttural. Maybe he spoke like that to compensate for his relatively diminutive stature. He was a short arse, measuring only 167 cms (5 foot 6 1/2 inches) from his thongs to his curls, but he could swear like he was ten fuckin' foot tall and he could drink for Australia.

Still he was more diamond than coal, a bloke who was more likely to cry than fight. More likely to help you than hurt you.

Pricey's drinking was legendary. Once he fell onto the railway line and broke his leg taking a shortcut home from the pub; another morning he woke up further up the highway in Narrabri after apparently deciding to hitch 500 m home from the pub. The life of any party, he wouldn't leave until he'd made friends with every single person in sight.

Still, there was this gruff front which you had to get used to. His youngest daughter remembers riding up to the front of the St Andrews Street house one day with a mate when Pricey came out and launched into a tirade at her overweight friend.

—Get ya fat fuckin' arse off that poor fuckin' horse. Ya gonna break it in fuckin' half.

Pricey's daughter was horrified. Any mention of the girl's weight usually ended in tears, but this time the girl laughed and laughed—it was just Pricey being Pricey and he seemed to be able to get away with it. You had to know that about him. He could abuse you like he hated your guts, but in true contrary Australian style it just meant he liked you more.

He fell deeply in love with Colleen. The tomboy and the hard but light-hearted little guy. They were meant for each other and knew they would get married. Only problem was they had to wait until he turned 18. When he did they had a big slap-up wedding in Wee Waa. She was pregnant, but that wasn't the issue. They were in love and straining the leash to start a family, create the loving environment they both craved. The newly weds initially lived with his parents but decided to get away from that and moved into the local caravan park. A few years after the first child, Johnathon was born, they had a second child, Rosemary. They moved up to Queensland chasing work and for a while lived on the mainland while

John worked at Stradbroke Island, before putting the van on a barge and shifting across. It wasn't a refined life, but it was a lot of fun.

The company he was working for folded in 1974 so they decided to take the opportunity and hit out north to Darwin. It was a real frontier town in those days and it appealed to the adventurous spirit in the pair. The family planned to be up there in the week before Christmas, but a couple at the Caboolture Caravan Park told them there was no work that way so they travelled back home to the Smith's Caravan Park where they'd lived before. In the early hours of Christmas day that year Cyclone Tracy hit Darwin, killing 65 people and destroying 70 per cent of its buildings. A caravan wouldn't have had a hope.

Pricey and Colleen thanked their lucky stars, but were wondering where the next job would come from. Somebody said they were looking for drivers. Colleen and John left the kids with his parents and headed to Muswellbrook and he got a job at the Howick mine.

After three weeks at a council caravan park in Denman the new family found a permanent site at the Aberdeen Caravan Park. They had a big van, with a $3000 annex, tinted windows and all the mod cons. Pricey loved caravan parks, because he had a readymade audience at hand. He revelled in the open community living, the beer and country music. The mateship. There was always somebody to have a drink with or somebody who needed something done to their car. Colleen loved the parks even more than John. There's a bit of gypsy in her. She enjoyed the freedom, the way you weren't concreted to the spot. The parade of people.

The family stayed there for the next decade, before deciding, reluctantly, to move on. Pricey's parents reckoned a family should have a home and he was determined they should get one, especially after the third child, a girl, arrived. With $12 000 she'd saved from Johnathon and Rosemary's child endowment—she did all the paper work and saving for the family—Colleen organised a loan from the bank and they bought a block of land on a small subdivision in Aberdeen on the eastern side of the railway line. A few blocks south of the abattoir. Just up the street from Ted Abraham's camp. In those days housing was at a premium in Muswellbrook, Scone and Aberdeen because the mining boom had dumped hundreds of wealthy miners and their families in the area. Rents and housing prices went through the roof. It was the area's first real estate boom since the abattoir had opened 80 years earlier.

Colleen and John built a modest, rectangular three-bedroom brick house and over the next few years the street began to fill up with other miners and their families. Their youngest girl was two when they shifted into the home Pricey had always wanted his family to have. Colleen missed the caravan. She wasn't too keen on the house and she was even less keen on the fact that Pricey always had somewhere else to be, something else to do. It was the usual domestic complaint. She had to run the house and raise the kids and he wasn't around to give a hand. Always had somewhere else to be. A mate needed his driveway laid, or car fixed. And there was always the pub. She buttered his toast and put the sugar in his coffee and then one day she left. Colleen was in her early 30s and figured she still had a chance at the life she wanted.

I know he loved me but he couldn't come home from work and have a cup of tea and say, 'What did you do today, Col?' All the years I was married with him he'd be best mates with so many people. At the caravan park he was always off with somebody, helping them out and socialising with them. He was never with me and the kids. He associated with everyone, he gave himself to everyone else but he just didn't give enough to me and that was it.

Anything we wanted we had, but the only thing I never had, I never had his love. I had him but never had his love. He never knew what my favourite colour was, my favourite number. He never knew anything like that. He never got into my circle with me.

She took $7000 to buy a car and moved the three kids into a flat in Aberdeen. A lawyer said she could probably hit him for $30000 or the house, but she wouldn't have a bar of that. He worked too hard to make money and she wasn't motivated by those things. It wasn't too acrimonious, but things got a bit tough for a while when she took up with another bloke. That eventually blew over and they got back on an even footing. Stayed mates. Later Johnathon moved back in with his father. He didn't get on with his younger sister and wasn't happy that his mum had left his dad. Pricey wasn't happy either, but he learned to live with it.

It was January 1988 when Colleen left, two years after they'd built the house. For the next twelve years the place didn't change that much. It had the same curtains, the plates were in the same cupboards, his shirts were where she had hung them and while Pricey had built a shed outside and she had started a garden, the work seemed to stop there.

I used to go down there and I'd say 'Pricey, if I was here I'd have a carport on the side now and a cement path out to the mailbox and I'd have such and such out the back' and he'd say, 'If you come back you could do it' and I'd say, 'No, if I came back nothing would change, Pricey, would it?' and he'd say, 'Maybe, for a little while, ha ha.' We were still able to laugh about it.

Pricey had always been a man of habit and he didn't like change. He would work, go to the pub, come home, have a few more beers and then say, 'I'm off to bed, Col', putting his watch, ciggies and lighter in the same place every night. And she'd ask him if he had a hangover in the morning and he'd deny it with a big 'Nooooo', or confess with a 'Fuckin' oath, I fuckin' have', but he was always cheery. A happy drunk. There might have only ever been two arguments in the whole marriage and he never stopped loving her. In the early 1990s she went on a holiday to Perth and found he'd slipped $600 into her bank account. Another time she asked to borrow $200 to buy a second-hand fridge and he drove all the way up the highway that same afternoon towing a new one. By this time Colleen and his youngest had moved to Tamworth. 'Be happy, Col,' he'd say. 'Be happy.'

With no women in the house, Pricey and Johnathon were lone males on the tear in Aberdeen. John stuck to his routine, the pub or the club, work and the mates.

Pricey's house became a bit of a local institution. He had a pool table in the lounge for a while and it all got a bit blokey round at St Andrews Street. It needed a woman's touch and so did John. He had a few girlfriends over the years, but couldn't seem to find the right one.

On 8 October 1994 Katherine Knight gave John a card to mark their first anniversary. It's got candles, flowers, store bought sentiment and these hand-written words:

I love you Price. e.
with all my hart
Kathrine.

There's a few Xs and Os, symbols of kisses and hugs, to finish off the clumsy gesture, but it's a nice thought and Pricey wasn't the sort of guy who was going to pick you up on your spelling. Probably didn't even notice that she couldn't spell her own name.

Katherine Knight and John Price had teamed up together in late 1993, as John Chillingworth found out so painfully that New Year's Day. The date on the card suggests it was two months before Chillingworth knew anything about it.

Kath was absolutely, totally in love. This was the big one for her. There was no room to play around with wandering drunks, good time boys or the like. She was getting on and needed a life partner. Needed it real bad. Of course, she couldn't see that she'd chosen one just like all the others. Pricey loved a drink, a good time, had a bit of the wandering spirit ... He could have been any of the previous blokes. God, she'd met him in a pub, the same place she'd met the last three. In some ways John and Kath were a perfect match. Divorcees in their late 30s, they were both outgoing and a little over the top. Kath loved to dress up and dance and Pricey would dance with a chair if nobody was available. They hit the pub and the club with a vengeance. Living the night life in Aberdeen.

His daughter, Rosemary, knew Kath through her friend Tracy, Charlie Knight's daughter, and told Michelle Coffey of *Who Weekly* that she had thought Kath was good for her dad.

When Mum left Dad he was always totally pissed and at the pub ... He had a couple of girlfriends after that, but Dad was lonely, and I think that was how it all started off. I did get on really well with her at the start.

Rosemary said her dad loved Kath and her husband Brad agreed.

Yeah, he did. He called her babe, and I think he really liked having her round, even though she'd fly off the handle for nothing. He was affectionate and he'd go up and give her a kiss, or whatever.

The couple came to a comfortable arrangement. She would stay nights there—there were spare rooms for the little kids—and then she would go back to her old place at MacQueen Street in the morning and the children would get ready for school. There was hardly a sign of their occupation at St Andrews Street; they had their pyjamas under the pillow and little else. After school they'd reunite at Kath's before heading back to John's. It was an arrangement that protected Kath's welfare situation. Over the years she did move more stuff into the house, but it was always in the face of some opposition. It was never really her home, as she discovered once when she tried to move the crockery around. She got a right revving up over that one. Colleen put those things there and that was the way John liked it. His kids never really took to her either and that was the source of a lot of ongoing conflict. Johnathon was still living there and he was openly resentful. He told the police they never got on.

I was still living with Dad in St Andrews when he first began seeing Kathy . . . things seemed okay between them. They would have the odd argument. I remember on one occasion, about nine months into [the] relationship there was an argument between the two. Kathy got abusive and started throwing things around the house and smashing things. She was scratching at Dad and hitting at Dad. Dad yelled out to me and I grabbed hold of Kathy and pushed her out of the house . . . I know that the police were called many times to the house about domestics.

John's account of the fight gives another indication of her

temper and also her strength—it took two men to calm her down. The tension between himself and Kath and Dad led to Johnathon moving out and sharing a home with a mate.

> During the time I would see Dad a lot of the times. I would see Dad at the pub. We would never talk about Kathy. I would visit him at home, and Kathy and her kids would be there. I never spoke to her. I knew they were fighting a lot ... From the time I knew Kathy, she would seem okay but after a few drinks she would just snap. It didn't take many drinks for her to be drunk.

The Price kids were protective of their dad and always had been. After Colleen left, Rosemary, the eldest girl, remembers a couple of girlfriends including a woman called Helen, who had three kids, who moved in for a while.

> Dad and Helen got on well together and I never knew of any problems between them. I do not know of any physical violence between Dad and Helen. I am not sure why Helen and Dad broke up, although I did have a confrontation with her which may have had some effect.
>
> I did get on with Helen but it was just a bit of jealousy on my behalf that caused our problem. My brother Johnathon also had a run in with her about her removing things from Dad's house. It was about 1992 that Helen and Dad broke up.
>
> Dad did have a brief relationship with another woman after Helen, but I think it was just a physical relationship; there was nothing much to it. I can't even recall her name at this time.

Naturally Pricey was keen on a physical relationship and he liked having a woman there to come home to, but the idea of being tied down again didn't appeal. He loved Kath and put up with her outbursts because he was a softie, but his heart wasn't totally in the relationship. And that stung her. She gave him as much as she could. Cooked his meals, did his sewing, kept the house tidy and kept him happy in bed, but she was increasingly frustrated because she knew he was holding back. There was part of him mortgaged to his first wife and the kids, and she couldn't change that. She never really did make any inroads on that house. His shirts hung where Colleen had hung them, the plates hadn't moved, the curtains were the ones she'd chosen.

Kath still had the three kids around at this time. Melissa had moved out to a caravan park in Muswellbrook, yet she was still under Kath's control. One young local says he was drinking in the front bar of the Aberdeen Hotel with her one afternoon when her mother appeared at the door in one of those moods that sent the whole town scurrying for cover. Kath was furious. She raced up to Melissa, grabbed her by the hair and smashed her head into the bar before knocking her to the floor, where she began to punch and kick her, telling her to get outside, but not giving her any chance to get up. The man says Kath dragged her across the floor by her hair and out to the red van parked outside where she smashed the girl's head into the side of the van a few more times, before throwing her into it. The cowering drinkers had worked up the courage to watch from the window and could hear her bellowing from behind the wheel. Could see the fury in her face as she looked back at the bar before driving off. And nobody did a thing. Not one of those big men in the bar was willing to step in and stop Kath when she was like this. They all knew what she was capable of.

Melissa says this did not occur, that it's another small town story. It's hard to know the truth, but all the locals in Aberdeen will tell you they would never cross Kath Knight when she was angry.

Like Barbara, Katherine was a strict mum and when Natasha left school she became house cleaner and tenant at MacQueen Street, paying the rent out of her welfare cheques. She would have to keep the place spotless. Neighbours remember Natasha copping terrible verbal abuse if Mum came home from Pricey's and found something not to her liking. And, she would be punished in some way. Kath always figured that if you did the wrong thing you had to pay. One local remembers driving home one evening from Muswellbrook and finding Natasha by the side of the road. She was only in her mid teens at the time and it was already dark. She told the woman she'd been arguing with Kath and she'd been thrown out of the car miles from town, just as Saunders had been years before. Kath hadn't come back to pick her up. The kid needed to learn a fucking lesson and you keep right fucking out of it. I'll bring me kids up the way me parents brung me up.

Nobody dared cross her. A couple of the local boys recall being at the MacQueen Street home chatting with Natasha when they were about 14. Kath came home and went berserk, grabbing a pole and chasing them. The boys ran for their lives, the larger one helping his mate over the back fence before jumping it himself.

Her smaller kids were kept on a short leash too. A neighbour remembers the youngest boy getting into terrible trouble because he'd left his jumper at school. An enraged Kath dragged him by the neck from the backyard to his bedroom and locked him there. He screamed and pleaded for five whole hours but she would not let him out. He'd stuffed up and he had to pay. You did wrong, you got punished. You deserved it. There's talk that he was once hung from the clothes line. It was harrowing for the neighbours to listen to that boy scream all that time over a forgotten school jumper.

Kath was always after a bit of extra money and on top of the money she was taking from the kids' fathers and the rent from Natasha, she started picking up a bit of extra by charging her nephew, Jason Roughan, rent to live in a pokey old caravan in the backyard. That enterprise came to an end when Kath came home and thought she smelt marijuana smoke in the van. She threw him out on the spot.

Pricey's youngest daughter would make trips down from Tamworth to stay with her father in Aberdeen. It gave her a chance to do some horse riding in the hills around town and catch up with her old man who loved her with abandon. She found it was never uneventful with her dad's new girlfriend. They got on well enough. Kath would pick her up when she came down, take her out for a feed and make her feel welcome before Pricey got home. She could be a bit demanding at times, didn't like the way the young one ran a bit wild when she was in Dad's care. Sometimes they clashed, but it was never over anything major. The kid just reckoned Kath couldn't tell her what to do and Pricey would agree when he got home. Once the older woman demanded the teenager do the dishes after she'd been out all day, otherwise she wouldn't be allowed out again. The kid told her where to go and when Pricey got home he supported her. Kath wasn't used to such easy-going parenting and thought he was letting the girl run wild.

As time passed the daughter began to see another side of Dad's girlfriend. She was a strange one. One night when they were camping Katherine said she'd been abducted by aliens; a story she would tell to others as well. The alleged incident occurred in about 1983 and Kath says other members of the family also saw the UFO. Katherine believed in ghosts. She'd seen Uncle Oscar, the one who shot himself. Barbara, her mother, saw ghosts too, visions of her grandmother and a

naked boy on the lawns. Pricey's kid thought she was weird.
She even used to put the gravy on the back step to settle.

One day the teenager and a friend dropped into the old
house at MacQueen Street to get some money for cigarettes—
they said it was for food—Kath agreed. but said she'd be
getting it back off Pricey that afternoon. Always careful with
money. The girls were waiting in the cluttered living room
where there was 'all this old shit on the wall, push mowers on
the roof', when Ken arrived. Kath was in the kitchen cutting
something up when her dad said something she didn't like.
Ken could be pretty abrasive.

> She had this big frigging knife and she came out and she started
> getting up him with the knife in the hand, pointing the knife at
> him and yelling and the way she was doing it. I shit myself; full
> on shit myself. I was scared and he said, 'I've had enough of you'
> and walked out sort of thing and I said, We're going now', and
> my mate said, 'She's weird, man, . . . she could've put the knife
> down and used her finger. That's what everyone else would do.'

Snapped like a dry twig, Kath. Rosemary remembers that
she and Dad would be all lovey-dovey and affectionate and
then: bang. One time they were sitting on the front verandah
when Kath came out and did some sweeping. When she
stopped, Pricey picked up the broom and touched her on the
bum and 'she went absolutely mental. Don't treat me like a
slut! It was just bizarre. Then five seconds later, it was as
though nothing happened'.

She was good at the domestics though, would wash up
after dinner. She loved Rosemary's kids, Pricey's grandchil-
dren, would sew for them and indulge them. Kath made a
video of Rosemary's wedding to Brad. She loved making
movies, was always shooting the kids' concerts or the new

babies. Rosemary's kids called her Nana Kath. She only had her family; she didn't really have any friends.

Katherine didn't care what the world thought or did. In 1994 Geraldine Edwards bought the shop next-door and got to know her neighbour reasonably well. She was in earshot of her terrible temper and foul mouth. If somebody parked a car outside Kath's place on one of her bad days then God help them.

Gerrie liked her, but learned that you didn't cross her. One Friday night she went across to the pub and didn't get home until midnight. She rarely went to the pub and while she was gone her dogs became agitated. The next morning Kath stormed into the shop, ignoring the customers, and launched into her neighbour.

> She went right off. Said those fucking dogs barked and barked and barked and I banged on the wall and they barked more and it was f.u.c.k this and c.u.n.t—a word I hate—that, and there were customers in the shop, but it didn't worry her.

Gerrie apologised and said she didn't know they would bark and if she ever went out again she'd leave a number so Kath could call if there was a problem. In an instant Kath changed from banshee to human and said, 'Okay, then.' Walked out and the whole shop took a deep breath.

> I was frightened of Katherine in a way but I didn't know what it was that I was frightened of. It was just that she was just the kind of person I would never want to have a run in with. She was the sort who would say exactly what she thought. It didn't matter to her what people said or thought about her, she would say what she wanted, wear what she wanted and she just did not have any tact. She just didn't care. It was like she'd say, 'Stuff the lot of

'em, I'm going to say what I want, do what I want and I don't
have to put on any appearances for any of them.'

Katherine had become increasingly over the top. She
didn't have any sense of protocol or decorum. She was nice
enough. Friendly and good fun, but if something annoyed
her she knew no reason or control. Sewing had became a passion. She'd make clothes and show them off and they were
gaudy and inappropriate. There was one pair of shorts that
were cut so high they were indecent. Aberdeen still talks
about the day she washed the front of the house down
wearing them and a bikini top. The town laughed behind her
back. But not too loud. She would be all over fellas in the pub
and they took to calling her the Red Squirrel. Pricey called
her the Speckled Hen, or the Speckled Fucking Hen, or the
Mad Cunt. Over the years he became increasingly derogatory
and it wasn't always in jest, but he loved her and she could put
up with it.

One day she came into the pub to pick him up after she'd
been on one of her regular long walks. She was boasting
about how tight her leg muscles were. 'Pity it's not your cunt',
Price said. The others there were horrified and there was a
terrible moment of silence when she could have gone either
way, but she laughed it off and said that he kept coming back
to it no matter what it was like.

With John, Kath changed a little. Through all those years
with hard-drinking men she had kept pretty sober, but with
Pricey she began to drink more. She liked rum with cola and
chocolate liqueurs, sickly alcoholic women's drinks. They
didn't agree with her, just as Pricey's children didn't. She'd
have a few and start to stew. Get real nasty. In the early days of
their relationship she would go out some nights with a girlfriend and would often sit and have one or two when she was

trying to get John out of the pub, which was a bit like trying to get a mollusc off a rock. Usually though, she'd have an orange juice. Now she was getting drunk every week or so.

Things took a bad turn for Kath in March 1995, about fifteen months into the relationship. She was making no progress with this bloke and it was frustrating her. He was holding back. It was starting to really get to her and one day she'd been drinking rum and some liqueur and he'd been drinking and they started to get nasty. She wanted him to commit. She wanted him to marry her and he was squirming around. Refusing to be nailed. Things got really heated and Pricey said he was only in it for the sex and she should get used to it. It was nothing serious. Just a bit of fun. Katherine was hurt and furious and got herself into a right state. She stormed out. She'd show him. With Natasha watching, she gulped down an overdose of pills and told the kid not to call an ambulance, she wanted it all to end. She wanted to be with her mother and to be rid of those kids and the bullshit. In truth, it was all about attention and sympathy. It had worked before and, like all her suicide attempts, it was not that serious. Natasha rang her aunt and an ambulance took Kath to the Scott Memorial Hospital, where she continued to be obnoxious and maudlin.

She was kept overnight and was much better in the morning. But Pricey's words would always ring in her ears and she knew his kids were actively keeping him from her. The resentment between the Price kids and Katherine was an open wound that began to fester. Young Johnathon and Kath were bitter, bitter enemies and over the years Kath began to bad mouth him and the two girls. Kath reckoned Pricey's son had been out of line with her daughter and Melissa told the police about an incident Kath would not let go.

I knew John Price junior from primary school at Aberdeen—not as friends, I just knew him. Rosemary was the year above me and I knew her through my cousin Tracy. She would come out and stay at the farm with us. When I was 17 I was living in a caravan park on the river at Muswellbrook. I had been in contact with Mum, and John and her were going to lunch to the club at Aberdeen. We had lunch then went into the pool room. Johnathon was my step brother. I needed to get back to Muswellbrook and he said he would drop me home. He dropped me back at the caravan. I let myself in and he came in behind me. I don't remember any conversation. He walked down to the end of my caravan and sat on my bed. He undid his pants and began touching himself. He even grabbed dish-washing liquid and began touching himself. I freaked and told him to leave and threatened him to leave. I left the caravan and came back and he was still there and I told him he was sick and I was going to tell his father and my mother. He then left after I picked up a camera and said something like, 'If you don't get out of here I'm going to show your father what you are really like.'

There are a number of versions of the story, but Johnathon didn't want to tell his.

When Bob Wells and Victor Ford interviewed Kath, she put her spin on it.

—Are you able to tell me about your relationship was [with] John Junior. How you got on with him?

—He hated my guts.

She reckoned that Johnathon had shouted out in the pub that he had had anal sex with Melissa, but she set him straight and told him he'd only ever got to masturbate in front of her. Johnathon hated her and on the day before his father was killed he visited the house. His account indicates the level of antipathy between the two.

The last time I saw [Dad] was on the Monday. He was on the
back verandah. I was down there looking for some parts for my
car in Dad's shed ... She was there, hanging out clothes on the
line, but I didn't even acknowledge her and she walked straight
inside when she saw me.

Kath didn't endear herself to Pricey's kids. One of the
more spectacular conflicts involved his youngest and paternity issues. The recurring theme. The girl was about 13 at the
time and visiting for school holidays. Knight sat her down for
a friendly chat and explained that her father was not her bio-
logical father. The kid bawled her eyes out—the world had
just slipped from under her feet. How could she have been
fooled about something so important for so long? When
Pricey got home she launched into him. Tears streaming
down her cheeks.

—I'm not your daughter.

—What the fuck are you talking about?

—Kath said you're not my dad.

—Kath wouldn't know jack shit. Of course I'm your
father.

The girl was not totally reassured but felt a bit better.
Then Kath arrived and continued with the lie. Pricey was real
cranky about this.

—You don't know shit, Kath. Shut the fuck up and keep
out of this.

Katherine was always looking for a wedge between the
kids and their dad, but when it came to her own family she was
the connecting point. Without her, they would probably have
all drifted apart. Despite all the anger and confrontations
between them, the blame for misdeeds past, she was the one
who kept in touch with all of them, passed on the updates.
Was first on the phone if a grandchild was born or a relative

died. She resented them, but could not reject them. For some reason she threw herself into other people's families, elbows and all. Kellett's mum showed her kindness, so she headed up the highway with a suitcase full of bandages and knives and scissors. She denounced Kellett's, Saunders', Chillingworth's and Pricey's mum. Calling them all terrible names. Prostitutes and sluts the lot of 'em.

Colleen Price was furious when she found out what Katherine had said to her youngest daughter and that finished any relationship the two mothers had.

It appears Kath was developing a small drinking problem and around 1995 she checks herself into an alcohol rehabilitation centre in Queensland. Price's daughter says that John told her one day she was an alcoholic and she was so gullible she ran off for help. Katherine spent three months up there getting help, although there's some confusion about why she did it.

'I actually went to Queensland for the mental abuse side of it. I actually had to say I was an alcoholic—I went to the AA meetings—it's a big AA in Queensland.'

Pricey had told Kath he didn't want a serious relationship and now was telling friends he wanted her out of his house.

Trevor Lewis, a miner who lived in St Andrews Street and a friend of Pricey's for about twenty years, was helping build a shed in the backyard of his mate's house and witnessed an interesting exchange between the couple. John asked Kath to get them a couple of beers. She refused. He told her to fuck off out of his house then and she said, 'You'll never get me out of this house, I'll do you in first.' Everybody who knew them knew this sort of banter. Him calling her every name under the sun and her giving it back in spades. However, her tenure in his house was a common theme of niggling between the pair and the heat seemed to increase over the years. She was pressing him to divorce Colleen and marry her, and he was reluctant to do so. A mate, Laurie Lewis, remembers many arguments between the pair on the subject. He was often called in to break it up.

They became engaged, but Pricey told his mates it was nothing too serious; something to keep the peace. His kids reckon she took his money and went out to buy a diamond ring. It was a joke. He would never marry her. He told Laurie he felt she wanted to get her hands on his house. At this time Colleen was urging John to put the house in the kids' names for that reason. He told Ron Murray that she'd bought the ring. 'That keeps her happy, but we're not getting married.'

Sometimes it could be so petty. In October 1997 Pricey called the police because Kath was pissed and playing music too loud. He was drunk too, he wanted to go to bed and if she kept this up there'd be violence. The cops came and Price greeted them in a dressing gown. She'd turned the music down, but she was still driving him up the wall, then she came out in a see-through nightie. The police made a record of the conversation. Eyes on the notebook.

Kath: What's going on? What's all the fuss about? Why are you here?

Police: John is saying you won't let him go to bed and the music has been too loud.

Kath: What do you want to go to bed for?

John: I'm tired, I want to go to bed. That's all I want to do is to go to bed and you won't leave me alone.

Kath: There is no problem here. We have been having a good time singing and dancing. We just had a shower together and we were going to go to bed to make love.

John: I just want to go to bed. Will you let me go to bed?

Kath: Yes, let's go to bed.

It was a rough time. Five days later she fronted at the

hospital alleging Price had assaulted her in the car outside the house, hitting her in the jaw and the wrists as she held the steering wheel. There were no charges. Another time Pricey got a little confused and called out the barmaid's name when they were having sex. That was the cause of a major falling out that even some of his mates heard about. Got a bit of a laugh in the pub. They all knew Pricey was a pants man and would chase anything if he had a few in him. Kath knew that too and was particularly suspicious about a local widow. God help him if he got caught talking to her. She told Gerrie Edwards, her neighbour in MacQueen Street, that he would pay for any infidelity.

'If I ever catch Pricey playing up on me I told him I'd kill him and cut his dick and balls off.'

By this stage Kath probably figured he owed her the house. She cooked, she cleaned, she ran him back and forth to the pub, she was owed something in return. She was entitled to it. Then he got jack of it. He asked her to go for good after an argument about the house. It was the start of the great schism between Kath, John, his family and their friends. Gerrie Edwards remembers a conversation over the back fence at this time. Kath told Gerrie that Price had asked her to leave and she told him she wanted $10000 (Pricey later mentioned the same sum to Bowditch) because she'd discovered that he'd left the house to his kids. He told her there was no way she was getting any money. She told Gerrie she'd got the bastard back.

She had kissed him goodbye that morning, knowing he was in for a hell of a shock when he got to work. As soon as he'd left, she called the family in. They had to get her possessions out of St Andrews Street before he got home. Joy, Shane, Barry Roughan and his wife Val came around and took things out of the shed and the house and down to MacQueen Street.

Pricey was getting his house back.

Kath had taken her favourite video camera and had filmed first aid boxes and the like that John had taken from the mine. He didn't mind a bit of petty pilfering and it was a constant problem on the sites. Kath sent a copy of the video to the mine management and one to the police. While she was doing a runner with all her precious possessions, Pricey was called in at work and questioned about the theft. He denied it and then they produced the video. He was gone. He was suspended and eventually dismissed, losing his $100000 a year job, superannuation and long service leave in the process.

When John got back from work he threw her out of his home, or at least that's what people think, but Barry Roughan helped her shift and he remembers the haste of trying to get everything done before Pricey got back. There was no need to throw her out.

Kath's revenge shocked everybody. Gerrie Edwards says there was a quiet irony in that when she bought Kath's house and knocked down the garden sheds they were filled with property from the mines. Laurie Lewis was infuriated by what happened. He'd picked John up for work that morning and remembered Kath had given him a kiss as if there was nothing going on at all. Talk about Judas. Kath was never one to have a guilty conscience. You messed her round, you paid. All was fair in her love wars. Laurie told her that he never wanted to speak to her or have anything to do with her again. Young Johnathon was incensed at what had happened and refused to let his wife or child have anything to do with Kath. Family functions became almost impossible. For a while Rosemary refused to speak to Kath too.

Later Kath told Dr Milton that she had sent the video 'after the very first time he hit me'.

Henry Perry, one of the youngsters involved in the Caltex service station incident 20 years earlier, remembers talking to

Pricey around this time. He thinks John might have been applying for a job at the abattoir. He knows he was looking for work at the time. Henry told Pricey about what had happened to him and his family back in the 1970s. He said, 'If you go back to her you're history.' Pricey said he wouldn't be getting back with her.

But Pricey went back. About three weeks later Henry saw them together and made a mime with his hands like he was videoing the couple. John laughed, but nobody else did. Laurie Lewis noted that John started to drink at a different pub after that time because he couldn't face his friends. Trevor Lewis remembers saying to Pricey that Kath would kill him if they stayed together. Pricey agreed but said he loved her. Ron Murray says he lost a lot of respect in town over that and his mates cut him out a bit. John said he'd lost his job, there was nothing else to lose. Both sides were unimpressed. Barry Roughan still reckons it was a waste of time shifting her out.

And so they began the second major chapter in their relationship. Kath told Natasha that this was an end game. It either worked out or somebody was going to pay.

'I told him that if he took me back this time, it was to the death.'

Pricey told her if she killed him he'd come back to haunt her. Oh, and don't bring that fucking camera anywhere near my house. Kath lent it to her sister and borrowed it from her when necessary. John Price was 43 years old and unemployed. He was at a loose end. It wasn't a good situation and he took to hanging out at the top pub a bit more regularly while picking up a bit of work here and there.

The new licensee, Paul Farrell, moved in in June 1998 and found Pricey came with the bar. They became best mates and the customer would drive his ute down to help them with the renovations. Farrell helped him fill in job applications, although he suspected Pricey read and wrote better than he let on. Kath was back on the scene by now and Farrell remembers her dropping Price off at the pub and coming back two hours later to pick him up. Often he'd put her off for another hour or so.

Kath was a good bird like that. Ron Murray says she used to run him down to the pub on a Friday afternoon to meet John and sometimes pick him up later. He says she was good hearted. He recalls them verbally jousting, Pricey calling her a mad cunt, or the Speckled Fucking Hen and her responding in kind. He often spoke harshly to her and about her, but the publican says he got the feeling it was a show of bravado in front of mates. Pricey would sometimes say he loved her.

Kath would get out too. Amanda Pemberton, a 29-year-old from Muswellbrook, was a friend of hers. They'd hit the pub Thursdays, Fridays and Saturdays up until about the time Pricey lost his job. After that they got together on Tuesdays and Thursdays at the RSL and workers' clubs in Muswellbrook.

Amanda was well aware of Kath's frustrations. She remembers she was extremely jealous and worried that Pricey would leave her, once threatening to cut his balls off in front of her if he did.

> The one thing that I did see in Kathy during the time I spent with her was that she had a very bad temper. If it was one thing that I could tell about her was her bad temper. From seeing her temper I would not like [to] be on the wrong side of her if she got cranky with me. The slightest thing would set her off and she would swear, yell and get away from things. She would also sometimes go to the pub and drown her sorrows. On a number of occasions she did this with me, especially in the early stages of her relationships with Pricey.

The main thing that seemed to upset Kathy about Pricey was that he was not home on time. Things like going to the pub after work, talking to other people. Kathy seemed as though she wanted Pricey all for herself and did not want to share him with anyone else.

Sometimes Amanda would be invited to come in for a chat or have dinner with the pair, but it was Pricey that invited her most of the time. She liked Pricey. He was a nice bloke.

Gerrie Edwards remembers her in the pub one night, flaunting her jealousy and anger like a homicidal peacock. It was July 1998 and the shopkeeper was having a Christmas in July celebration at the bowling club with some friends, when she saw Katherine in the front bar. She was very drunk, red-faced, swearing and screaming. Going on about that cunt Pricey and how she'd cut his fucking balls off. Gerrie tried to calm her down. Kath said some old girlfriend of Pricey's had given him a hug at the pub or something and things had spun out of control from there. She was just so jealous and insecure.

One night Kath and John went up and had dinner with Dave Saunders and Glenda Reichel. Dave and Price shared a love of cars and beer; in fact, Dave had introduced Kath and John. It was years before, back in Segenhoe Street, and Saunders was pulling down the twin cam Corona. The one she vandalised another time. Anyway, the car had been in bits for months and Saunders was saying one night at the Commercial that he was sick of the slow thing he was driving and he was going to get that Corona back together. Pricey showed up 9 am the next morning and they spent the day drinking beer and getting the car running. They were too drunk to take it out when they were finished so Pricey came back the next day and they took it for a run. This night Pricey and her showed up for dinner he was telling Glenda about maintenance and the kids, and Kath started to get real shitty. Jealous. Didn't like seeing him talking to another woman. They had to talk her down and then she was right again.

So life continued in its own fraught, frustrating and self-defeating manner. Katherine wanted to be Pricey's wife. She had her eyes on that house and while he loved her, he would have given it all up to have Colleen back. It was Col's house, he used to tell her that. Nothing had changed.

He was always a bit lighthearted. He'd say, 'You can have the house, Col,' and I'd say, 'No, I don't want it.' You see, he worked his arse off and his dad and mum always used to say, 'Buy yourself a house,' and he always wanted one, and that's why I let him have it. It was a nice home and I loved it, but to me it was bricks and mortar.

I told him for years after he got with her that whatever he did he had to put the house in the kids' names because you're not letting her take it, because I didn't give it to you to give it to her, and for years I was on at him all the time about it and saying have you put it in the kids' names and he'd say, 'No, I was going to put in yours,' and I'd say 'No, do it for them.' I said, 'It's not her house.' I said, 'You worked your arse off for this and she's not getting it.'

If only all the women he met were like Colleen.

By 1999 Kath was running out of options. She thought this was the last shot and it was all falling apart. She couldn't pry him away from the ex-wife or the kids and he was becoming more distant, pushing her away, testing her limits. Pricey was feeling like a man who has got nowhere to turn. They'd painted themselves into a corner and it was becoming increasingly obvious to both of them that there was only one way it was going to end.

His mate Paul Farrell had left the pub and moved on, but Price used to keep in touch and late in 1999, maybe it was Grand Final time, Paul got a call at a pub he was looking after in Camperdown. Mid conversation Pricey broke down. 'I've got to get rid of the bitch.' He started to sob. 'What's happened now, mate?' Pricey had trouble getting the words out and what he said shocked the publican. 'She stabbed me the other night, I don't know what to fuckin' do.' Farrell told him to ring the police but Pricey wouldn't. If she couldn't get him she'd get the kids; that's what she had said she would do.

John didn't show anyone the stab wound. He hid it under his shirt until the day he died. Everybody would just say the same thing, they were already saying. 'She's gonna kill you, mate.' He didn't need to be told that. At the same time, she ran around town telling the authorities. Kath claims she told the police and her lawyer. She was always looking to protect herself, cutting off avenues of complaint. She got in first and told the police it was an accident. She wasn't wearing her glasses and he came too close.

He gives me heaps for when I actually cut him with the knife, I was actually pointing [it] at him. I went to my solicitor. I went to the police about it. I didn't know I had a knife in my hand. He gave me heaps that night. He put his arms around me that night, told me I deliberately did it.

She had all manner of excuses for the incident. She'd tripped. It was his fault. She wasn't wearing her glasses. It could just as easily have been a spoon as a knife. Anyway, he'd dumped her in it when he got picked up for driving under the influence *after he went to court and lost his licence and he told the judge it was my fault. It was all lies.* He deserved it. Kath reckoned she was going to leave him. He didn't deserve her. And he could only tell Paul Farrell, couldn't bring himself to tell anyone else.

John's daughter remembers catching a glimpse of a big bruise on his chest a few months before he died. He said it was nothing and to forget it. She thought he might have been fighting with her brother and later, when she made the connection, she cried bitter, awful tears. 'He said, "It's nothin', darl. Don't worry about it." I just wish he could have told us. I wish we could have been there for him.'

I'll kill Pricey
29 February 2000

The camera is rolling and for a minute nobody is in the room. Katherine takes the chance to record her thoughts. 'I love all my children and my grand-daughter.' She sighs heavily. 'And I hope to see them all.' There's only a few hours left. 'Pick up all those cups.' It's already 6 pm. She's calm and ready to take this situation in hand. She's had the knives sharpened, had her last blue with Pricey, and now it is time he got what he deserved. She'll show him. The dead don't give you any grief. You can hang them on the wall and they never call you a cunt or the Speckled Hen or take the good years of your life away and then expect you to leave with nothing to show for it. She's got bruises on her tit and he's going to pay for that. All the others have got away with hurting her and her kids. And she'll get away with this somehow. They can't blame her if she's mad, and anyway all men are cunts and rapists and they fuck you round. From the first one that climbs into a little girl's bed, to the last one that tries to stick his dick up your arse and throw you out of his house. They've fucked her around, destroyed her life and her confidence. She's made his bed, cooked his meals, cleaned for him, driven him around and what does she get? Abuse and scorn. Her self-esteem is shot and it's his fault.

She feels some calm at last. A little tingle of excitement. Time's running out, she's got to say goodbye to people.

Earlier she had the boy to do the filming, got him to get the two daughters and granddaughter in frame. The women kissing and hugging. She loves her kids and they'll all be together again. And it's been such a lovely day with the grand-daughter who has been giving her the biggest smiles. It's good to get all this packaged up and contained on tape. It's like pre-serving the moment in a jar of formaldehyde. Put it on a shelf, sit back and look at it forever. Pricey wouldn't let her keep the video camera at his place after he lost his job at the mines.

Life has been getting out of control. Kath is brooding. Things turning to shit like they always do. It's him and his kids against her. She's collecting grudges against those kids and Pricey's terrified about what she might do to them.

Things came to a head when the youngest daughter was down again and a jumping castle had been parked in the vacant block next to the house. Pricey had paid the bloke a case of beer to pump it up for the kids in the street. There was a lot of coming and going and Kath was getting sloshed and aggressive. When the youngest came in her eldest sister Rosemary had news for her, 'You know what this bitch just said? She reckons you've been interfering with her kids.'

This was a big call, even for Katherine. She was trying to tell John and his eldest girl that the 14-year-old girl had sexu-ally assaulted her two. Just another chapter in her lifetime of abuse accusations, but perhaps the most ridiculous. It was another piece of grit she would use to nurture a pearl of resentment. And payback. She was in a right mood that after-noon. Drunk and niggling and bitching for all she was worth, but she wasn't getting far enough so she resorted to a tried and proven method for getting a bloke where it hurts. She turned on his mother. Nobody talked about John's mum. Everybody knew it was just too sensitive. Kath got the reaction she wanted.

> You should have seen Dad. He saw red. Rosemary grabbed him. He wasn't going Kath, but he was furious and Rosemary got her husband to take him out the front. Then Rosemary grabbed a plate and said, 'This is a nice plate. Who owns it?', and Kath said it was hers and Rosemary said, 'Well, fuck off or I'll break it over your head.'
>
> Then they went out the front. I took off, but they said she still kept going on and on, and Rosemary kicked her off the porch but she grabbed the pole which saved her.
>
> Then Rosemary said, 'Get out of me dad's house or we'll call the cops', and she wouldn't and the cops come, but she was acting unconscious in the front room.

The next morning Kath woke and got breakfast like nothing had ever happened. Except now she had two of his kids down as abusers as well as him. In her head the whole bloody lot of them were at it. Pricey had a harmless game he played occasionally with his grandson and Kath's little boy. When they got out of the shower or bath he'd make a laughing lunge for their penis with his finger and thumb. Pullin' their tail. He'd do it in full view of everyone. It was a little coarse but it made the boys laugh and nobody saw it as inappropriate. Except Kath. She got herself right worked up about that and told her daughter and a few others. There were whispers that some of her male relatives had a fondness for little boys. It had caused a lot of grief in the family, but it was another of those dark secrets.

After Pricey had lost his job at the mine, Kath got in her

head that she might need to get ready to play hard ball with him. In her mind he was now a threat to her because he had good reason to be. Later, after the job was done, she said he threatened to kill her. Which is highly unlikely. She said lots of things. He smeared shit on her face. He stuck his foot up her vagina. He wanted to have sex with other blokes and make her participate.

She often thought of getting even. A year before, Kath contacted her nephew, Jason Roughan, and there was talk of breaking Price's legs or burning his car. She told Roughan he called her a slut and bought other women drinks to scorn her. She'd considered putting a snake or spider in his bed, but she gave up on that idea. She and Jason discussed throwing battery acid in his face so he could know how she felt. Scarred inside. The conspirators went over and over their plans. Jason had taken on Pricey once before. Went him and Shane for abusing her. 'She loved me like a mum. I wouldn't let anyone hurt her.'

Katherine was forming a plan but it was no state secret. She dropped down to her brother Charlie's place in Muswellbrook and said she was going to kill Pricey. She'd said this before, but this time she added she'd kill Pricey and the two kids. Charlie took her to mean her two kids and told her to wake up to herself. He was angry. She said she'd get away with it because she would pretend to be mad. Charlie's daughter Tracy was there and remembers her aunt saying that if she couldn't have him nobody could. She remembers her saying about how she'd get away with it by feigning madness.

She was creating problems everywhere she went. She was in her mid 40s now, might even be menopausal. She'd had lots of problems with skin cancers and lumps and a reddening of the face. She looked older than her years, but she'd been trying to keep fit. Almost every morning she and Joy and their

half-brother Barry and his wife Val would get together at the
top of the street and go for a long walk toward the garbage
dump. The family roaming the outskirts of town. Sticking
together. Wandering out the back of town, past the colliery on
the meatworks side of the railway line.

There were a few people just wandering around.
Aberdeen's going to the dogs. It wasn't uncommon for the
abattoirs to shut during quiet periods but in 1999 it closed
down forever. After a century the meatworks was gone. Four
hundred people lost their jobs. Apparently the bottom had
fallen out of the overseas market. There's not much call for
local killers now that the animals are exported live. It tore the
heart out of the little town. For 100 years the slaughterhouse
seeded the district with meatworkers and their families. It
brought them to town, in some cases gave them housing and
then gave their kids and grandkids jobs. And now nobody has
to put a bullet through the beast's head, or cut its throat.
Nobody need hang it by a hook and open its guts, strip off its
skin and cut the meat off the bones. Put it in neat little
vacuum packs.

It hurt the town. Housing prices dropped dramatically,
people had to look further afield for work. Some of the men
starting commuting to Newcastle and even Sydney. The
women struggled to find casual work, especially in a town
where there's only a handful of shops and two pubs. There's
no bank, no hospital, no industry apart from the tannery and
the coal mines down the road which weren't interested too
much in hiring the locals—they were a union crowd.
Aberdeen still doesn't even have a McDonald's and probably
never will. After the pub closes you've got to drive to
Muswellbrook to find an ATM.

Early in 2000, Natasha and Kath's granddaughter left
MacQueen Street and moved to Muswellbrook, although it

appears she took some convincing. The kid was in no hurry to leave but Kath wanted her out. It wasn't that Kath didn't love her granddaughter. She had made a video of the child when she was born. She made her a little squaw's outfit out of chamois-like material for her christening, but she couldn't put up with Natasha around the house any longer, even if she was paying rent. She and the baby left for the big town down the road.

Natasha wasn't married when her daughter was born and there had been issues of paternity involving two brothers. A blood test proved conclusively that one of the contenders was indeed the dad. The daughter was a chip off the old block. She would tell people that she loved knives more than her mother. She has a blood chilling temper and a foul mouth.

Before Katherine's trial, Donna Page of the *Newcastle Herald* caught up with Natasha at her Muswellbrook home. the journalist was offered an exclusive insight into the mother-daughter relationship and the murder.

Pricey was always a good fella [but] he started to change a bit. I never saw him hit her, she told me it was more of a mental abuse.

She was a good mum and there is no doubt about that. I could not have asked for a better mother. I used to get smacked hard, Mum grew up that way so that is the way things were. With the younger kids she started to change. Mum was starting to learn as we got older that things were different in terms of discipline and punishment.

She made sure we never went hungry. Mum was never the person to help with homework and she hated sports. She had trouble reading and so couldn't help with school work and stuff like that but I remember once we had got to Maitland or Newcastle for a soccer game and we stopped off at McDonald's. There was a whole bunch of us in a van and Mum shouted us all.

It was great, she was always thinking of someone else. I just thought she was under a lot of pressure. You would have to hate someone to do something like that.

Natasha wasn't surprised by the details of the murder.

If that is what you're trained to do then of course that is how you would kill someone if you were going to do it. If there were three knives used they all had a different purpose. So I would have to say that she would have stabbed him, cut his head off and skinned him. Is that what happened?

Page thought that Natasha felt some guilt about her mother, she told the journalist 'Mum was asking me for help and I did not click on'.

The second daughter said her mum was a bush girl who loved camping.

My mum really wanted to kill me once. I was teasing her real bad, calling her stupid names and things and she just went off. Mum was always very sensitive, she always followed her heart. She fell in love fast. It's hard to understand why she would have done that. There is no excuse for it. I think that one day the bottle got that extra bit full and the lid came off. It was a whole heap of shit really.

Natasha believed her mother would do her time in jail and come home to live with her, saying 'once she gets out I would like her to come and live with me, because I would do anything for my mum. If somebody hurt her they would have to get through me first.'

*   *   *

During the day Kath would try to keep active, sewing and visiting mates, but there were so many hours between the time
the kids went to school and when they would come home
again. It was starting to get her down and she was starting to
spend a lot of time at MacQueen Street by herself. A lot of
time with her dead things, all those inanimate objects. Stuffed
wombats and peacocks and fawns, a plaster collie, spurs,
cowboy boots, leather jackets, skins and skulls. An electric
organ and an antique pram her mum had given her when she
was 11. Dust falling from the ceiling and the rumbling from
beneath the foundations. She would sit in one chair then
another to get different views, she was having nerve troubles
again and was on antidepressants. The dead cheered her up.
She described it as her dream home. Those things helped *to
keep the past as a future ... I loved all of that. I loved it. That was my
escape ... Just looking at everything on the wall. I'd swap sides on the
lounge and watch the old things I had there. Time stood still and
I owned it ... I didn't see the peacock killed; it was beauty and the
horns ...*

It was at times like these that Kath really missed Barbara,
but she had her spirit in pictures and mementos and she
could arrange them and sit with Mum in a peace rarely experienced during Barbara's life. The dead lived in totems. It
gave her control of her environment that she'd never had
when things weren't dead.

German psychiatrist Eric Fromm says that this behaviour
is consistent with necrophilous, a form of necrophilia, or the
love of the dead. He says that certain personality types, the
narcissistic and anal, who gain control over their threatening
environments with violence, can worsen over the years. They
discover a sadistic joy in hurting and eventually killing.
Beyond this comes a love of handling death, dealing with it.
Transforming the living into the dead. Carrying a sticky, skin-

less head from the lounge to the soup pot. Hanging the skin on a butcher's hook.

Katherine had always been somewhat sadistic. She controlled her environment with violence. She loved the abattoirs because it was a place where the living were turned into the dead. She loved scraping out the carcasses. She was obsessively materialistic, collecting things and nailing them to the walls. Collecting mementos of people living and dead. Hoarding things.

According to Gordon Burn in his book *Happy Like Murderers*, English mass murderer Fred West showed a similar fondness for things over people. He preferred inanimate objects. They turned him on sexually. His home was populated by the pieces of the many people he had murdered and he got comfort from that. He liked the deadened and dehumanised over the alive and responding. He loved to video things. Package them and put them on a shelf. West also had dealings with abattoirs, collecting skins and hides in his van. He used a sharp knife to dismember and behead his victims, working carefully and cleanly.

V S Naipaul wrote about the casual cruelty of English farmers who could tenderly raise a calf all the time knowing the hand that reared it would one day cut its throat. An abattoir worker only knows one end of this equation. Katherine's and Fred West's cruelty knew no boundaries. She would slash the throat of a rabbit out of necessity, a puppy out of anger. The next step was to kill a man and when she did it, she found it wasn't enough. There was further to go.

Kath was getting down in the dumps. She'd get quiet at times like this and would bury herself at home with the videos and the television. She had an enormous collection of videos. That video collection was something else. She loved the horror ones. The bloodier the better. They were all carefully catalogued in a little diary and the family—Shane and Barry and Joy and Natasha and a few others—would dub them off and pass them around. Even Barbara had liked a good horror flick. They had hundreds and hundreds. Their video collection was probably the biggest in town. Some of the movies were extremely disturbing. Some days she'd watch the soaps too. Her favourite was 'The Bold and the Beautiful'.

Come Sunday 27 February 2000, John Price has three days left to live. Three days and two nights. It was hot and bright. Mid summer in the valley Aberdeen is a long way from the cooling breezes of the coast. Kath had a stye on her eye and she couldn't stand the light. They'd been at a party the night before and that had ended up in a screaming match—something about her dancing and, of course, his mum. Dave Saunders had been there too and Pricey came up and told him he just wanted to get rid of her.

Ronny Murray and Pricey got together for their Sunday constitutional just before lunchtime. They parked themselves on the small front porch that looks across at Keego's place and had a couple to clear the cobwebs. They used to have their Sunday drink at the top pub but the new owner, who hasn't fitted in that well with the locals, doesn't open early enough so the boys drink at home. Ronny stuck his head inside and saw Kath lying on the lounge, wearing a small eye mask. She came out later and asked how they were going before ducking back inside because the glare and the dry summer winds were hurting her eye. Ronny left at about half past one after they'd had about four beers. He liked Kath. She'd been caring to his wife who had lost her speech faculties because of a brain tumour, and had come up to her with a woman's magazine step-by-step guide to sign language, and showed them the intricate American eagle she'd stitched onto a bedspread. She ran him around to the pubs and he'd never really seen them fight. It was something John didn't talk to him about.

Johnny Collison came over later and Kath had gone to the pub to buy a carton of Tooheys stubbies. Pricey had complained because they cost $30 not $27. It was shitty weather, windy and hot and the two kids were there along with a niece and when Collo left the couple started to fight. They were tired and irritable and who knows how it started. There's only one left to retell the story. This is how Kath described it to Bob Wells.

—He was rubbishing me having different fathers for my children again, and I just said to him, 'Hang on', I said, 'You said last night at a party that your parents were married and they're, they weren't,' and he just went off his brain and said, 'Don't say anything about my mother.' And then he attacked me.

—Can you tell me how he attacked you?

—He stood up beside the, in between the two lounges, the big lounge and the little lounge and that's when he grabbed me by the throat and on the breast.

—Right. Can you recall about what time that was?

—No, I don't. It was still daylight.

—All right. Do you recall what John did after that?

—He, I got away from him and went out to the kitchen and when I was going out there I noticed my necklace was broken. I then grabbed his smokes and broke 'em all up. He told me to get out and I told him to get out and he went.

—Do you know where he went to?

—And then the police came . . . I presume I told them that he attacked me . . . He told, told them that I had a knife, went to the kitchen and got a knife. And I never, 'cause the three children could verify that. I told the police to go out and check the drawers themselves and they couldn't see the knife, so I went out to look and it was in the kitchen sink. I asked the

policeman to take the knife away 'cause it didn't have my fingerprints on it whatsoever. I didn't know whose fingerprints
were on it at the time. And then my [youngest] daughter ...
said that [the young son] cut the tomato and onion up with
the knife for tea that night. So, if they would have took it away
it would have his fingerprints on it.

It was a yellow-handled boning knife that belonged to
Price, according to Knight, who admitted she had a knife that
she 'only cut up hot meat with'. She couldn't remember
where the children had been. 'The pain in me breast was just
too agonising to see or think of anythink.'

Pricey had broken her necklace. She went off over that.
Something was going on with that necklace. Rosemary Biddle
remembers at her son's fifth birthday the week before that the
little boy was playing on Nana Kath's knee. He liked to open
the locket she wore and look at the picture of Kath and Pricey
in it. Kath told him not to bother trying to open it. 'There's
nothing in there.'

Kath's youngest daughter was interviewed about what
happened on the Sunday. She'd been staying with her dad
and his new wife in Scone and had returned on the Sunday
about 5.30 pm and had just put her bag down when things
started to get violent. 'Pricey and Mum were having a fight.
And Pricey went over to Mum and tried to strangle her and
nearly ripped off her breast.' She hadn't seen the struggle,
but had been in the bedroom with the other two when 'Mum
screamed and Mum told us and she showed us the bruise and
the red mark'. The girls said it had been a long time since
their last fight and she had kept out of the way.

—They were just starting to fight, and then I went into the
kitchen to get a drink and then I went into my bedroom ...
Mum and Pricey [were] sitting on the lounge. Mum was
laying on the big lounge and Pricey was just sitting on the

rocky lounge. Then Pricey was drinking beer. Mum was watching her show . . .

—How did Pricey bruise your mum's breast?

—Grabbed it and started pulling it.

—Why did he grab and start pulling your mum's breast?

—'Cause Pricey was trying to get at her throat . . .

—How do you know he was trying to get at your mum's throat?

—Oh, because Pricey said he was sorry and he didn't mean to get her breast, he meant to get her throat.

Later on, the girl said that Pricey too had lost a necklace in the unseemly struggle.

—Did you ever see any marks on Pricey from any cuts with a knife?

—No. Except for the scratch that Mum did when she pulled off Pricey's necklace because she was trying to defend herself from Pricey . . . a crocodile tooth that Mum gave him for a present when we were up in Queensland with my sister.

Kath would maintain that she was about to leave Price, but her daughter recalled her saying something quite different on the day.

—Did your mum ever tell Pricey that she was not going to leave?

—Yes.

—What did she tell Pricey?

—That she was not going to leave.

—When did she tell Pricey that she was not going to leave?

—When Pricey went across the road [to Keegan's house].

Katherine and some of the family made statements to the police that she had made up her mind to leave him. There was a lot of disinformation peddled in the ensuing months by her support group. Whatever the truth, the fight happened and the police came.

Michael Steele, a senior constable with Scone Police, found Price at Keegan's that night with a scratch on his cheek that had been bleeding a little and a stubbie of beer in his hand. He was 'slightly affected by alcohol', to use the police language. Pricey told him he'd grabbed her by the throat and wanted to punch her after an argument. Steele and Constable Amanda Doyle went over to the house and found Katherine Knight smoking a cigarette on the lounge chair.

Steele asked her what happened.

—He grabbed me by the shirt and pushed me down and grabbed me by the throat, but there's no problem. He's let off his anger and he'll be right now.

—John said that he grabbed you by the throat and that he let you go and you went into the kitchen and grabbed a knife. You then came out of the kitchen and threatened him with the knife.

—No, I never grabbed any knife. You can ask the kids, they were here.

The daughter backed up her story and Kath showed the female police officer her bruise. Doyle thought it looked like a love bite. Steele spoke with Price again before returning.

—John said that you grabbed a knife out of his work bag.

—No, I didn't. You can have a look if you like.

Doyle found the yellow handled knife in the sink. She said it was his and she never touched it. Doyle asked her if she wanted to press charges against Price.

—No, I don't have a problem with him. Now that he's got his anger out he'll just come home and go to sleep.

—Well, for the kids' sakes you might like to go back to your house for the night.

—No way. This is my house as much as his. I told you I don't have any problem. I never called the police.

She said she wouldn't give a statement or take any action unless he did. Doyle again said she should leave for the night, told her to think of the kids.

—No way. I'm not leaving, The kids are settled. They have their own bedroom. I'll put them to bed and he'll come home and go to sleep. There won't be any problems, I can tell you.

Steele told her the courts would be left to sort this one out. They then went back to Price and told him if he wanted her out, he should go and get a court order. The only way she was leaving was if they dragged her out and they weren't going to do that. Pricey was stuck with her and her pig-headed conviction that it was her house as much as his. Hers by right.

The next morning Steele went to the Scone Courthouse and saw clerk Glenn Dunning, the man Pricey would visit on his last day. He handed over two AVO complaints and summonses that he had prepared. The summonses were issued for a court date on 22 March 2000. Later that day he gave them to Senior Constable Simon Gallen, but says he then realised he couldn't deliver cross summonses. Price had admitted grabbing her by the throat and as it was usually the woman who needed protection, Steele said Gallen could serve the order on Price and forget Katherine's.

It was to prove a fatal move. Not because an order would have saved John Price, but because Katherine was left wondering what was going on with the order against her and started to get paranoid.

Gallen went to St Andrews Street with Senior Constable Heath Boswell at 9 pm. Kath answered the door and they asked for Pricey. She got him out of bed. John was told they had an AVO summons for him. He wasn't surprised, but asked if he could speak to the officers in private. They were reluctant—it wasn't their business—but they agreed to follow him to the bedroom. Kath asked if she could come and listen. He

said no. Pricey told the cops he wanted her out. They told him
he'd have to go to the Clerk of Courts the next day.

When they came back to the kitchen Kath was keen to
know what was going on. Had he been telling them about the
knife? She seemed agitated that they'd issued an order when
she hadn't wanted to take any action. The police weren't that
interested in explaining the ins and outs of it and wrote down
Steele's number on the AVO and left. The document says that
Steele believed 'that the protected person (Katherine Knight)
is in need of protection and fears the commission of a personal violence offence or conduct amounting to harassment
or molestation by the defendant'.

It gives a brief 'general history of violence and harassment':

The de facto couple have been in a relationship for around the
last 6 years. In 1997 police were called to the defendant's home
for a report of a verbal argument. The couple still own their
respective separate homes and the victim with her 2 children
have been sleeping at the defendant's home for about the last 6
months. According to the pinop [person in need of protection]
the defendant has not previously engaged in acts of violence but
has lost his temper, usually after drinking. The pinop however
stated she did not have a problem with his behaviour. On the
day in question, Sunday February 27, 200 [sic] the pinop and
the defendant were sitting in the lounge room watching television. Both parties then began to argue and the defendant
grabbed hold of the pinop and scuffled on the lounge.
According to the defendant the pinop then went to the kitchen
and grabbed a boning knife and returned to the lounge room
and threatened the defendant. The defendant has then left the
home and attended a neighbour's home and telephoned the
police. When spoken to the defendant had a scratch to the left
side of face which had been bleeding. When speaking to the

pinop she showed a female officer her right breast that the defendant had allegedly grabbed during the scuffle, however the bruise appeared to be that of a 'love bite' rather than a fresh bruise and there was no redness to the area. Both stories of the pinop and the defendant differ in relation to the knife. It was obvious that the defendant had been drinking when spoken to. It was suggested to the pinop she take her children and return to her home. The pinop refused and stated she did not have a problem with the defendant. Both parties were reluctant to initiate proceedings against the other so police have initiated this A.V.O. Application as a means of controlling the behaviour of the defendant toward the pinop.

It was a mass of senseless type to both Knight and Price.

Gallen made a note on the Affidavit of Service of Summons of Price's reaction: 'I just want her out of here but she won't go', and swore it before a Justice of the Peace the following day—John Price's last day on Earth.

Poor Pricey. She was chasing him around with a knife and she was refusing to leave his house and then they served him a summons. It just wasn't right. But Kath was toey too. She figured he'd worked something out with the cops and that they were about to serve her with a summons asking her to leave his house. She was waiting for them to knock on the door and throw her out of the house that was half hers. She had a right to it. She wouldn't let him get away with it.

Pricey didn't know it, but she'd taken some old pieces of his clothes and fashioned them into a little suit for a doll. She'd taken his semen too and smeared it on the doll. Witchcraft might work. It was her voodoo doll. But the situation had become more serious. She got a relative to sharpen her knives.

Katherine was in a corner and she only knew one way to respond. This was the end game.

The murder
29 February 2000

Kath knew the end was near. She believed she would get a court order and it played on her mind. He was kicking her out. He'd used her up and was throwing her out of the house. She'd said numerous times she'd kill him and tonight she was going to do it. This morning she'd stood at the end of his bed, hands behind her back, knowing it would scare the living bejesus out of the bastard. God, he jumped when he saw her there. Petrified. And, in that moment she came to understand that she had so much power over him, she could snuff him out just like that and it was a magnificent feeling to have that power. But there were a few things a girl had to do first.

He scampered off. His nerves shot. No doubt swearing he was going to get rid of her, whatever it took. She headed out for her morning walk with the family. On Monday she showed her twin Joy the bruises as they walked out to the colliery. She told their sister-in-law Val about the fight too. Joy said she should leave him. Kath said she'd do it when she was ready. Her sister knew about the fight the day before because her daughter had been there playing with Kath's daughter.

Kath was ready to head off on Tuesday as usual for the walk but found Joy and Val had been up all night at the hospital for the birth of Val's grandchild. Joy and Val were tight like that. In fact five months later Barry, Joy and Kath's half-brother, would discover the two women kissing in his house. His wife then left him for his half-sister. But that's another story.

That morning nobody was up for a walk, so Kath went back to St Andrews Street and took the kids back to her home and got them off to school, stopping at McDonald's in Muswellbrook to get the boy's breakfast and grabbing a bacon and egg McMuffin for Natasha before popping around to see her. The granddaughter was achingly cute that morning, but Kath had to go. She made a mental note not to forget the video and take some film of the child.

She headed up to Scone to see her solicitor, Mr Noonan. Surely, she couldn't just be thrown out of his house? She could. She talked about the bruises. She couldn't just let him get away with this. She was getting worked up and had to keep moving. There were goodbyes to be said, but not in so many words.

Glenda Reichel was just leaving her flat in Scone at around 10.30 in the morning. She remembers the time because the soap 'Sons and Daughters' was on the television before she left. As she pulled out of the driveway she noticed a red van pulling up. It was Kath in a pair of blue denim shorts and a small, sleeveless blue blouse. Glenda put the car back and went inside with her. She noticed that Kath wasn't herself. She didn't want a cuppa.

Glenda pulled out a ciggy and Kath showed her a small tear around the button of her blouse. 'Look at that. That's where he grabbed me.' She showed her the small bruise on her breast. 'This is what Pricey did to me.' Kath said she had been to a solicitor. 'He told me I may as well pack my gear and go from Pricey's. The bastard has done this to me. I've got nothing.'

They talked for about an hour, Kath going on about how Dave Saunders and John Price had been so cruel to her. Glenda was used to this stuff and switched off a bit, but noticed that Kath was unusually sombre and then she had to go. On the way out she said, 'I love you, Gurt.'

That was strange. Gurt didn't love Kath. It seemed so inappropriate.

Kath got back in the red van and headed to the police station, where she told the story all over again, how he'd attacked her and the police woman thought the bruise was a love bite. They fobbed her off, told her to see her doctor. She made an appointment with Dr Cook for 5 pm and kept moving, down the road, past Aberdeen and on to Muswellbrook, where her mate Amanda Pemberton saw her going past towards Kath's niece's place in Wollombi Road, two doors up from hers. Later, Pemberton headed out to Woolworths with her daughter, where she bumped into her friend. Kath nursed Amanda's baby and they chatted for about 10 minutes, Kath telling her all about her granddaughter, Natasha's baby.

Her brother-in-law, John Hinder, Joy's husband, was at his Aberdeen home in the early afternoon when Kath showed up to return three videos and wanting to borrow another, but he wouldn't let her without Joy's permission. It was one of her good ones. She left and went to pick up the girl from school, coming back an hour later with the girl. Joy was home. She borrowed the video and picked up the video camera that John Price wouldn't have in his house.

Kath had some things to get down on tape, moments to preserve. She picked up the boy at her house, where the bus dropped him off. One of the ladies from the shop next-door, where she bought milk and bread every day, walked past her in the street and noted that Kath was in one of her moods. 'She just looked through me and I thought, "What's up your nose today?"' She dropped the two children off at Natasha's house, then she was back on the road, heading up to Muswellbrook to see Dr Cook about the bruises. The consultation was brief. The doctor got the impression she just wanted the injury documented. And she was back in the car again and off home where she picked up some money before heading to Natasha's for the third time that day.

Kath set up the video on Natasha's television set and plonked herself in an armchair mid-frame, a naked grandchild on her lap, her two younger children coming in and out of the shot. The matriarch on her throne, weighed down by heavy responsibilities she cannot share. The child opens her shirt and plays with her breasts. She leaves it open. *Nana's titty bops.* She sings nursery rhymes in a shrill voice and complains, *She's not going to smile like she did this morning for me.* The scene ends and the film starts again in another room with the boy holding the camera. Natasha doesn't want to be filmed, but Mum is keen. *Tash, be in the picture please. . . for your mother's sake . . . because I want all of us on it.* The three women hug and she kisses them time and again. *Mummy loves ya.* The boy comes in too close. *Git back, will ya.* Tash says that the baby has taken its first steps off screen. *Ya fuckin' missed out the first steps on video!* The moment passes and she goes back to kissing. It seems so strained and unusual. She's not a mum given to shows of affection.

Then the video camera is back on the television set again and the kids are playing around. She wants a shot with the youngest daughter. She tells her she loves her and asks her to say it back. The girl is affectionate with her mother and they have a prolonged kiss. *I love you very very very much, my darling daughter . . . I love you* [*sic*] *in the whole wide world. Don't forget that old cane pram that my mum owned. I own, you own.* They kiss again and the girl leaves the room.

Katherine looks at the camera. Alone for a moment with her situation. She speaks an aside to the future. *I love all my children.* Music playing nearby makes the next bit almost inaudible. It sounds like 'and my granddaughter.' She feels a terrible sadness and sighs deeply. Then Katherine can be clearly heard to say *and I hope to see them all.*

The moment is cut short when the others re-enter and she is back in full voice. *Pick up all these cups!* Off-camera the young daughter bumps Natasha's breast. Kath looks up from the chair. *Did she hurt your breast like Pricey hurt mine?* The granddaughter plays on a small rocking horse and Katherine is back in the material world. *Look at this. Nan only paid $10 and look how good it is . . . Are we gonna go out and enjoy ourselves now and have some tea?* She's picked up a sewing machine for Natasha at the welfare shop in Muswellbrook, where she also bought a sexy black nightie. For the big night.

It's a telling few minutes on film. The materialism. The discourtesy to the male child. The sense of a last will and testament. The scene ends when the young daughter insists on placing a toy in front of the camera. Katherine gets out of the chair and angrily turns off the camera. Fade to black.

Natasha thought it was odd that Mum was shouting them Chinese from down the road, but was happy to go along. Mum didn't usually do this. Naturally, they have a screaming blue in the car, but that didn't ruin the dinner, although Kath was preoccupied and distracted for most of the meal. She was upset too because the granddaughter was again achingly cute, playing with the drink straws. She should have brought that video camera along. Captured the moment for eternity.

Katherine told her youngest daughter that all the children have to stay together.

Amanda Pemberton ran into them again. She was going into the Valley Motel Indoor Sports Centre near the restaurant.

> Kathy seemed to be a bit different. She appeared to be in a rush, asking me all sorts of questions ... I saw her driving away and she was driving real fast. It would have been about 10 pm by this time.

It was late and Kath wanted to get back home and watch the video of the grandchild she'd made earlier. It gave her a sense of calm, like when she sat among the dead things at home. She was reluctant to let go. The three kids got in the bath together. Then she did another strange thing. She asked Natasha if the kids could stay with her. They didn't have their things with them and it was going to be a hassle in the morning. Natasha started to wonder what was going on. Mum was 'confused, frustrated and tense, although she also seemed relaxed and calm at the same time'. They stopped at the door. Natasha voiced her concerns.

—I hope you're not going to kill Pricey and yourself.

—Oh no no no no. If Pricey starts on me I'll go to my house.

—I love you, Mum.

—I love you, Natasha.

Kath hesitated, offered her a cigarette, then jumped in the van and drove back towards John Price who was already at home in bed, wondering what the night held in store. Wondering where she was.

Katherine was tired but she knew she was going to kill him. She'd done all she had to do. Well, almost. She hadn't seen her sister-in-law Val since her grandchild had been born.

She arrived at their place in Aberdeen around 10.30 pm, Barry remembers because he was watching 'Third Watch' on television. The two women sat at the table and had a chat. Val was exhausted but pleased to show a video of her new grand-child. Katherine was keen to talk about the bruises. Barry showed her the renovations to the bathroom and she left before 11.30 pm.

Katherine went home to her place at MacQueen Street again. The neighbours know she wasn't there at 10.30 pm, but a little later Gerrie Edwards heard Kath open the gate between their houses. She assumed she was putting the bin out. She wasn't. Kath was just preparing to protect her assets from the forthcoming storm. Like when she moved all the stuff out of Pricey's before he found out about the video.

Katherine drove the van back over to St Andrews Street. A curtain opened across the road.

—The Speckled Hen must be home.

She lit a cigarette and let herself in. John was asleep, with the airconditioner on. She watched some television. She remembers that 'Star Trek' was on the telly.

*   *   *

But memory has failed, or been hidden like a bloody knife in the garbage. Katherine crossed the threshold. She has glimpses. She showers. Slips on the sexy black nightie from the welfare shop. The short one with buttons. Pricey's asking where the kids are.

> He turned over with his hands across my tummy. He wanted sex so we had it. He was gentle and kind. He undone my buttons on my nightie. He got me on top of him ... I came because he was kind. He went to the toilet. He was walking back to bed and that's it ...

Her memory is in the garbage bin again. Lost among the shit of her life.

He's two metres away and the movie cuts and the images jumble.

Sometimes there are flashbacks.

She's walking down the hallway in the nightdress. She's on the couch and her skin is crawling, like there are maggots all over her. White and wriggling, looking for a corpse. Maggots and hot flushes and sitting on the couch. Looking at a picture of Johnathon. He'll get his way, get the house and his dad and he abused Melissa—she has to live with that— abused her and yelled out in the pub that he took her up the arse. And Pricey's going to leave, like David Kellett did all that time before. Leave her alone. It's terrifying and it's infuriating. She has to take control. Then a sensation like her waters breaking.

She's come at him when he's lying in bed; the seat's up in the toilet and his bladder's empty. He did have a pee. She starts to lay into him with the boning knife. One time. Two times. Blood spraying up the walls with each thumping heartbeat. Three times. Four times. She stabs and slashes and he's jumped up in a crimson terror and he's trying to get past her. Trying to get the light switch on but she won't stop. Five times. Six times. John's just trying to get away. He staggers down the hallway towards the door and she's relentless. Seven times. Eight times. Nine. Ten. Eleven ... She doesn't stop. Twelve. Thirteen. Fourteen. At some stage he reaches the front door. Fifteen. Sixteen. And he's opened it and he's got a hand outside and she pulls him back in to the hall. Seventeen. Eighteen. Nineteen. And he's got his back to the wall. Twenty. Twenty-one. Twenty-two. But still he doesn't raise his arms. Twenty-three. Twenty-four. And still she's stabbing. Twenty-five. Twenty-six. Big vicious blows through the rib cavities into the lungs and the organs and he's slipping down onto the floor. Into a pool of his own blood and its all over the place. Twenty-seven. Twenty-eight. Twenty-nine. In his eyes. Spraying on the walls with each fading heartbeat. Thirty. Thirty-one. Thirty-two. And she doesn't stop. Thirty-three. Thirty-four. She keeps on stabbing. Thirty-five. And stabbing. Thirty-six. And stabbing. Thirty-seven terrible wounds. Thirty-seven blows before she stops. There could have been more. It's a bit hard to tell.

And John Price dies on the cork tiles, his body a shredded mess, wounds feeding an ocean of blood. His heartbeat fading.

She's got him now. Try calling me a red-headed cunt. Try squeezing my breast. Throw me out of your house. Ya can't. Ya can't leave. Ya can't hurt me.

But she's not finished with her revenge. She's not leaving without money and if he won't give her the $10 000 then she'll get what she can. At some stage she's in the shower, a bloody footprint on the bathmat, hair and flesh in the drain. Washing it all off like you would after a day at the abattoir. The bloody nightie draped over the bath. Back into the denim shorts and sleeveless blue shirt. She grabs his ATM card and then jumps in the car. There's no machine in Aberdeen so she drives to Muswellbrook, where Natasha is with the children, and she stops at the machine. Punches in his four digit PIN number and withdraws $500 at 2.32 am. A voice says you can get more. You can get $1000 a day. It used to be $500. She puts in the PIN again, takes out another $500 at 2.35 am. Price has $12 456.74 in the account. Enough to pay her off. The $1000 disappears into the night. There are many theories about where it went. Her relatives point fingers at each other.

Katherine drives back to Aberdeen, on the deserted country highway, a murderess and a robber and a scorned woman, glowing and plotting what to do next. Calm and in control. She drives the van back to MacQueen Street, where she's left the side gate open in preparation, and slips quietly into the backyard. Right up behind the shed. She never usually parks here, there's no room to turn and take it out again. It is another possession tucked safely away. She puts her keys inside the house and leaves her empty purse on the floor of the van by an ATM receipt showing her just how much Pricey has in the bank. Then she sets out back to St Andrews Street. She walks past Lisa Logan and her little dog at 3.30 am, never knowing she's being watched.

Back inside, Katherine continues her revenge on John Price and has some fun while she's at it. She strips. And gets the knives and the sharpening stones. Drags him from that sea of congealing blood into the loungeroom where there is room to work. Cuts across the shoulders and down the pubic hair line, around the genitals and down the legs, down the arms and across the top of the head. She begins to peel and tear, pull and roll, and then it is off. John's death suit. And she has a hook and she hangs him in the doorway between the lounge and the kitchen like the skins that hang in her home. It's heavy to lift but she's strong.

It's just like being back at work, back at the job she loved. A little like the movies she likes. Like *Resurrection*, where he cuts the limbs off the living and hangs them up on butcher's hooks. She likes that one. She's in control and she's showing him.

Don't rush. There's plenty of time before the sun comes up and there's more payback left yet. She's going to get that daughter and son. They won't let her have John or his house. Well, she'll show them. She peels and slices the vegetables. She cuts through the flesh of the neck, working the blade through the vertebrae and carries the sticky, skinless head to a soup pot. Katherine's favourite cut of meat is a rare rump steak and she takes a few from John, bakes some in the oven. Throws one outside for a bit of a laugh. There's plenty of time so she makes some gravy. His youngest always liked gravy. John's watching from the doorway. Mute and twisted.

She serves up the dinner on plates. Vegetables and meat and gravy. She makes out a note for his eldest son and youngest daughter, and a little PS for Pricey too. She smashes their framed photographs. Collects the fat in a coffee mug. Has a coffee and a cigarette. Gets a bit of blood on the kettle. Puts the bloody faced watch on the shattered glass. Something for them to squabble over.

The morning is approaching and she washes, takes a selection of pills from the bedroom and the kitchen, puts her day clothes back on and lies on the bed waiting for them to come. The airconditioner droning away. She is satisfied. John is no longer a threat. He's a souvenir. A trophy. Dehumanised and diminished. And she has had her revenge against him and his children. She snores for the last time ever in the home she thinks should be hers. And she keeps her eyes tightly shut until it's safe to open them again. Whenever that is.

And the dinner goes cold on the bench. Fat begins to congeal, the gravy gets a skin and the soup cools.

*   *   *

Mass murderer and abattoir van driver Fred West had a fascination with exploration of the insides of the human body. In prison he recorded his memories of beheading one victim. 'I run the knife around the neck through the skin, and then just twisted the head round. And whatever bits was left, just cut that off.' In this case, he was referring to the mutilation of his daughter, Heather.

Dr Tim Lyons was impressed by the way Knight had skinned and cleanly severed John Price's head. It was almost an expert job. Right between the vertebrae. No knife marks on the bone. Like she was trained to do it.

Or born to.

The psychiatrists shape up
March 2000

Katherine won't open her eyes. Pricey's not dead. He's not. He's not. For the six days she is in the Muswellbrook and Maitland hospitals she pretends to have no knowledge of what she's done. She's told he's dead. She says he's not. She talks of going camping on the weekend. Kath monitors and manoeuvres. She claims no memory beyond John making love with her and a nurse waking her in the hospital, but somehow she is able to inform medical staff about which drugs she overdosed on. She tells the psychiatrists her partners have been abusive. She can see enough to know she has to start weaving a defence. Search for sympathy and mitigation. John's not dead, but she has to work hard to make sure she doesn't get nailed for what happened to him.

After being charged on the Monday, Katherine is taken to prison and locked up for the first time. It's not as bad as she thought it might be. A bit like the time Lloyd Lyne had her in the lockup at Aberdeen and Mrs Lyne came out with her lunch. Everybody seems concerned for her welfare. She quite likes that. It's been the same in hospital, the family milling around her bed, lawyers, doctors and nurses fussing about.

They didn't let her watch television in the ward because they didn't want her to know what she'd done. One night she dreams that the doctors were trying to kill Pricey—he was wrapped in bandages.

A staff member at Mulawa remembers her arriving at the jail. She is notorious after the newspaper stories and they all want to see the abattoir worker who cooked and skinned her defacto. They're struck by how ordinary she is. Polite too. She doesn't seem that hard. She is referred to the prison psychiatrist Dr Michael Giuffrida. The staff are told not to inform her of her crime for fear she may have a psychotic episode. She settles well into the swing of prison life and reports back to her family that she loves it. She is the centre of attention and everybody is caring for her. *I'm happy for the first time. I love it here, it's exciting, I like helping people.* Of course, you wouldn't want to spend your life here either, but she's in the Mum Shirl Unit and they let her work as a sweeper and she does lots of craft and the like. It's unlikely she'd be put on kitchen detail.

At times Katherine is glowing. She tells visitors she is being complimented for the first time in her life and it's just so wonderful. She tells people how bad her life was and how bad John Price was. She tells somebody she wants to donate her Aberdeen land to the local soccer club. The last claim would appear to be an absolute lie but gives an indication of how hard she is working to spin her story. Katherine's cunning, always working an angle.

She is being treated with kid gloves and has to prepare for a mention at Muswellbrook Court in early April. Prison staff are told that she is to be watched closely, apparently she became hysterical, throwing a sort of fit when an inmate informed her that not only was John Price dead, but that she had killed, skinned and decapitated him. It's all a thousand times worse than she thought.

The day at court—back in the town where she married David Kellett—dissolves into farce. She doesn't make it into the courtroom because police are worried about her safety. Two of Price's brothers, Ray and Bob, are threatening to kill her and cause a disturbance out on the highway, stopping cars and lashing out. To get Katherine away from the place safely a dummy prison van is sent out and a compliant television journalist pretends to interview the Price brothers while Kath is hurried into another van. Prison psychiatrist Dr Michael Giuffrida provides an assessment to the court, saying she is suffering amnesia and dissociation and was suffering dissociation on the day of the murder, although she has shown no signs of psychosis.

She's fit for trial, but he's indicating she's not guilty of murder because she was in a trance-like state at the time. The *Daily Telegraph* newspaper reports the next morning that

> a woman accused of the decapitation murder of her 44-year-old defacto smiled as she was led away from Muswellbrook Local Court . . . She was transported to Muswellbrook from the psychiatric ward at Long Bay Jail but not taken into the courtroom . . . due to security fears.

She has told visitors at prison she will never return to Aberdeen again because his family would hunt her down. She could be right, but John Price's daughter Rosemary Biddle and some of the other relatives want to see her because they want to know why. What happened?

While John Price's brothers drink and plot a revenge, Katherine Knight's family realise they are going to have to pay her legal fees and decide that the house in MacQueen Street needs to be sold, along with the caravan out the back, which had housed her nephew Jason Roughan. Melissa seems to be coordinating the sale, while Barry Roughan moves her things out of the house.

Geraldine Edwards pays $25 000 for the home, with some cladding that was in the back shed thrown in, but she has to pick up the conveyancing and legal fees for both parties in the deal. She wants to convert it into a cafe. Gerrie gets some idea of just how high passions are in the town when somebody comes in and abuses her for financing Katherine's lawyers in the court case. She also gets an idea of how materialistic the family is when she realises that they've taken the insulation out of the ceiling when cleaning the place out. It is returned after some inquiries are made. Gerrie's defacto buys the caravan for a few hundred dollars but its rotten and ends up being taken to the tip. The money for legal fees gets eaten up before Knight gets to the final court hearing and she ends up being granted legal aid.

Katherine had hoped for more money from the sale and is upset to lose her home. There is some irony, perhaps justice, that by feeling so entitled to a share in Price's house her actions have resulted in the loss of her own *dream home*. Her possessions are packed into a trailer and taken up to Queensland to Melissa's. The elder daughter takes just about everything, keen not to let the undeserving fathers of the two younger siblings get their hands on anything that might be Mum's, which means a lot of the kids' gear disappears over the border.

Despite being informed on a number of occasions about the details of John's death, Katherine continues to close her eyes and profess ignorance. Anyway, life is too nice in prison to let it be ruined by such thoughts. Visitors note that she is content and calm. She tells them she loves it here. The kids call and occasionally visit and she sends them money and gifts. At Christmas she sends out cards and presses a big lipstick kiss on the back. Ken says he loves her. She's overjoyed.

In the meantime, Wells is still limping around, running here and there, and all the time worried the case will never get to court. He becomes aware from the mention at Muswellbrook that she has a sympathetic psychiatrist in Mulawa. It's at this hearing that he first meets David Saunders and starts to understand that any argument of battered woman syndrome by the defence will be easy to counter. Saunders can show them the scars if they like.

Kylie Henry, a solicitor at the Director of Public Prosecution's (DPP) office in Newcastle, keeps reassuring Wells that her boss Mark Macadam will see the case through. A copper's always cynical about support from the DPP; too many times they see plea bargains done to save the government money. And, he's never met this Macadam.

In the meantime, Wells is chasing down all sorts of minutiae: records of television programs to correlate the timing of events on the day of the murder, medical files from all over the valley, obscure leads that go nowhere. Always at 100 miles an hour. Fussing and obsessing. Wondering if it's a waste of time.

Mavis Paulger, Kellett's mother, remembers Wells' visit. The detective with his black briefcase that never leaves his side, lap top computer and sense of mission. She realised he was a man consumed by the task at hand.

> I just thought, I hope this man gets some peace when this is done. I hope he had something good in his life apart from this. He was just so focused and determined. So dedicated.

Wells' work has resulted in an extraordinarily good brief. It's pretty clear Katherine Knight killed John Price at some stage between Tuesday night and Wednesday morning. You don't have to be Sherlock Holmes to get there. Also, Wells has found a number of witnesses who will testify that she has a history of violence against men, when, in fact, she is claiming they were violent to her. Any hope of mitigating the crime by presenting herself as a battered woman would be up against the testimony of Kellett, Chillingworth, Saunders and a score of other witnesses.

The most damning evidence comes from her brother Charlie and the others who heard her say she would kill Pricey, and the implication any reasonable person would take from the last videotape was that she was planning to kill him, possibly even that night. That evidence goes a long way towards proving intent. Then there's the talk of wanting $10 000 to get out of the house. It's all looking pretty grubby and clear cut. Still, if you're a cop trying to get a conviction you've got to keep closing imaginary gates that might lead a jury into dismissing a crime or developing misplaced sympathies with a criminal. Or a DPP's office deciding it's too hard.

Aware that the defence will probably attempt to suggest Knight was not of right mind during the crime, the DPP authorise Dr Robert Delaforce, a Coffs Harbour forensic psychiatrist, to interview Knight and prepare a medico–legal assessment. Delaforce is given a copy of the brief of interviews prepared by Wells, the medical records and videos of the crime scene, the interview with Knight and footage of evidence being removed from her home. The prosecution want to find out what they're dealing with. They want to know what psychiatric issues might be raised as either defence or mitigation of the crime.

Delaforce spent eight hours and 46 minutes with Knight at the Mulawa Correctional centre over two days in June 2000 and compiled a 66-page report from the interview. It's a mix of autobiography, psychiatric and legal opinion. Basically he says she's odd, but knew what she was doing. He even thinks she might have enjoyed it.

Kath was bright and smiling at times during the interview and at other times she became openly distressed. She had a lot to say, but Delaforce notes:

> On numerous occasions she made self-manipulating gestures (that can suggest giving misleading information) such as scratching herself, including when I was questioning her about events related to Mr Price's death. Her intelligence was estimated to be at best in the lowest region of the average range. Some difficulty reading, but not a difficulty understanding my questions, was noted.

The report is instructive to Wells and the prosecution as it flags, further to the initial interview conducted two months before, the sort of defence Knight will be running. They already have a fair idea: all the men in her life were violent, all her relationships were dysfunctional, she has no recollection of the murder and had no intention of killing John Price. In fact, she wanted to get away from him and was going to leave. Knight wants the jury to think, as she previously told relatives, that she killed him in a moment of madness and he got what he deserved, being the last in a long line of bastards, wife-beaters and sexual deviates who preyed on her children and her. She even tells Delaforce that Price threatened to kill the kids; a claim she has never made before.

Delaforce made a summary of Knight's life, a ghost-written autobiography. It's an interesting assessment of Katherine Knight's life as told by Katherine Knight:

> Her childhood, much of which could not be recalled because of bad and sad events, was characterised by repeated physical violence by her father to her and other family members, especially her mother, his forcing sexual activity onto her mother, Ms

Knight receiving 'beltings' from her mother, during her primary school years, repeated sexual abuse of her by her half-brother and brother, and her fears of being raped. Her mother died in 1986 following a good relationship with her. Ms Knight continued to have negative feelings towards her father. During her primary school years her uncle died following suicide.

At school, where she attended to partway through Year 8, she was in the lowest or second lowest class, achieved only very minimal reading and writing skills, was called 'uncontrollable' by one teacher, had few friends, and tended to keep to herself.

Between age 16 years and 1985 she loved her work at the meatworks, initially doing the final cleaning of the animal carcass and subsequently slicing the carcass, work that was more exciting than her year working in a clothing factory. She loved to spend time at the meatworks with a man who would knife pigs to make them bleed, although she denied she was aware of the details of his work. Overall she had been a good worker and had not been employed since 1985 because of her back problems.

At age 18 years she left home 'to get away from the violence at home'. There was only one relationship with a male prior to her marriage to David Kellett, her only legal marriage, that resulted in her 2 children, Melissa Kellett aged 24 years and Natasha Kellett aged 20 years. Her defacto relationship with David Saunders resulted in her 12-year-old daughter, ... The 9-year-old ... resulted from the non-defacto relationship with Mr John Chillingworth. In about 1994 she commenced a defacto relationship with John Price. During all her relationships she feared getting raped and she would always give in to requests for sex rather than having forced sex. In all of her relationships she was the victim of physical abuse. She realised she picked the wrong male partner because they 'were all drunk and violent'. There were numerous separations during her relationships.

During the relationships she was sometimes sexually involved with other males. Sometimes her children were physically abused by her partner. Her daughters had been sexually abused by adult males. Ms Knight's overall experience with males meant that they abused females.

An alleged incident where she sat on Mr Kellett's chest and held a knife to his throat was denied. In response to his involvement with another woman, Ms Knight was admitted to Morisset Hospital (psychiatric) after she used a knife and demanded that a woman drive her to Mr Kellett's mother so that Ms Knight could kill Mr Kellett's mother, she thought to pay back Mr Kellett, and kill herself. The allegation that she had at about that stage (1976) swung her infant around by the legs was denied, however, she recalled at about that time she swung an axe around. At another stage she burnt all of Mr Kellett's clothes following his involvement with another woman.

There was a lot of violence to her from Mr Saunders with police involvement, including for apprehended violence orders. During the worst incident (1987) they were each violent to one another, she killed his dog by cutting its throat, something she had not been able to recall, and was hospitalised after taking an overdose of medication.

Because Mr Chillingworth hit one of her children she deliberately smashed his false teeth set . . .

The negative aspect of her relationship with Mr Price, a 'pisspot', was his sexual involvement with other women; other aspects of his sexual behaviour, such as his eventual cruel sexual acts to her, his homosexual-type talk, and inappropriate public sexual/social behaviour; his physical abuse of her; and conflict with him about the sexual abuse of her children by his children. After Mr Price was violent to her for the first time and the police would not charge him she videotaped recorded items he stole from his employment and his employment was therefore

terminated (in about 1998). In November 1999 she accidentally stabbed him in the chest.

She escaped from the abuse by Mr Price by 'all of the time'
watching television and videotapes, including violent videotapes. Her own home was like a museum with items hung on the
wall or ceiling, including a cow skin, animal horns, animal
skulls, and coats made of leather and fur. Also displayed were a
stuffed deer and peacock. She loved to watch these items and
did not regard the animals as dead.

Mr Price kept threatening to kill her children, and also
threatened to kill Ms Knight. The only other persons she may
have told about Mr Price threatening to kill her children were
the 2 prison health care workers. About 6 times overall since Mr
Price's employment was terminated because of her videotape
recording, and last about 2 weeks before his death, she talked
with her nephew, Jason Roughan, about him being violent to Mr
Price or his property, for example, breaking Mr Price's bones or
burning his motor vehicle.

Mr Price called police to his home on 26 February 2000 and
claimed Ms Knight came at him with a knife. He was served with
an apprehended violence order the following day. Ms Knight
stated that if she were to again overdose she would never die
alone and would take another life with her, and presumed that
included Mr Price. However, she denied her plan was to kill Mr
Price. Instead she talked, but inconsistently, of her plan to in
early March 2000 cease living with Mr Price and move back to
her own home after going camping with her children.

On 29 February 2000, a day she did not use medication or
alcohol, she spent time with Natasha and Natasha's daughter . . .
'the apple of my eye', including some time trying to record a
videotape of [the granddaughter] That night they went to a
restaurant, something that Ms Knight did not do with her
family. Afterwards at Natasha's home she found it peaceful

watching a videotape of her family. She had no recollection of Natasha asking, when Ms Knight was leaving, if she was going to kill Mr Price and herself.

Mr Price was already in bed when she arrived at his home on 29 February 2000. Her last recall before her hospitalisation was him about 2 metres from her on his way back from the toilet after they had just had sexual intercourse. She did not know what happened to Mr Price but was told in prison that she had killed him, removed part of his skin, and cooked his head in a pot. Also she presumed she cut off his penis. There was no recall of notes left at the crime scene. Her relationship with Mr Price, which always had its ups and downs, was said to be satisfactory up until the night he died. It was her wish that someone was around when she became aware of all the details of his death. Her current fear was that she would repeat her behaviour if released from prison.

Although she denied ever being (other than related to his death) violent to Mr Price she referred to her violence to her father, Mr Kellett, and Mr Saunders, and smashing Mr Chillingworth's false teeth.

To date she had not experienced emotion about the death of Mr Price and still thought of him as alive, even though part of her said he was dead.

Inquiry about mental health problems noted chronic low self-esteem, shyness, much difficulty coping with the end of a relationship, unstable emotions, difficulty controlling her anger, anxiety when re-experiencing childhood abuse, continued fear of being raped and of her children being sexually abused, avoiding talking about her sexual trauma, and difficulty coping with injury to humans. There had never been a period of significant depressed mood. Her maximum depressed mood followed the permanent or temporary end of her relationships with males. There had been reduced pleasure from life since

1998. Deliberate self-harm involved overdoses in 1976, 1987, and 1995. There was no recollection of her drug overdose in 2000 or that she in hospital in March 2000 talked about her overdose prior to that admission. It was difficult for her to believe that she would have overdosed after Mr Price's death because she had lived for her granddaughter that she described as 'my world'. Ms Knight experienced 'visions' of ghosts, heard bells that she thought meant someone would die because that had happened after hearing the bells, but had not heard voices other than her name being called. People would tell her that she was mad because she had difficulty remembering everyday things.

Mostly she would not take psychiatric medication, which was first used during her marriage and last some months prior to March 2000. Al-Anon and Alcoholics Anonymous had both been attended because of her partners' alcohol problems. When she attended her general practitioner she did not talk much about the problems in her life. Twice since imprisonment she had taken a tranquilliser.

I administered parts of the Structured Interview for DSM-IV Personality (SIDP-IV) which identified especially Borderline and Avoidant Personality Disorder traits. I utilised the Structured Clinical Interview for DSM-IV Dissociative Disorders—Revised (SCID-D) and noted again her reference to difficulty recalling the bad things in her childhood and some problems with identity confusion . . .

Delaforce's diagnosis suggests that Katherine was suffering from post-traumatic stress disorder that was chronic but in partial remission and borderline personality disorder.

The Post-traumatic Stress Disorder refers to the outcome fol-lowing her experiencing repeated childhood trauma related to witnessing the alleged physical abuse of her mother by her father and the alleged sexual abuse of, and sexual activity with, her by her half-brother and brother. The symptoms include re-experiencing the sexual abuse/activity during her childhood as suggested by her play with her dolls, during her childhood her isolation from her peers and not expecting to have a future, the continued anxiety associated with thoughts related to the abuse and sometimes re-experiencing the abuse, avoiding talking about the abuse ... avoiding males and sexual activity during her early adulthood, fear of being raped, her continued excessive anger and irritability, and the extent to which she remained very vigilant about abuse of her children and has been in Partial Remission since about her early adult years.

The Borderline Personality Disorder has been present since adolescence or early adulthood. The features present here are ...

There are nine symptoms that may be seen in somebody with borderline personality disorder. If you have five of those you are deemed to have the disorder, according to Dr Delaforce—and this was later supported by other psychiatrists—Katherine Knight suffers from eight of the nine symptoms, which are: (1) frantic efforts to avoid real or imagined abandonment; (2) a pattern of unstable and intense interpersonal relationships, characterised by alternating between extremes of idealisation and devaluation; (3) identity disturbance: markedly and persistently unstable self-image or sense of self; (4) impulsivity in at least two areas that are potentially self-damaging (e.g. spending, sex, substance abuse, reckless driving, binge eating), but excluding suicidal or self-mutilating behaviour; (5) recurrent suicidal behaviour, gestures, or threats, of self- mutilating behaviour; (6) affective (emotions) instability/marked reactivity of mood; (7) chronic feelings of emptiness; (8) inappropriate, intense anger or difficulty controlling anger; (9) transient, stress-related paranoid ideation or severe dissociative symptoms.

The boot seemed to fit Katherine's foot perfectly. Delaforce's footnotes from DSM-IV state that a personality disorder is:

> ... an enduring pattern of inner experience and behaviour that deviates markedly from the expectations of the individual's culture and is manifested in at least two of the following areas: cognition, affectivity, interpersonal functionings, or impulse control. This enduring pattern is inflexible and pervasive across a broad rage of personal and social situations and leads to clinically significant distress or impairment in social, occupational, or other important areas of functioning. The pattern is stable and of long duration, and its onset can be traced back at least to adolescence or early adulthood.

The standard definition of post-traumatic stress disorder is:

> the development of characteristic symptoms following exposure to an extreme traumatic stressor involving direct personal experience ... The person's response to the event must involve intense fear, helplessness, or horror ... the characteristic symptoms resulting from the exposure to the extreme trauma include persistent re-experiencing of the traumatic event, persistent avoidance of stimuli associated with the trauma and numbing of general responsiveness ... persistent symptoms of increased arousal.

Delaforce also noted that there was some correlation between an abusive childhood and picking abusive partners, but suggested that 'some aspects of Ms Knight's borderline personality disorder, her moodiness, problems with anger control, and her lack of trust, caused her male partners to become uncharacteristically violent to her or to increase the level and frequency of violence'.

He ruled out battered woman syndrome, saying he believed that the main basis of Katherine's psychiatric problems were 'repeated victimisations in childhood and in adulthood', and noted that here there was some uncertainty as to whether she was beaten by her partners. He also addressed her apparent amnesia about the killing.

Dr M Giuffrida, visiting psychiatrist to Mulawa Women's Correctional Centre, in his short report dated 28 March 2000 diagnoses the mental disorder 'Dissociative Amnesia' for the period related to Mr Price's death and her overdose. I do not support that diagnosis. For a start there are too many inconsistencies regarding the details she reports related to the death of Mr Price and her overdose to begin to support the diagnosis.

He noted that she could give adequate information to medical staff about the overdose. He also contradicts the prison psychiatrist's diagnosis of hysterical disssociative fugue and amnesia, claiming 'it is completely inappropriate'.

Delaforce dismisses any diagnosis of a psychotic disorder. He makes a note regarding Knight's suggestion that Price threatened to kill her children, claiming the story was 'vague, inconsistent and unconvincing'.

Addressing the legal issues associated with the case, he says he does not support a diagnosis of dissociative amnesia, that a defence of automatism is probably inappropriate and there are no justifications for a defence of mental illness. He concedes she could use a defence of diminished responsibility but the 'difficulty with a successful defence of diminished responsibility would increase if the facts during the trial showed she wanted to carry out any extremely violent fantasies'.

Delaforce conceded some possibility of a dissociative state in his draft report, but an overlooked piece of the puzzle caused him to change his mind. Executor of John Price's estate, Laurie Lewis, received a bank statement from Price's account in November and noticed two withdrawals made on the morning of Wednesday 1 March of $500. It was obvious Katherine had gone out on the night of the killing and robbed her dead defacto of the money. The psychiatrist changed his earlier conclusion slightly, noting that this was the 'lowest state of her motivation', demonstrating 'grubby and malicious intent'.

How informative footage from the ATM would have been. Although it didn't matter to the overall case, it would have been fascinating to view Katherine in the middle of the crime. What was her demeanour? Was she calm, in the zone, as you think you would have to be to remember somebody else's PIN number? Was she a zombie in a dissociative state as some suggested, and was she alone? As it turned out that machine did not have a camera.

Katherine appeared to enjoy the experience of talking about herself over two days with the psychiatrist. She took him by the hand at the end of the second interview and with tears in her eyes gave him a sudden hug and thanked him for not being critical of her.

Delaforce then went to see Katherine's Corrections Health Services file. He had earlier alerted the staff that he had written permission from her solicitor and from Knight herself, but what happened next was very odd. Staff at Mulawa informed him that items had been removed from the file following a request by Dr Giuffrida. Dr Delaforce was astounded; it was highly unusual to remove things from a medical file, and he told the staff that he couldn't accept this and would take the matter further. He went away to read what he was given when the head nurse appeared and grabbed the files from him, saying he should not be reading them and they were Dr Giuffrida's notes.

Delaforce told the DPP what had happened and Wells began to make inquiries, taking a statement from one staff member. He headed out with a subpoena to try and get the files himself and got the same run around. Later Delaforce was given an incomplete record with parts of the medical files from prison deleted.

Then in September Giuffrida submitted his report to the solicitor Brian Thornton, who had requested the forensic psychiatrist respond to Delaforce's findings. Giuffrida thought that a defence of automatism was possible and that Knight was suffering genuine dissociative amnesia. He went to great lengths to find holes in the other psychiatrist's report and concluded

> I would perhaps make the general comment about Dr Delaforce's report that it is extremely lengthy and seemingly comprehensive. I find it interesting in that it goes far and beyond what I would consider to be the relevant clinical expertise of the psychiatrist in the forensic setting. I rather gained the impression that I was reading a brief prepared by the Department of Prosecutions than a report by forensic psychiatrists. I make no criticism of that other than to say Dr Delaforce makes a large number of comments and conclusions that seem to me to go beyond the relevant skills and expertise of a clinical psychiatrist.

The two psychiatrists were clearly at odds and openly hostile. It was shaping up for a good court battle.

*   *   *

By this time Bob Wells has hit a wall and taken three months off work. The pills he has been given seemed to make things worse. The medication is changed and he starts to feel better, but the nightmares and anxiety persist. He is starting to think he may never work again. He knows he is in no state to be back in the office chasing crooks. A rehabilitation officer comes to visit him at home and asks when he thinks he'll be ready to work again. Wells gets tearful. 'I was just fucked. I was rat shit. I couldn't go back. I was completely and absolutely worn out.'

There's an irony here: both Knight and Wells have been diagnosed as suffering post-traumatic stress—Wells from his exposure to her crime. It would have been funny if he wasn't so sick and he is further irritated to hear news from work that he's letting the side down.

The psychiatric trauma is dredging memories from Wells he doesn't realise are there. Names of car crash victims from the 1980s just pop up. Images of the carnage. 'It was like a videotape being replayed. Things would just come back to me.' A terrible car accident at Collector on the old Federal Highway between Goulburn and Canberra. A car rolled with three kids in it, killing them. Wells was working alone and when he got there one of the girls had her face ripped off by a wire fence. Another died in his arms. Her name just pops into his head like she was an old friend he hasn't thought about for a while. And all the time he keeps thinking the DPP is going to pull out and accept a plea, that all the work is being wasted. He thought he was going mad.

Then in June of 2001 he meets Mark Macadam for a moment at a police funeral. The prosecutor is climbing into a car, about to drive away, but says not to worry and to meet him the following month. They are going to get her. Wells watches him drive away and is slightly reassured.

A peculiar meeting takes place on 14 July 2001 at 84 St
Andrews Street, involving Bob Wells, a trainee detective, Mark
Macadam and Kylie Henry from the DPP and lawyers Brian
Thornton and Peter Thraves for Katherine's defence.

The detective walks the prosecutors through the crime
scene. Pricey's house still reflects the residue of murder.
There is a hole where a bloody footprint had been cut out of
the floor coverings, blood splatters on the walls and smears on
the floor. It is still empty. On the kitchen bench are a set of
Stay Sharp knives; there is a Mexican hat and a mug that says:
'To my wife and sweetheart. May they never meet'.

The defence indicate they are happy to cop a plea for
manslaughter, that their client is illiterate and of low intelligence. Macadam asks Wells what he thinks. Wells says, 'It's
your call,' but is quietly praying they wouldn't accept. The
prosecutor says, 'No, it's your call, Bob. It's your brief. What
do you reckon?' And Bob Wells begins to tell the defence all
that has been on his mind, everything that has made him sick
to the guts about this.

Mate, some of the most brilliant people in the world that have
had major achievements have had low IQs but what this woman
survives on is rat cunning, mate. She may be low IQ, but still
owns her own home—worth next to nothing—but she owns it.
She's reared two adult children and rearing two others, they
were clean, well dressed, she had once been employed and held
down a job. Here's a woman who wasn't living destitute, mate.
You don't need high intellect or high IQ to be successful in life.
I classify myself as average or below average IQ, I was never a
good student, no good at maths, I did the school certificate and
left high school because basically I was told to leave, but I've
made a reasonable go of my life and she survived with rat cunning. That's what she was all about. She was never without a

bloke, she would have lived to 85 or 90 and been all right as would her kids. I don't reckon we should cop a plea.

It's good enough for the DPP and they tell the defence to forget it and to prepare for a murder trial. The job is on.

At a committal hearing in August, Knight's barrister, Peter Thraves, indicates that despite the meeting the defence will be arguing she was provoked into murder and will be looking at a plea to manslaughter. The defence keep saying this to the prosecution, but the Crown won't play ball. They will not accept manslaughter. Knight's defence team keep holding out for them to cave in.

The trial
October 2001

Up in Queensland David Kellett is on edge. He gets a sick feeling in the stomach every time the mobile phone rings and Bob Wells' name appears on its screen. Coppers have been calling around with subpoenas, seats are booked on planes but the trial dates keep changing so he's been let off a couple of times. He doesn't want to go to court, doesn't want to see his teenage bride again, doesn't want to stand in a witness box, doesn't want to see his in-laws and doesn't want to cross her one last time, nor does he want his daughters Natasha and Melissa to go through the trial.

Nobody is looking forward to it. John Price's family is bracing itself. They already know too much. The brothers are angry and are drinking themselves into tragicomic states of rage. Slurring oaths of vengeance. Katherine Knight's family is on egg shells, throwing about threats and accusations against fellow family members deemed to be for or against the troubled twin. Tearing itself into ever smaller pieces.

Bob Wells and most of the police are looking forward to their day in court. A chance to prove it has been all worthwhile, but as the date approaches the trauma returns and

Wells starts to get crook all over again. The headaches and nightmares are back. He can't sleep properly.

Katherine Knight has also become anxious and agitated. She breaks down one day in a conference with her lawyers when she realises that she will have to sit in court and look at a video of what she's done and what she's been avoiding ever since. She is happy to take a plea to manslaughter so there wouldn't be a trial, but the DPP has played hard ball and her day in court has arrived.

Justice Barry O'Keefe, a small man who is well respected among his colleagues, is the presiding judge for the trial at the Maitland Courthouse and begins the hearing on 16 October 2001, nineteen months after the murder. There's a lot of interest in the trial and a degree of reservation among the lawyers over what the jury will be put through. Mark Macadam QC for the prosecution expressed reservations about jurors' reactions.

> The nature of the case and the evidence that is potentially such as will go before the jury [is] of such a horrific nature, and that is perhaps an understatement in this case, being unusual as it is.

Defence barrister Peter Thraves says he too is concerned about 'undue reactions'. Justice O'Keefe agrees that they do not want people taking 'ill of fainting or some equivalent'.

The following morning, 60 nervous men and women from the local area are given a pre-empanellment address by the judge.

> The evidence will be graphic and grisly. The evidence as to the circumstances of and surrounding the death of the deceased will involve the members of the jury being exposed to quite explicit material; it is material which is quite gruesome and such

as to be likely to shock and upset even those who may be fairly pragmatic by nature. It may be capable of causing significant distress to anyone who is squeamish or made ill by the sight of blood or human remains, even in pictorial form, or who may be affected by the graphic verbal description of such matters.

Justice O'Keefe says they may seek to be excused now if they have any concerns. Five take the option and leave the gore and drama to the others. And, because Maitland is only 90 minutes from Aberdeen and is a mining town, a few more are excused when they recognise some of the 60 plus names on the witness list, including one who remembers her son was good friends at school with a young boy called Bobby Wells. She doesn't recognise the harassed looking policeman sitting a few metres away.

Empanellment is completed but further delayed when, just before lunch and after discussions with Knight's defence, O'Keefe adjourns the hearing until the following day.

The next morning begins with high drama and anticlimax. The charge of murder is read out and Katherine Mary Knight announces she is guilty. O'Keefe asks her if she understood the effect of the plea.

—Beg your pardon?

—You understand the effect of the plea—that is, that you are admitting to the charge of murder?

—Yes, your Honour.

—You have taken counsel's advice, have you?

—Yes, your Honour.

—I understand that you have had the opportunity to consider the matter overnight?

—Yes, your Honour.

—And you're content to lodge the plea. Is that correct?

—Yes, your Honour.

O'Keefe reluctantly accepts the plea and thanks the jury, explaining that he has to be wary of accepting the plea automatically following rulings by the Court of Criminal Appeal, especially in a matter that is 'the most serious crime in the calendar'. He explains to them that the prisoner may get a sentence discount for a plea because it saves the court money and the jury the 'horrific details' of the case. He thanks those who did not take the chance to 'skip out . . . That was very public spirited of you.' Some members of the jury are disappointed and one stays to watch the sentencing, becoming a permanent fixture in the public gallery and striking up a relationship with some of the Knight family.

What the jury doesn't known is that Knight's barrister, Peter Thraves, indicated to O'Keefe the day before that Knight wanted to change her plea. The judge arranged for a psychiatric assessment overnight to ensure she was fit to understand the consequences and a local psychiatrist was satisfied that she did. It was an extraordinary change of mind that has never been fully explained. Everything Knight has said and done since the killing indicates she takes no responsibility for her actions, and those around her, particularly her mental health team in prison, have supported her in that belief and her claims of amnesia and dissociation.

Had her legal team indicated they thought she didn't have a hope? There were major problems with the psychiatric reports, as a few days before the trial the prosecution sought a second opinion from highly respected forensic psychiatrist Dr Rod Milton, a man who had been called on by police back in 1992 to do a profile of the killer in the backpacker murders. His findings wiped out any remaining hope of Knight defending herself on psychiatric grounds. At the same time the defence was having trouble with Dr Giuffrida's report and in the end did not put him on their witness list, possibly because he may be asked questions that would not help himself or the case. Perhaps there was a belief by the defence that she had no hope of beating the murder charge and that a plea of guilty would at least gain her some discount.

There is some belief that she did not have the stomach for a trial. Her lawyers indicated that she didn't want the families to go through the trauma, but this does not seem likely to have swayed her. Melissa said her mother had run out of money, but she'd been granted legal aid and would receive it no matter how long the case ran. The most convincing explanation for the guilty plea is that she just could not stand the thought of what she did being aired in public, and particularly did not want to sit through an examination of the gruesome detail. There is some indication of this in her attorney's later requests that she be excused during presentation of some of the facts, suggesting that she had become hysterical during discussions with her barrister about certain evidence.

Kath was shutting her eyes again. She didn't want to know. Her guilty plea could well be seen as an act of cowardice to spare herself further distress.

*   *   *

The change of heart transfers the trial into a simple sentencing hearing and is a great relief to the scores of witnesses scattered up the valley and beyond, none of whom have relished having to cross Katherine, even when she is in the dock.

O'Keefe then says he will give the prosecution time to prepare for the sentencing and in the meantime puts it on record that Katherine Mary Knight is a convicted murderer.

—Would you stand please, Mrs Knight? Mrs Knight, you have pleaded guilty to a charge of murder and I have accepted that plea. As a consequence, I judge you to be guilty of murder and a conviction of murder will be recorded accordingly. Do you understand?

—Yes, your Honour.

Knight remains even toned and emotionless throughout. In the gallery there is a sense of disbelief. Katherine is led out the side of the court for her first night behind bars as a convicted murderer.

Friday morning the prosecution begins its case and is obviously aiming high. The Crown wants life, the toughest possible sentence, announcing it will first be presenting select witness statements, then two psychiatric reports, a set of photographs and a collection of videos. Free of the need to be circumspect with the graphic evidence, Macadam tells the judge, 'The photos that I place before your Honour include a large number of photographs that I would not have placed before the jury.' He continues on about the order and detail of exhibits and statements but O'Keefe seems more interested in the folder of photographic evidence, interrupting to ask, 'Were the genitals of the deceased intact?'

O'Keefe decides he should watch the crime scene video first but Thraves asks if his client can be excused 'in view particularly of the experience I had earlier in the week with my client when I gave her certain information'. O'Keefe agrees.

After a short adjournment, the court and depleted public gallery watch one of the most disturbing crime scene videos imaginable. The scenes begin outside the house and become increasingly horrific. The camera goes up and down and up and down John Price's skin on the butcher's hook, zooms in on the truncated neck and gaping wind pipe at the end of his skinned torso, and shows a yellow-gloved hand removing the lid from the pot on the stove, revealing his head in its sick soup. That takes them to lunch and court is then adjourned until Tuesday morning, almost as if nobody has the stomach to carry on.

On Tuesday morning Bob Price is causing trouble. O'Keefe begins with a warning.

Ladies and gentlemen, the prisoner has pleaded guilty to a charge of murder and is entitled to have her sentence hearing conducted without unnecessary stress. The law will take its course and no one, whether related to the deceased or otherwise, should even contemplate anything different than the law taking its course. I say no more than that.

The animosity between the Knights and the Prices has been causing headaches for Bob Wells, who has had to tell Jason Roughan, Kath's nephew, to pull his head in or he'll be spending the trial in a cell. Bob Price has an esky in a car in the carpark and is topping up constantly. It's becoming a circus and some of the Price relatives are embarrassed.

Forensic pathologist Dr Tim Lyons is called to the stand and begins to explain how the skin was removed and how it was of considerable weight, possibly about fifteen kilograms. He says it's impossible to say if the wounds to the back and legs were inflicted when Price was running or lying down and that it had been hard enough just to match up the 37 entry holes in the skin to the ones in the body and limbs. Lyons says the death would have been fairly quick. He also suggests the blood stains in the bedroom may have come from the carotid artery in the neck. Macadam is interested in more emotive responses.

—Doctor, in your experience of years of attending crime scenes and the like, I imagine that even in your past experience you would never have come across a case such as this before?

—I have never seen such an unusual case as this before.

After lunch discussion revolves around the decapitation, with Lyons explaining how there were no marks on the bones and the knife had to cut through muscles, tendons, ligaments and neurovascular bundles. It had to be a sharp knife, but it also had to be a skilled hand. Macadam suggests:

—It is one thing to chop a person's head off with an axe or meat cleaver or something like that with brute force, but this was a much more delicate operation, if delicate is the right word?

—Yes, it appeared to be, if I could use the word, [to] have been anatomically dissected.

They move on to the subject of skinning, which only Lyons has had any experience of.

Knowing how long it takes to carry out certain dissection techniques which I do, I mean, I can say to you I think it would not have taken just a few minutes, but it is something that could probably been completed within 30 minutes to an hour, but beyond that I would not like to say.

He estimates it would take five to ten minutes to remove the head with a sharp knife. O'Keefe struggles to understand the evidence and says to Thraves, 'I am just trying to ascertain what you do. I have never cut a head off.' To help him understand, Lyons draws a diagram with a pencil and is then excused. The court is then played the video of Bob Wells and Victor Ford interviewing Katherine Knight at the hospital. O'Keefe says he is 'anxious to see the mien of the prisoner'.

On Thursday they play the video Knight made on the night of the murder and after lunch Peter Muscio gives evidence about the crime scene, producing the knives and a glove for the judge to handle them with because they are still bloody. The policeman gives his opinion that Katherine has had to carry the head through the arch with the skin hanging from it when Thraves suggests there is something wrong with his client. Katherine is sitting in the box. Eyes closed. O'Keefe says they should continue. She begins to moan and rock and kick the partition and scream. Shane Knight yells from the gallery that she needs help and O'Keefe adjourns the hearing. Katherine is carried out screaming, 'No...no...no.' It's a chilling interruption. Bob Wells thinks she was crying 'John ... John ...'

The next morning the judge explains that the previous day's episode was over in a matter of minutes. 'Mrs Knight was given a cup of tea with lots of milk and sugar in it and then removed to the prison.' She was later given a mild sedative. Dr Delaforce is called to the stand. He is asked about the diagnosis of borderline personality disorder. Macadam wants to know if this is behind what happened on the night of the murder. Delaforce doesn't think so.

> What she did on the night was part of her personality, her nature, herself, but it is not a feature of borderline personality disorder. It is not even slightly connected.

He is asked whether her post-traumatic stress disorder has anything to do with the murder. He says again he thinks it is more her nature than the disorder that caused the murder. Macadam pushes it further, asking if she took pleasure from the defilement of John Price's corpse.

> There is much to indicate that and that is why I say that she probably enjoyed what she did ... It is probable that she thought about doing things like that for a long time, perhaps many years. Remember, up until the mid eighties she worked at the abattoirs, and if you of course introduce the idea of dealing with

animal parts, and she told me how she enjoyed getting out the blood from the bone marrow, cleaning that out; she enjoyed slicing, she enjoyed that work. Not many people do, or would, but she enjoyed it. She particularly enjoyed going to the old man who was involved in killing the pigs.

She particularly enjoyed, especially enjoyed, it was a wonderful peace for her to sit at home and look around her room, and she has told me, she has described her room at home, the lounge room and living room area, and I have seen a video of what is hanging on the wall, and there were horns from animals, there were animal skins . . . other dead animal parts and some of these skulls had a little bit of skin still hanging on them and it was all around her and she would tell me she would move from one chair to another so she could get a different view. She loved that. It gave her so much peace and that was important to her.

Knight had crossed Price's legs and propped his arm on a bottle after killing him. Delaforce offers the opinion that the arrangement of Price's body was a demonstration of 'the control and power usually present in crimes of this nature. It is a fundamental feature of it.' The issue of the video *Resurrection* is raised by Delaforce. It was one of the movies found in her house. O'Keefe says he found it disturbing to watch and it is. The movie was released in 1999 and follows a serial killer who zaps his victims with an electric stun gun like they use in abattoirs and then removes their limbs while they are conscious. At one stage bodies hang from meat hooks in a cool room. Delaforce finds the movie highly significant and her taste in movies equally so. 'For some people I think it is harmless escapism, but for some people it is an absolute morbid interest which excites them.' He says that just as in the movie, some people are excited by being sprayed by blood and if Katherine had stabbed Price once or even 30 times and

walked away claiming she had lost control, that could be
understood.

> Well, she had a lot of anger in her life. Maybe she just totally lost
> control, but it is more than that. It is more than just stabbing,
> cutting, the knife going in and out, many many times. The skill,
> the time, the focus that must have been required to cut the
> head—and I have been told it was cut with considerable skill—
> to be able to take virtually all the skin off, again with
> considerable skill, must have shown her purpose, her intent and
> her desire, I would say. It must have taken considerable time to
> do that and to continue doing that one would want to do that. I
> can't find any other explanation, that it was pleasurable, and I
> think that is a critical thing. She has done more than is required
> just to kill. We know because it is fairly common ... that one
> partner will kill another because of problems in the relationship
> and the sudden loss of control. But this to me is different. As I
> say, I can accept the 30 or more stab wounds; maybe she just
> totally lost control over the time which was required to inflict
> those wounds. But just imagine the time, the skill, the purpose,
> the intent, the motivation behind cutting the head off with sur-
> gical precision of considerable degree—skinning the body, the
> time, the skill, the purpose. Why would anybody do that? That is
> not about killing, that has got to be about something else.

He finds the cooking of the body parts harder to explain
and wonders if Katherine wanted to cook the flesh off the
skull. He suggests there is an element of payback and degra-
dation, saying it is a 'very pathological example of payback.'
He equates this revenge with the time she sent the video of
the stolen goods to Price's employer and the destruction of
John Chillingworth's teeth. Saunders' dingo, however, was
more a heat of the moment thing.

Macadam asks about another possibility.

What I am just wondering, doctor, is your view as to whether or not the prisoner is perhaps possessed of sufficient, dare I say it, cunning to realise that anybody looking at this incident would immediately jump to the conclusion that whoever did that would have to be mad.

Delaforce concedes it could be possible but thinks that the payback and gratification of fantasies go together. The prosecutor wants to know if Jason Roughan's evidence that she wanted to hurt Price monetarily for calling her a slut and buying other people drinks is relevant. The psychiatrist says that she is an

absolute vindictive, retribution, payback person in operation. It gives a basic reason for hurting Mr Price, even to kill Mr Price, but then, as I have indicated, why not one blow to the head or poison or one stab wound? It becomes more than that. It becomes an opportunity to carry out these perverted interests related to what I call the probably fantasies she had about this gruesome conduct.

Delaforce explains that his position hardened against Knight when he learned she had robbed Price.

The significance of the money is paramount, pivotal I have called it in my second report. It is grubby. It is a personal intent to go and get some money. This comes down to money, to go off to the bank teller, to withdraw the money for herself or whoever, whatever, obviously is purposeful behaviour for personal gain. If she is that controlled at that stage to be able to do that, to me that is a reflection more so of how she must have been in the rest of the night.

Katherine has sat through the evidence with no show of emotion apart from the one outburst, although she seems to be fascinated by the discussion. Dr Delaforce's assessment has been totally damning and just gets worse when he is asked about her future prospects.

Anybody that has already caused problems to her or will in the future, and that would include some members of the Price family, his children. I don't rate that highly but it is a matter of significance to look at that. I would think it would be more to do with what would happen in the future.

In a moment of levity the judge wonders if this would include the prosecutor. Delaforce doesn't think so but he believes she is a future threat.

To get a taste of what she has done here, what she has done can increase the risk of it happening again, and that has been proven over and over and over again with murders of this grue-some nature, that it does not stop at one; but in doing what they have done, they were motivated to express those perverted fan-tasies, they get a taste of it and they want to do it again. That is a particular concern I have.

Dr Rod Milton is then sworn in and says he does not believe Knight's claims of amnesia, suggesting it was 'simu-lated' and undermined by her 'ordered behaviour' on the night indicated such. He also discounts the suicide attempt. 'I think on balance it was not a genuine suicide attempt. It fitted I think with the pattern of covering in certain ways things that had been done.'

He reads an extract from his report for the court and echoes some of what Delaforce has said:

The personality problems demonstrated in the history of Mrs Knight's life are not in my view psychiatric disease—they are her nature. These personality problems did not stop her from knowing what she was doing, or whether it was right or wrong. Nor did they stop her from exercising control over her actions when she chose . . .

Milton's expert opinions are not good for Knight. He refers to her 'ruthlessness' in getting Price sacked from the mine, her sense of 'entitlement' to his home and the fact that 'there is no guilt; there wasn't any shame. She blames others for what she does.' He mentions her attitude to the youngest son as suggesting 'some underlying hostility towards the male sex'. Like Delaforce, he thinks that she may have pretended to be mad to get away with the crime. 'It is consistent with other aspects of astuteness that Ms Knight has demonstrated.' Unlike Delaforce he does not think she is suffering post-traumatic stress, nor is he convinced about borderline personality disorder.

The cross-examination by Knight's lawyer bears no apparent fruit and O'Keefe adjourns the court until Monday October 29 to discuss issues of possible rehabilitation.

Dr Delaforce is recalled on the Monday as the defence wants to revisit the issue of Katherine's taste for horror videos, particularly *Resurrection*. Thraves asks if it would matter if she did not watch that video and the psychiatrist says it does, as the taste for such material ties in with the decorations in her house and is relevant to her personality. There is some suggestion of a 'copycat' element related to the video. He paints a grim picture of the house on the main street of Aberdeen.

It is a place to me of death, of destruction. She is not in the garden and growing things. I am not aware there is a pet budgie or something like that. It is a theme of death and some writers in psychiatry have made a lot of significance of this. They have given it a term in fact of necrophilous, and it literally means a love of death. She is surrounded by it, all of these dead things. She enjoyed her work at the abattoir, then comes the violence in the various movies, and the selfishness, grubbiness of taking the money. It is all there. It is all there. It all adds up ... The wall hangings were incredibly significant to me.

O'Keefe seems intrigued by the psychiatrist's evidence and offers his own observations for analysis, wondering why Knight did not want to watch the crime scene video but 'appears from observation where I sit in relation to the Bench to have given rapt attention to the evidence by both psychiatrists of which she is centre'. Delaforce replies, 'I think she needs to know what people think of her, the good or the bad, because she gets a lot of bad throughout her life.' He says that maybe she doesn't need the video to aid her memory. 'She could have such a rich fantasy life that continues every day, every night, the fantasy of violence.'

Thraves has his first potential runs on the board with admissions that the video is relevant to Knight's state of mind, but the next witness that is recalled is concerned with more concrete things.

The crime scene detective Muscio takes the stand at 3.15 pm and begins to talk of congealed fat, water temperatures and cold steaks. The scientific officer says he cannot completely reconstruct Knight's movements on the night, but thinks she washed before preparing the vegetables and the footprint that had almost sent Wells and Dellosta into a panic eighteen months ago is still causing problems. Muscio is baffled by the appearance of just one bloody print.

I have searched and searched and searched my mind, your

Honour, as to how it got there. I did expect to see a left foot or
another right foot impression, but it was not to be.

The following day the defence call John Hinder to the
stand, Katherine's brother-in-law and former husband of her
twin sister Joy, and the defence plays its hand. He testifies that
Katherine had only picked up the video with *Resurrection* on it
on the day of the murder and explains that the family is constantly swapping and dubbing tapes. They are implying that
any suggestion of copy cat intent is rubbish.

After lunch Joy is called and Thraves asks if she is John's
husband, which causes some mirth and an explanation from
her that the pair separated in July. She says in evidence that
Barry Roughan had dropped the *Resurrection* tape at her
house on the Monday and Katherine had borrowed it on the
Tuesday when she came to say she'd take the children
camping on the weekend. Macadam's cross-examination is
stern. He puts it to her that her story is 'pure fabrication ...
absolute, utter fabrication'. Joy denies this, but her evidence
looks weak during further cross-examination.

Hearing the twist in the case, Bob Wells has rung Barry
Roughan to ask him if what the family is testifying is accurate.
He goes down and picks up the half-brother, who appears
later in the week and testifies that it is Katherine's tape
and he's borrowed it and left it at Joy's weeks before the
murder.

The defence also call its psychiatrist, Dr Leonard Lambeth,
who interviewed Knight in prison the previous month and produced a sixteen-page report—both Delaforce's and Milton's
ran over 50 pages. He concludes that she has borderline personality disorder and post-traumatic stress. The judge says
that many people have personality disorders but they do not
stab, cook and decapitate. Lambeth agrees, but says:

I think, your Honour, that the personality disorder very possibly determines, if you like, the decision—'I will do this'. The way the decision is carried out—if you like, the plastic part of the decision—is determined by other factors, not including the personality but also including experience, social mores and generally the way the person lives.

Lambeth thinks the fight between Price and Knight on the Sunday triggered the crime.

Lambeth doesn't seem to make too much of an impression on O'Keefe, who says,

I don't see a great deal of difference, quite frankly, except in semantic terms, between what the doctor, this witness, has said and the outcomes postulated in the final analysis by doctors Delaforce and Milton. On the night in question none of them have this borderline personality disorder as the final operative factor.

An exchange between the judge and the defence lawyer late in the afternoon gave some warning of what sentence O'Keefe was considering.

—We have got all this material and I have got to do something with it in relation to the sentence that I impose on this lady.

—I understand that, your Honour, and I have to do something with it to try and persuade your Honour in a certain direction.

—Not to do what you fear I might do?

—Fear is probably the appropriate word in the circumstances, your Honour.

Knight gives no indication that she understands the ramifications of this exchange and continues to sit, straight-backed and passive in the dock.

On Thursday 1 November O'Keefe adjourns the trial to give the defence and prosecution time to prepare their final addresses which they deliver on Monday 5 and Tuesday 6 November. As the East Maitland court has already been booked, the sentencing moves to Newcastle.

A sentence and a smile
November 2001

atherine Mary Knight climbs from the cells in
the bowels of the Newcastle court and emerges
in the dock before Justice O'Keefe on Thursday 8
November 2001 to learn her fate.

On Monday her barrister, Peter Thraves, struggles to find
any grounds to argue for compassion from the judge, but
knows his client is facing a long time in jail.

It will be the defence submission to give a very long sentence but
one which is finite, allowing the possibility that in the future this
offender could be assessed as being able to be released. When
the court comes to its final decision, I ask that the plea of guilty
preventing a long trial, her lack of prior criminal record and her
personality disorder at the time be taken into account and a life
sentence not be imposed.

O'Keefe tells Thraves he has seen no remorse from
Knight and any claims of amnesia are doubtful.

On Tuesday Mark Macadam's submission for the prosecution is searing. He says any discount because of the plea to
murder is negated by the fact it has been entered so late in the

process, thus saving little money or time. He argues that she will continue to be of danger to the community and that this is a murder clearly in the worst case category.

> The murder of John Price, accompanied by an extreme level of cold-blooded callousness, is fairly to be described as an atrocious and gravely wicked act. The evil displayed by the prisoner is such that it defies adequate description—the more so as the motive was vengeance and payback because Mr Knight intended to separate from her, something she would not accept.

Macadam points out there is absolutely no evidence of any contrition and an enormous amount which indicates premeditation.

> The unspeakable violence perpetrated on a defenceless man and the degradation visited on his body make this beyond any doubt the worst conceivable killing in every respect. Only one sentence is appropriate. That Katherine Knight spend the rest of her life in jail.

On the day of sentencing, Knight sits straight-backed and still, her face reflected in the perspex around the dock. She wears glasses and a floral print dress. Behind her to the left sit her brother Shane and father Ken, but she did not see them when she entered. The Price relatives sit on the other side of the court. Bob Price is making a nuisance of himself again and is eventually arrested outside the court with a piece of broken glass in his hand.

Justice O'Keefe begins to read his sentence from the 40-page document he has prepared. He meanders through the legal details and then outlines the murder, describing the stab wounds in graphic terms.

Many of the wounds were deep, and extended into vital organs.
These included the aorta, both lungs, the liver, the stomach, the
descending colon, the pancreas, and the left kidney, the lower
pole of which had virtually been sliced off.

The Price family squirm. Reporters in the court take notes
furiously.

Mr Price's head was in place at the time he was skinned.
However, at some time between the time the body was moved
into the lounge room and skinned and about a time before 7.30
am on 1 March 2000 the prisoner decapitated Mr Price's body
and at some stage arranged it with the left arm draped over an
empty soft drink bottle, and the legs crossed. This was said in evidence to be an act of defilement demonstrating contempt for
Mr Price's remains.

O'Keefe comments on the 'steady hand and grisly
methodology' Knight demonstrated during the skinning and
beheading. He reads a biography of the prisoner's life, taking
extracts from the statements of David Kellett, David Saunders
and John Chillingworth. He accepts that the murder was premeditated and rejects claims of amnesia.

Every word seems to spell doom for Katherine Knight.
After nearly an hour the judge reaches his summary:

The prisoner has pleaded guilty to a murder which falls into the
most serious category of murders. I am satisfied beyond any
doubt that such murder was premeditated. I am further satisfied
in the same way that not only did she plan the murder but she
also enjoyed the horrific acts which followed in its wake as part
of a ritual of death and defilement. The things which she did
after the death of Mr Price indicate cognition, volition, calm

and skill. I am satisfied beyond reasonable doubt that her evil actions were the playing out of her resentments arising out of her rejection by Mr Price, her impending expulsion from Mr Price's home and his refusal to share with her his assets, particularly his home, which he wanted to retain for his children. I have no doubt that her claim to amnesia forms part of her plan to affect madness in order to escape the consequences of her acts and to provide a convenient basis on which to rely to avoid detailed questioning by the police and escape punishment.

As I have said, the prisoner showed no mercy whatsoever to Mr Price. The last minutes of his life must have been a time of abject terror for him, as they were a time of utter enjoyment for her. At no time during the hearing or prior thereto did the prisoner express any regret for what she had done or any remorse for having done it: not even through the surrogacy of her counsel. Her attitude in that regard is consistent with her general approach to the many acts of violence which she had engaged in against her various partners, namely 'they deserved it'. In addition, the prisoner's history of violence together with her flawed personality cause me to conclude, along with Dr Milton and the other psychiatrists called in the case, that she is without doubt a very dangerous person and likely, if released into the community, to commit further acts of serious violence, including even murder against those who cross her, particularly males. A crime of the kind committed by the prisoner calls for the maximum penalty the law empowers the court to impose.

An examination of the cases referred to by counsel supports the view that I have formed, namely that the only appropriate penalty for the prisoner is life imprisonment and that parole should never be considered for her. The prisoner should never be released.

Katherine Mary Knight, you have pleaded guilty to and been convicted of the murder of John Charles Thomas Price at

Aberdeen in the State of New South Wales on or about 29 February 2000. In respect of that crime I sentence you to imprisonment for life.

John Price's family breaks into applause. Katherine shows no response, but as she rises and turns she sees that Ken, her father, has been sitting behind her. Their eyes lock for a moment. He seems to try and mouth something to her. Perhaps he cries. Her eyes take in the others, the Price family getting to its feet. She is led away, then pauses.

Katherine Knight smiled and took the first step down into the cells.

Epilogue
November 2002

Katherine Knight has appealed against the length of her sentence. Her former partners and the people of Aberdeen anxiously await the outcome and live in fear of her getting out.

In June 2002 she sent David Kellett a card with an FJ Holden on it. Inside it read, 'I forgive you from Katherine.'

Her two youngest children are with their fathers and have visited their mum in prison. Other family members also visit but sometimes she turns them away because it interrupts her sewing classes or other activities.

Recently Katherine was making signed sculptures of claw-like hands until the prison authorities told her she could no longer do it. She has told her family she still loves prison but does not want to die there.

Bob Wells still has trouble sleeping, is still seeing a psychiatrist and will probably never return to full duties as a police officer. Many of his fellow officers who attended the crime scene are in similar position.

Katherine's Aberdeen home has been turned into the Oasis Cafe while John Price's home is still on the market. In mid-2002 tenants moved in.

ENDNOTES

Chapter 1

Direct quotes are attributed in the text and taken from Katherine Knight's interviews with Dr Robert Delaforce, Dr Rod Milton and Dr Leonard Lambeth and quoted from their psychiatric reports; John Price, Geoff Bowditch and Peter Cairnes quotes taken from police statements and author interview with Peter Cairnes. Additional information from Anthony Keegan and Jill Simmons' police statements and author interview with Jill Keegan and Frank Heap.

'I was always ... drunk and violent.' Katherine Knight interview with Robert Delaforce August 2000.

'I always wanted ... loved doing all that.' Katherine Knight interview with Robert Delaforce August 2000.

Chapter 2

Direct quotes are attributed in the text and taken from Lisa Logan, Peter Cairnes, Jill Keegan, Jon Collison, Ron Murray interviews by author with additional information from police statements;

'It was weird ... and that was it.' Johnathon Price interview with Michelle Coffey of *Who Weekly*.

Chapter 3

Direct quotes are attributed in the text and taken from Bob Wells, Lloyd Lyne and Victor Ford interviews by author. Historical information from Muswellbrook Visitors Centre and Les Parsons.

Chapter 4

Direct quotes are attributed in the text and taken from Bob Wells and general information from interview with author, court records and autopsy report.

Chapter 5

Direct quotes are attributed in the text and taken from David Saunders, David Kellett and John Chillingworth interviews with author.

Chapter 6

Direct quotes are attributed in the text and taken from David Kellett, Mavis Paulger, Colleen Ryan, Barry Roughan, Melissa Knight and anonymous sibling interviews with author and police statements; childhood friend (anonymous) interview with author; Brian Conlon police statement; Katherine Knight interviews with psychiatrists Dr Robert Delaforce, Dr Rod Milton and Dr Leonard Lambeth. Bus-train crash information from Macleay River Historical Society, researcher Pam Parmenter.

'The personality problems ... court to decide.' Dr Rod Milton 14/10/01.

'What she did ... must have been required.' Dr Robert Delaforce 26/10/01.

'Barb was hurt ... it was always there.' Anonymous sibling interview.

'When she was good ... in your family.' Anonymous sibling interview.

'I used to get ... remember the beltings'. Katherine Knight interview with Dr Leonard Lambeth.

'Her mother and father ... no love.' Anonymous childhood friend.

'If there was a fight ... ever backed down.' Anonymous childhood friend.

'Suddenly they were at it ... and vice versa.' Anonymous childhood friend.

'One doll used to ... world I suppose.' Katherine Knight interview with Robert Delaforce August 2000.

'I know it ... afraid of being raped.' Katherine Knight interview with Dr Robert Delaforce.

'They rape them ... They're helpless.' Katherine Knight interview with Dr Rod Milton.

'Her personality problems ... intellectually lacking.' Katherine Knight interview with Dr Robert Delaforce.

Chapter 7

Direct quotes are attributed in the text and taken from Lloyd and Betty Lyne, David Kellett, Mavis Paulger, Lorna Driscoll, Les Parsons, Margaret MacBeth, Henry Perry interviews with author. Additional information from Melissa Kellett's police statements, court records and Tom Barrass's interview with Ted Abrahams, *Newcastle Herald*, 14 Oct. 1985.

'This lady is of ... of all concerned.' Katherine Knight, Record of admission, Morisset Psychiatric Hospital.

'This young lady ... Mrs F Paulger.' Discharge summary compiled by M. Elmoff, Medical Officer, Morisset Psychiatric Hospital.

'I pick the wrong ... drunk and violent.' Katherine Knight interview with Robert Delaforce August 2000.

Chapter 8

Direct quotes are attributed in the text and taken from David Kellett interview with author.

Chapter 9

Direct quotes are attributed in the text and taken from Bob Wells interview with author; Natasha Kellett, Joy Hinder and Barry Roughan police statements.

Chapter 10

Direct quotes are attributed in the text and taken from Bob Wells interview with author and Katherine Knight interview with police.

Chapter 11

Direct quotes are attributed in the text and taken from David Saunders, Melissa Kellett, Glenda Reichel, Ron Wilton, Dale Fittock, Gerrie Edwards author interviews and police statements; Katherine Knight interviews with Dr Robert Delaforce, Dr Rod Milton and Dr Leonard Lambeth, and police; Rosemary Biddle interview with Michelle Coffey of *Who Weekly*; Natasha Kellett and Brian Conlon police statements. Additional information from court records.

'She had all this . . . for dying too.' Katherine Knight interview with Dr Robert Delaforce.

Chapter 12

Direct quotes are attributed in the text and taken from Dr Tim Lyons interview with author and autopsy report; Bob Wells interview with author; Charlie Knight, Tracy Knight and Jason Wilson police statements.

'The house is . . . measuring 170 mm.' Dr Tim Lyons, autopsy report.

'This is a . . . body was reconstructed.' Dr Tim Lyons, autopsy report.

'There are a number . . . 15–17cms in length.' Dr Tim Lyons, autopsy report.

'Multiple internal . . . and decapitation.' Dr Tim Lyons, autopsy report.

'There are . . . defence wounds.' Dr Tim Lyons, autopsy report.

'Here was a story . . . of a Stephen King.' Phillip Adams, 'Hypocrites shop horror', *The Weekend Australian*, Sat. 27 May, 2000.

Chapter 13

Direct quotes are attributed in the text and taken from David Saunders author interview and police statement; John

Chillingworth author interview and police statement; Melissa
Knight author interview and police statement; Natasha Knight
police statement.

Chapter 14

Direct quotes are attributed in the text and taken from Colleen
Price, Paul Farrell, Price's youngest daughter, Gerrie Edwards,
Dave Saunders and Henry Perry interviews with author; Rosemary
Biddle interview with Michelle Coffey of *Who Weekly* and police
statement; Johnathon Price police statement and interview with
Michelle Coffey of *Who Weekly*; Katherine Knight police interview
and psychiatric interviews (see Chapter One endnotes); Amanda
Pemberton police statement.

'all this old ... on the roof.' Rosemary Biddle interview with
Michelle Coffey of *Who Weekly*.

'She had this ... everyone else would do.' Rosemary Biddle interview with Michelle Coffey of *Who Weekly*.

'she went absolutely ... nothing happened.' Rosemary Biddle
interview with Michelle Coffey of *Who Weekly*.

Chapter 15

Direct quotes are attributed in the text and taken from John
Price's youngest daughter and Ron Murray author interviews;
Katherine Knight police statement and pyschiatric interviews with
Dr Robert Delaforce, Dr Rod Milton and Dr Leonard Lambeth;
Katherine Knight sentencing report; Rosemary Biddle interview
with Michelle Coffey of *Who Weekly* and police statement; police
statements from Katherine Knight's children, Michael Steele,
Amanda Doyle and Simon Gallen and interview by Donna Page of
the *Newcastle Herald*.

'to keep ... as the future.' Katherine Knight interview with Dr
Leonard Lambeth.

'I loved all of that ... and the horns.' Katherine Knight interview
with Robert Delaforce.

'there's nothing in there.' Michelle Coffey of *Who Weekly*.

Chapter 16

Direct quotes are attributed in the text and taken from Val Roughan, Joy Hinder, John Hinder, Natasha Kellett, Amanda Pemberton and Anthony Keegan police statements; Barry Roughan and Glenda Reichel author interviews and police statements; Katherine Knight police and psychiatric interviews with Dr Robert Delaforce, Dr Rod Milton and Dr Leonard Lambeth. Additional information from author interview with residents (anonymous) and court records.

'He turned over ... and that's it.' Katherine Knight interview with Dr Leonard Lambeth.

'I run the knife ... just cut that off.' Fred West quoted in *Happy Like Murderers* by Gordon Burn, Faber and Faber.

Chapter 17

Direct quotes are attributed in the text and taken from author interview with prison sources (anonymous); Geraldine Edwards, Bob Wells and Barry Roughan author interviews; Dr Robert Delaforce's psychiatric report on Katherine Knight with references to the *Diagnostic and Statistical Manual of Mental Disorders*, 4th edn, American Psychiatric Publishing Inc.; Dr Michael Giuffrida psychiatric report on Katherine Knight; Sharon Young police statement regarding medical records.

'a woman accused ... due to security fears.' *The Daily Telegraph*, 'Accused kept in cell', 5 April 2000.

'that the doctors ... in bandages.' Katherine Knight interview with Dr Rod Milton.

'I'm happy for ... helping people.' Katherine Knight interview with Dr Rod Milton.

'the development of ... increased arousal.' *Diagnostic and Statistical Manual of Mental Disorders*, 4th edn, American Pyschiatric Publishing Inc. CD ROM.

Chapter 18

Direct quotes are attributed in the text and taken from court records – transcript of the sentencing proceedings Regina v. Katherine Mary Knight 16/10/01–8/11/01 NSW Supreme Court; Bob Wells interview with author.

Chapter 19

Direct quotes are attributed in the text and taken from author's court reports; Court records – transcript of Justice O'Keefe's sentence, 8 November 2001 NSW Supreme Court.

Other sources

The author interviewed the following people:

Detective Sergeant Bob Wells
David Saunders
David Kellett
John Chillingworth
Colleen Price and her youngest daughter
Margaret MacBeth
Henry Perry
Melissa Kellett
Barry Roughan
Mavis Paulger
Henry Perry
Geraldine Edwards
Dr Tim Lyons
Glenda Reichel
Ronald Murray
Detective Senior Constable Victor Ford
Paul Farrell
Ron Wilton
Lloyd and Betty Lyne
Lisa Logan
Peter Cairnes
Jon Collison
Jill Keegan

Les Parsons
Lorna Driscoll

Medical sources:
Dr Chris Dullard

Katherine Knight psychiatric profiles were written by:
Dr Robert Delaforce
Dr Rod Milton
Dr Michael Giuffrida
Dr Leonard Lambeth

Journalists:
Michelle Coffey and Donna Page have been quoted.

The NSW Supreme Court granted the author access to the police brief prepared by Det Sgt Bob Wells, which included statements from Sharyn and John Chillingworth, Amanda Pemberton, Sharon and James Simmons, Wayne Hampton, Dale Fittock, Paul Farrell, Ronald Wilton, Sen Const Gallen, Sen Const Boswell, Jennifer Saunders, Sen Const Maude, Sen Const Doyle, Sen Const Steele, Brian Conlon, Tracy Knight, Jason Wilson, Robert Kembrey, Jeffrey Harrington, Sen Const Mathews, Sharon Young, Glenda Reichel, Ronald Murray, Laurence Lewis, Sgt Graham Furlonger, Det Victor Ford, Colleen Price, Rosemary Biddle, Sen Const Winn, Sen Const Dellosta, David Saunders, David Kellett, John Chillingworth, Glenn Dunning, Anthony Keegan, Natasha Kellett, Lisa Logan, Johnathon Price, Barry Roughan, Valerie Roughan, Melissa Kellett, Margaret MacBeth, Geraldine Edwards.

Photography credits

Aberdeen, Peter Lalor
Aberdeen road sign, Sue Lalor
Abattoir, Bob Barker, News Limited
Knight and Kellett, supplied by David Kellett
Knight, supplied by the Knight family
Knight and Price, supplied by the Knight family

Price, supplied by the Knight family
Price's house, Peter Lalor
Knight's house, Peter Stoop, *Newcastle Herald*
Graphics by Sue Lalor
Wells, Bob Barker, News Limited